NORWEGIAN CRUISING GUIDE

FROM THE SWEDISH SOUND TO THE RUSSIAN BORDER

Second Edition

John Armitage
and Mark Brackenbury

ADLARD COLES NAUTICAL
London

Dedication

For Ben, the best friend and first mate one could wish for
John Armitage

*For Gina, Claire and David, in grateful thanks for their
help at sea and, in Gina's case, patience ashore*
Mark Brackenbury

Second edition 1996
Published by Adlard Coles Nautical
an imprint of A & C Black (Publishers) Ltd
35 Bedford Row, London WC1R 4JH

Copyright © First edition
Mark Brackenbury 1978
Copyright © Second edition
John Armitage and Mark Brackenbury 1996

First published by Stanford Maritime
Limited 1978
Reprinted 1980, 1983
Second edition published by
Adlard Coles Nautical 1996

ISBN 0-7136-4115-0

All rights reserved. No part of this publication may be reproduced in any form or by any means – graphic, electronic or mechanical, including photocopying, recording, taping or information storage and retrieval systems – without the prior permission in writing of the publishers.

A CIP catalogue record for this book is available from the British Library.

Typeset in 10 on 12pt Sabon by
Falcon Oast Graphic Art
Printed and bound in Great Britain by
Butler and Tanner Ltd, Frome and London

Note
While every effort has been made to ensure the accuracy of the contents of the *Norwegian Cruising Guide,* neither the authors nor the publishers can take responsibility for any accident or damage.

Cruise planning maps
Some of the sources used in the preparation of the cruise-planning maps have been based on Mercator projections, others on land maps based on modified conical projections. Bridges have been omitted, and owing to the small scale of the maps relative to the complexity of the waters depicted, some navigable channels may not be visible on the maps. The purpose of the plans is to show the relative positions of the recommended ports and the distances from one to another, but apparently navigable channels may be closed by low bridges or other obstructions, so detailed cruise planning should only be undertaken with the relevant marine charts to hand. As space has only allowed the naming of the very largest islands, in many cases the passage notes are also only usable in conjunction with the charts. The authors hope that, notwithstanding these difficulties caused by the intricacies of Norwegian waters, the maps will provide a valuable overview of the different areas covered in the book.

Contents

Preface iv
Acknowledgements and Thanks vi

Part 1 Cruising in Norway 1

The Passage 4
*A Specimen Cruise of
  SW Norway* 6
*Cruising Alternatives in
  N Norway* 6
Tides, Streams and Currents 6
Charts 7
Buoyage 9
Mooring and Anchoring 11
Food, Drink and Water 12
Cleanliness 14
Miscellaneous 15

**Part 2 From Sognefjorden to the
         Russian Border 23**

1 Sognefjorden to Kristiansund 23
2 Kristiansund to Rørvik 33
3 Rørvik to Bodø 41
4 Bodø to Narvik 50
5 Narvik to Tromsø and
  Torsvåg 66
6 Torsvåg to Nordkapp 77
7 Nordkapp to the Russian
  Border 83

Part 3 Svalbard 87

8 Cruising Spitsbergen, Bjørnøya
  and Jan Mayen 87
9 SW Spitsbergen 99
10 W Spitsbergen 102
11 NW Spitsbergen 106

**Part 4 Sognefjorden and south to
         the Swedish Border 113**

12 Sognefjorden 113
13 Sognefjorden to Bergen 118
14 Bergen to Haugesund with the
   Hardangerfjord 124
15 Haugesund to Stavanger with the
   Lysefjord 132
16 Stavanger to the Naze
   (Lindesnes) 138
17 The Naze (Lindesnes) to
   Larvik 144
18 Larvik to Oslo and the Swedish
   Border 153

**Part 5 The Swedish Coast between
         Norway and the Sound 160**

**Part 6 Cruise Planning
         Information 167**

Sailing Distances between Principal
  Ports 167
Coastal Radio 170
Weather Forecasts and Ice
  Reports 174
Coastal Danger Areas 179
Glossary (words and abbreviations
  from charts and *Den
  Norske Los*) 182
Glossary of Wildlife 189
Bibliography 192

Index 196

Preface

In 1978, Mark Brackenbury's *Norwegian Cruising Guide, A Pilot for the Norwegian & SW Swedish Coasts between Sognefjord & the Sound* was published, and for several years this remained the only English language guide for Norway, until it finally went out of print in 1991. Mark's guide for southern Norway has now been comprehensively updated and combined with new material from John Armitage for northern Norway, to become the jointly authored *Norwegian Cruising Guide*, including SW Sweden, Spitsbergen and Bear Island. There are small differences in style and layout between the southern and northern parts of the new guide, but the general organisation is similar, except that the northern part is dealt with travelling north and east, and the southern part is dealt with travelling south and east, in both cases starting at Sognefjord.

This is much more a *guide* than a *pilot*, covering only a selection of harbours and offering mainly cruise planning information. Pilotage detail is provided only where there is an unusual hazard or an exceptional situation, and in general a fairly high standard of navigation is assumed.

Harbours and anchorages have been included for several reasons, both positive and negative:

- the harbours are especially fine, places one would not want to miss
- the harbours are pleasant or convenient, useful to be aware of
- after examining the chart, one might be tempted to stop at a particular harbour, but the harbour has proved to be unsafe, uncomfortable or otherwise undesirable

The density of coverage in a particular area is partly determined by the inclinations of the authors and their friends, and by vagaries of weather and time, and does not necessarily correspond to the quality of the different areas; this guidebook is only a starting point for further exploration.

Some harbours are included that the authors have not personally visited, nor obtained a trustworthy comprehensive firsthand description of them, and these are indicated with an asterisk (*) after the name; thus a perfunctory description in these cases does not necessarily indicate a mediocre harbour as in other instances. Qualitative information is given for each harbour to help the reader decide whether or not to make a visit there, but as this is such a personal matter there are bound to be discrepancies. This guidebook is oriented towards a 10–13 m (30–40 foot) sailing yacht drawing 1.7–2 m, so if cruising in a materially different vessel, allowance must be made.

Readers should note that the cruise planning charts included are sketch maps only, and that they are not suitable for navigation.

Hopefully this guidebook will be revised and reprinted from time to time; users are by far the best source of information for this purpose, and the authors will be most grateful for any correspondence sent c/o the publisher, Adlard Coles Nautical, 35 Bedford Row, London WC1R 4JH, UK.

The Blindleia, one of the prettiest passages on the SE coast.

Acknowledgements and thanks

One of the finest attributes of the international cruising community is a generous readiness to give help. This guidebook is much the richer for such assistance from those listed below – help both in contributing information and photographs, and in the tedious task of editing. We hope there are many occasions wherein those fortunate enough to cruise these N Nordic waters may find their enjoyment enhanced by this guidebook, and will join in our thanks.

Anneline, Per Bjarne and Signe Akselsen, Narvik
Anne Marie, Finn Engelsen, Bergen
Antonio Pigafetta, Jürg and Ali Andermatt, Asendorf, Germany
Arctic Explorer, Lofoten
Baal, Folkmar Ukena, Leer, Germany
Bagheera, Jean-Yves and Lawrence Hamard, Paris, France
Baluba, Ronny Åsheim, Narvik
Berg, Jan Tore and Eli, Liland
Bodø Radio
British Steel Challenge, Simon Walker, Shrewsbury, England
Cloud Walker, David and Judy Lomax, Upper Woolhampton, England
Dahle, Hjørdis, Bergen Radio
Dolce Vita, Frank Larsen, Bodø
Enhiørningen Emma, Peter Schmidt and Diana Boholm, Fanø, Denmark
Extasa, Ørje and Barbro Andersen, Sortland
Flyvholm, George Earle, Murroe, Ireland
Framanjo, Egil Lindberg, Voss
Gosken, Geir and Solveig Myhre, Narvik
Governor of Svalbard, Longyearbyen
Hart, John and Margaret, Barry Island, Wales
Hjoennevaag, Gabriel and Inger-Johanne, Fedje
Idun, Ola and Gunn Bergslien, Trondheim
Karisma, Thorvald and Laila Mathisen, Narvik
Kyrah II, Armand and Ginette de Mestral, Etoy, Switzerland
Lille Mor, Lars-Erik and Aase Karlsen, Hugo Svendsen, Lofoten
Macono, Reidulf Mathisen, Narvik
Mahedda, Yvonne and Ad de Roos, Prinsenbeek, Netherlands
Naomi, Owen Morgan, Horten
Nomad, Ed and Mary Arnold, High Seas
Nautisk Forlag, Hans Tryggve Eggen, Oslo
Nord-Norge Vervarslinga, Tromsø
Norges Sjøkartverk, Stavanger
Os, Harald, Narvik
Pegdon, Don and Peggy Campbell, High Seas
Pettersen, Hallgeir, Narvik
Royal Wiking, Rolf Jacobsen, Bleik
Saint Patrick, Paddy Berry, Dublin, Ireland

Samantha, Magne and Anne Skarbøvik, Ålesund
Sea Bird of Trondra, Bob and Carole Wilson, Cauldhame, Shetland
Shardana, John Gore-Grimes, Dublin, Ireland
Solvejg, Thijs Alle Zoethout, Harlingen, Netherlands
Terra Nova, Corri and Willem Stein, Eemnes, Netherlands
Tigre Mou, Hervé and Béatrice Legoff, Nancy, France
Vindia, Sten Björnberg, Spanga, Sweden
Xenia, H F Meyer, Tervuren, Belgium
Yeni Raki, Eivind and Kari-Ann Aase, Bodø
Zorba, Arnfinn and Synnøve Santi, Narvik

PART 1

Cruising in Norway

The Norwegian coastline provides one of the most delightful and varied cruising grounds in the world, and one to which the experienced sailor will find it well worth while making the considerable effort involved in organising a visit. Not only does Norway offer superb cruising, but visitors stepping ashore will find a warm welcome from a people interested in visiting sailors and eager to help make their cruising a success. And, except for the most populated areas in the south, the visitor will have it all to himself.

The S section of the *Norwegian Cruising Guide* covers the coast from Sognefjorden southwards past Bergen to Lindesnes, and then E and N past Kristiansand and Larvik to Oslofjorden and the capital itself. The SW Swedish coast is also covered as far as the Sound, as this may well be the best route home. The N section of this book goes northwards from Sognefjorden to the well known Lofoten islands, then round to Nordkapp (the North Cape) and to the Russian border. Spitsbergen, in the Svalbard archipelago N of Norway, is also extensively covered.

An amazing fact is that the total coastline of Norway, including the islands, would be long enough, if straightened out, to encircle the continent of Africa some four and a quarter times! This book therefore gives only a general description of each area, and includes only a selection of ports and anchorages – enough to enable the reader to form a cruise plan. There are thousands of other small harbours and anchorages shown on the charts which those with sufficient time may wish to explore for themselves.

The most obvious difference between S and N Norway is that the N part is much farther away! However, there are also many other dissimilarities. Surprisingly, the weather in the N is generally better than that in the S (certainly W of Lindesnes), as the S is on the main track for summer depressions. The sailing wind, though, may be more reliable in the S. Going N, the average summer temperature falls a little, but by less than might be expected because of the effects of the Gulf Stream, which keep the NW coast free from ice even in winter. Continuing northwards, the summer nights become lighter until, with the crossing of the Arctic Circle, we are in the land of the midnight sun. Coastal arctic Norway is not a bleak tundra inhabited only by reindeer and polar bears; it is a land of deep mossy forests, wild flowers in profusion, spectacular mountains, islands, fjords, villages, small cities and hospitable people, much like the rest of Norway. The coastal area around the Arctic Circle offers perhaps the finest cruising

2 CRUISING IN NORWAY

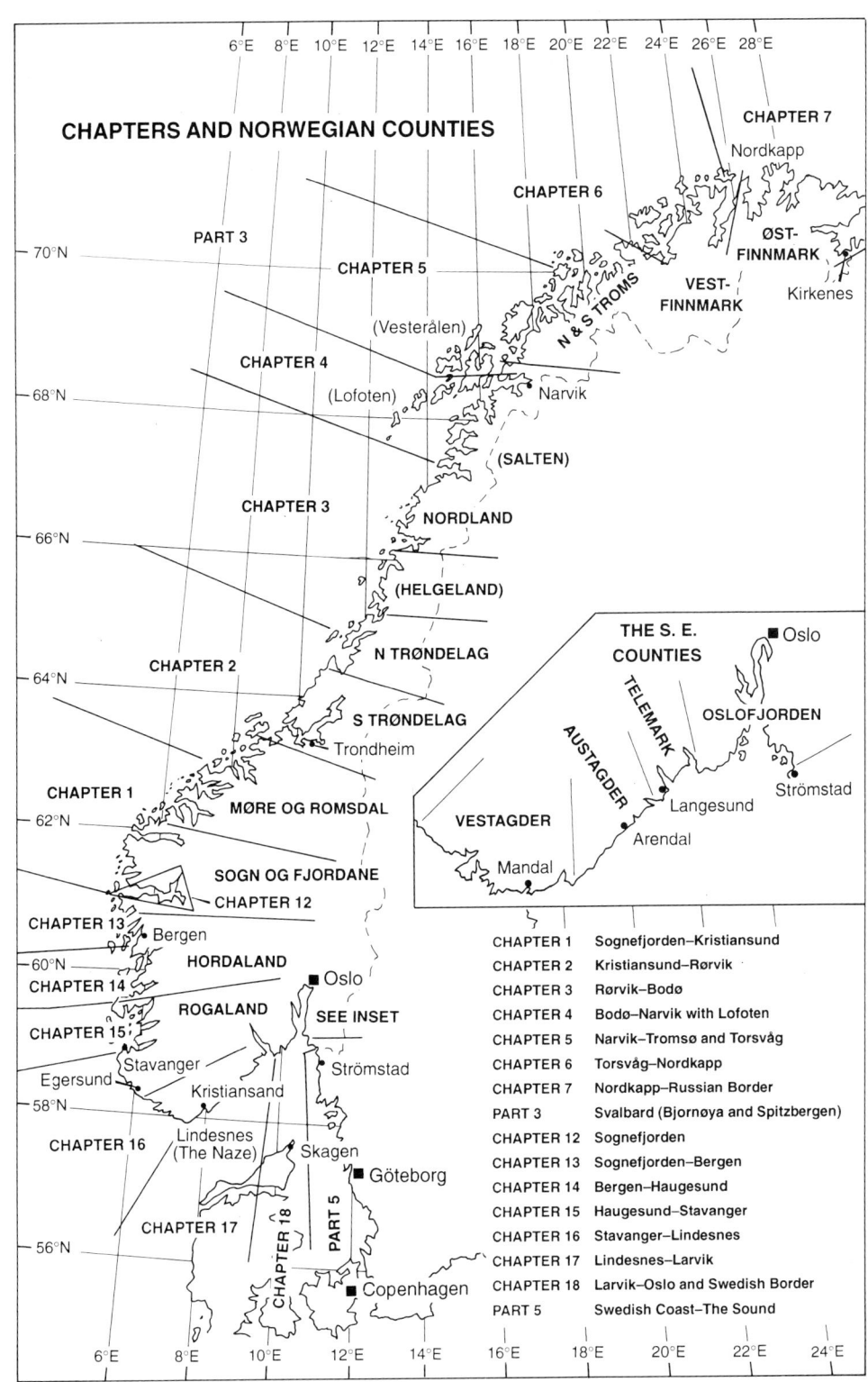

in Norway. The population density in the N is lower than in the S, there are fewer yachts and motorboats, and there is a feeling of being at the edge of the world: at the frontier. For those who have plenty of time and are not afraid of being alone, N Norway is ideal. And if the time allows an even longer trip, consider Spitsbergen.

Both scenically and climatically, the SW Norwegian coast is divided into two quite dissimilar areas at Lindesnes ('The Naze', as English sailors called it for many years). To the W, the scenery is grand, rugged and awe-inspiring, and the last two adjectives would often serve for the weather as well, which can be wild and stormy, and can change dramatically in just one hour. This is the land of the great fjords, huge gashes that run for up to 115 miles inland with inhospitable shores, incredible depth of water, and sometimes almost vertical cliff walls rising 1000 m or more from the surface. Here, savage squalls can be encountered, and a strong boat with really reliable power is vital.

Yet the SW coast also offers hundreds of miles of sailing in sheltered waters protected by islands, where one can enjoy the unusual experience of sailing day after day in strong winds, but through almost perfectly smooth water. This is the skjærgård (pronounced 'share-gore'), which means in Norwegian 'the waters protected by islands' (skerries). On the E coast the skjærgård is rather more broken, but then it is also of much less importance. Once round Lindesnes, the westerlies that bring most of the bad weather to the W coast in summer are broken up by the mountain barrier and, incidentally, emptied of their rain at the same time. The hours of sunshine are therefore much greater on average on the E coast, the winds are lighter, and the average temperature much higher. The scenery is softer:

Many photos taken in Norway look much the same either way up. (Try it!) This is of Fjærland in Sognefjorden.

rounded hills covered with deciduous forest rather than the jagged pine-clad mountains of the west. But for a foreign yachtsman on what may be a once-in-a-lifetime visit, it would certainly be a shame to miss the incredible grandeur of the west.

Bound N, it is possible to sail nearly all of the long distance from Tananger to Nordkapp inside the skjærgård, sheltered from the Atlantic. There are only five relatively short areas where the skjærgård is discontinuous, and thus where one must sail 'outside':

1 Between Haugesund and the entrance to Bømlafjorden
2 Around Stattlandet, notorious for rough and sometimes dangerous seas
3 Hustadvika, NE from Bud towards Kristiansund, where the skerries are too sparse to offer good shelter and the navigation among them is exceedingly intricate
4 Folla, S of Rørvik, a stretch where the skjærgård simply has a gap, and
5 Lopphavet, above 70° N, where the skjærgård gives way to more open waters as one approaches Nordkapp

Many of the coastal islands are quite large and high, with skerries outside, making a network of leads along the coast, with some more 'outside' and others more 'inside'. The high steep islands combine with the high coastal mountains to create spectacular scenery, and provide a superb route along the coast; even though the meandering involved adds to the miles to be travelled, one may be comfortable continuing in weather that would prove unpleasantly rough offshore. There are a dozen small coastal cities (large towns is probably a better description) and hundreds of tiny village harbours, making a nice counterpoint to the wild scenery and anchorages. The coast is cut by several deep fjords, most notably Nordfjorden and Geirangerfjorden, rivalling Sognefjorden in splendid scenery if not quite in length. The coast past Nordkapp, to the border with Russia, is lower than the W coast and not so steep; it is indented with deep fjords, but without sheltering islands – and so has quite a different character from the coast farther S.

THE PASSAGE

With the Straits of Dover as a point of departure, there are six main choices of route from England to Norway, or from countries to its S and W:

The direct route

This needs little comment. It is of course likely to be the quickest way, but it involves a longer unbroken passage than is perhaps desirable with, for instance, young children aboard. From Harwich to Tananger, which is probably the best landfall to aim at for reasons I will go into later, it is about 440 miles; Skudeneshavn is another excellent landfall and only a few miles further. The great advantage is that there is plenty of sea room all the way, and any strong winds will hopefully be quartering or, at worst, on the beam.

The Scottish route

Working one's way up to Scotland very much reduces the length of the long passage. Aberdeen to Tananger is only 265 miles, and from Peterhead it is further reduced to about 245 miles. On the other hand, Harwich to Aberdeen is itself 360 miles, so this route puts about 185 miles on to the actual distance involved. And there may be many who will feel that an extra couple of hundred miles or so of open sea passage is a small price to pay for avoiding the difficulties of a passage up the length of the E coast of England and Scotland. However, for those on the W coast of England or Scotland, the scenic Caledonian Canal may be a good alternative. The greatest advantage of this route is in the course: even a northwesterly gale will be well abaft the beam.

The Shetland route

For those who wish to absolutely minimise the offshore distance across the North Sea, consider that from Lerwick to Fedje (a good landfall near Bergen): it is 178 miles, and from Out Skerry it is 156 miles. Shetland is not much out of the way on a route from the W UK, but may be an unwarranted detour from the E UK. Orkney and Fair Isle provide good intermediate stops, but in waters that are strongly tidal and truly nasty in bad weather. None the less, the N Scottish islands do make an interesting intermediate destination in their own right, and good last provisioning at UK prices. For those with minimum time available yet wishing to see something of N Norway, the 600 mile offshore passage direct to Lofoten is a good choice; this has the further advantage of missing the NE winds common along the Norwegian W coast in early summer.

The Dutch route

This is much to be recommended for those who wish to cut down the length of the long passage without wasting too much time. From Harwich to Tananger via Den Helder is only 500 miles, so the detour adds only 60 miles to the whole trip, but still takes 80 miles off the long passage – Den Helder to Tananger being 360 miles. Another great advantage is that the approach to the Norwegian coast is at a very shallow angle, which enables one to stop off at Egersund if it becomes obvious that one is going to arrive at Tananger in the dark or in poor conditions. (Incidentally, this also reduces the passage by a further 25 miles or so.) The main disadvantage of this route is that a northwesterly leaves you close-hauled at best, and possibly unable to lay the course at all, but there is still plenty of sea room – and if the worst comes to the worst one can always bear away and run for shelter behind the Skaw (Skagen: the N point of Denmark).

The Baltic route

It is of course possible to reach Norway by the Dutch and German coasts, the Kiel Canal and the Baltic, without ever needing to be at sea in the dark! It is, however, a very long way round, and if the W coast of Norway is to be visited it means that the same coast will be travelled twice almost from end to end. For people with a deep dislike of long passages, and with plenty of time to spare, it is a useful route.

The route to avoid

The one route that I would advise against in the strongest terms is that from Helgoland to Esbjerg to Thyborön and then across to Norway. If all goes well, this can also be done by day sails, but it is a truly dangerous route. The W Danish coast is thoroughly bleak and inhospitable, and in a westerly blow Thyborön cannot be used, as the sea breaks heavily on the bar. To invite the risk of finding oneself on a shelterless lee shore in what is often very bad visibility seems to me quite unjustifiable when, as in this case, it is unnecessary.

A SPECIMEN CRUISE OF SW NORWAY

This is a risky section to include, as so many of the judgements that underlie it must be subjective. However, for what it is worth, I would suggest that a good way to make the best value of the available time is to arrive at Tananger or Skudeneshavn, sail up past Bergen to the entrance to Sognefjorden, explore the first few miles (Vikum offers a pleasant anchorage only 16 miles up the fjord, and the magnificent scenery does not change greatly after that for many more miles), and then return. If a little more time is available, the glacier at Fjærland and the stave churches mentioned in the harbour notes are but a few extra miles. Pay a visit to Kviturspollen, the beautiful yacht harbour of the Bergen Sailing Club, and then proceed S to Stavanger. From here, a day sail will allow one to explore Lysefjorden. This is one of the most beautiful and spectacular fjords in Norway, but with the great advantage of being only just over 20 miles long. Then back to Tananger, S to Lindesnes, and then NE to Oslofjorden. Oslo must not be missed; but, if time presses, the boat can always be left at Tønsberg, and a visit made by train.

Starting from West Mersea and returning by the W Swedish coast and the Baltic, MB logged some 2350 miles on such a cruise in 1976, using the Dutch route outwards. This is probably as much as most people have the time or inclination to do on a summer cruise, and indeed it would be perfectly feasible to lay up in Norway and complete the cruise the following year. Fuller details of the routes between the various places will be found at the beginning of each section.

CRUISING ALTERNATIVES IN N NORWAY

To most non-Norwegian yachtsmen, 'northern Norway' is likely to mean the Lofoten Islands. Lofoten is indeed a unique area, spectacularly and exotically scenic, with unusual villages and interesting people, and many good harbours sheltered from the open Atlantic. If time is very limited, it is possible to make an offshore dash directly to Lofoten, spend a week or two visiting the highlights, and dash back S again; this would provide only a bare sampling of N Norway, but would none the less be a notable summer's cruise. With more time available, the superb areas surrounding Lofoten, which are just as fine – Helgeland to the S, Ofoten to the E, and Vesterålen to the NW – could be explored, and perhaps more of the beautiful 'inside route' could be taken along the coast to the S. With even more time, Nordkapp, or Kirkenes at the Russian border, can be one's goal. If Spitsbergen is the objective, one will probably want to maximise the time spent there, and will perforce spend less time along the way. One of the fine things about the Norwegian coast is that it can serve as a cruising ground unlikely to be exhausted in a lifetime, or equally well as a splendid passage route as part of a longer cruise.

TIDES, STREAMS AND CURRENTS

E of Lindesnes there is no significant rise and fall of tide, and no tidal stream. Off the SE Norwegian coast there is a generally SW-going current, although this can be reversed inside the islands in places and is affected by strong winds. The maximum strength is from about 3 to 10 miles offshore. W of Lindesnes the current sweeps round the coast and up to the N. There is little tidal stream offshore, but a progressively greater rise and fall, with a spring range of around 0.6 m at Stavanger, 1.2 m at Bergen, and as much as 3.7 m at the Russian border. (More detail is given in the relevant sections.)

There is a considerable tidal stream in some of the inshore channels (dealt with in the sections concerned). There may sometimes be currents in the fjords as a result of river flow, wind and other factors; often these involve an ingoing current on one bank, and an outgoing current on the other, which can be most useful if spotted in time.

The small scope of the tide in the S allows one to lie alongside at the many quays with great convenience, but particularly going N along the W coast it is important to remember that there *is* a rise and fall, and sufficient slack must be left on warps to allow for it.

HW Bergen is approximately 1 hour before HW Dover.

CHARTS

The main Norwegian chart series, the 100 series, is on a scale of 1:50 000, and it would be hard to speak too highly of the clarity and excellence of the charts. Each chart has an index chart printed on the back. The series starts with chart 1 at the Swedish border, and works its way up to chart 116 at the Russian border. There are a few extra charts above 116, filling inland gaps along the coast that were omitted from the numbering system as originally established. The entire coast is also charted at a scale of 1:350 000 (1:200 000 N of Tromsø) in the 300 series, which are very useful for planning and route selection.

Although it is possible to navigate via the main leads followed by the Hurtigruten ships using only the 300 series charts, most mariners would consider the 100 series charts necessary both for safety and to do justice to the cruising quality of the Norwegian coast. The SW coast and a few other selected areas are charted at 1:75 000–1:150 000 in the 200 series, but – except for a few inland areas not covered by the 100 series – the 200 series charts are easy to do without. The 400 series charts cover several dozen cities in a very detailed scale; and although these charts are nice to have, it is a largely unnecessary expense. One exception, though, might be chart 456, for the sound SE of Ålesund, although the inset on chart 31 covers the most intricate part. Svalbard (including Spitsbergen) is charted in the 500 series, at a scale of 1:100 000 – 1:350 000. Charts of the coast from Sweden to N of Kristiansund are also available in groups of smaller 1:50 000 charts – *Båtsportkort*. (This series is being extended northward, so check for the latest coverage.) These are a convenient size on small boats, but since the area covered on each chart is quite limited there are many edges, and it is difficult to use the *Båtsportkort* for planning or overview purposes, making 300 or 200 series charts essential. Each group of *Båtsport* charts has a transparent cover, some extra information relevant to pleasure boating, and a sheet explaining the symbols in English. They are somewhat less expensive than the standard charts for the same area covered, and available only in larger towns. British Admiralty charts are useful for offshore work, but are not adequate for navigating the skjærgård.

Each chapter in this book summarises

the charts needed. A comprehensive and very useful *Catalogue of Norwegian Charts*, which admirably clarifies the above information, is available free of charge from: Norges Sjøkartverk, Postboks 60, N-4001 Stavanger, Norway. Also useful is the comprehensive publication entitled *Symbols and Abbreviations used on Norwegian Charts*, available from chart agents.

One great feature of Norway is the ease with which charts can be obtained. Even the most modest coastal town will have a bookshop with the sign 'Sjøkart' in the window, and a full stock of at least the local charts. One can therefore safely set off with only a few charts and buy the rest as they are needed, thus saving money if plans are changed. It is surprising how often it is possible to borrow charts from Norwegian sailors whom one meets along the coast, thus saving the considerable cost of buying new charts.

In England, Norwegian charts may be ordered through Imray, Laurie, Norie & Wilson Ltd of Wych House, The Broadway, St Ives, Huntingdon, Cambridgeshire PE17 4BT, Tel: (01480) 462 114, Fax: (01480) 496 109. For hiking ashore, detailed topographic maps may be very useful, and these can be obtained at most large bookshops in Norway.

In conjunction with the Glossary of Words and Abbreviations at the end of this book, the use of Norwegian charts should present no problems. Care must, however, be taken to distinguish between the symbols for commercial and yacht anchorages. The difference is not always all that obvious in poor light, but it is important, as commercial anchorages on the W coast may be as much as 50 m deep.

One other point to watch for is that on many older Norwegian charts the longitude W of Oslo is shown more prominently than E of Greenwich! And older Norwegian charts are likely to have longitude values too high by as much as 0.75′ relative to the European Datum (ED-50) or WGS-84 Datum. If one wishes to use GPS for intricate navigation with these older charts, it is necessary to establish the longitude error for each chart by actual measurement if the offset is not given by a note on the chart. Recent charts marked as being made to the European Datum or to WGS-84 can be used directly with GPS. In this book, coordinates are given with respect to WGS-84, and are given with a precision of 0.1′ where it is felt that this might avoid confusion; these coordinates should not be relied upon for navigation. GPS works well even in the deep fjords, but Decca is not reliable for inshore navigation, nor very accurate along the S coast of Norway. The term 'miles' in this book designates nautical miles, 1′ of a great circle (ca 1852 m), not the Norwegian 'mile' of 10 km.

The charts and markings are so thorough that it is easy to trust them excessively; however, a browse through the Notices to Mariners shows a number of perches missing for several years before replacement, and shoals of 1.5 m being found where a depth of 10 m has earlier been charted. These dangers are most often off the main routes, of course, so it is wise to be somewhat sceptical – especially when exploring in the skerries. If you find a discrepancy, your report to Statens Kartverk by post or through the coastal radio will be given prompt attention.

On the SW Swedish coast and NW Norwegian coast, the magnetic variation is small enough to ignore for most coastal yacht navigation, but on the SW Norwegian coast the variation reaches around 5° W, and as one sails E across Finnmark towards the Russian border it increases to around 12° E.

Overhead power cables are common in Norway. They are marked on the charts by a broken red line, with the lowest height in metres shown in red. These markings are usually conspicuous, but where they are printed over numerous islands and other features they can be missed; and it is also possible for a new cable to have been added since the printing of the chart, so it is important to keep a sharp lookout for them. Bridge heights are given in metres in parentheses, as 'Bru(15)'. You will want to know accurately your air draft before sailing into the skjærgård. Wavy red lines (continuous) denote underwater cables, and the symbol for underwater pipelines is a line of joined red dashes and spots, looking rather like a string of tadpoles!

BUOYAGE

Before dealing with the buoyage system in Norway, it is perhaps worth pointing out that one will spot more buoys in the course of an average weekend trip on the coast of England than one will see in a whole season cruising in Norway. The reason is perfectly simple: especially on the W coast, the water is too deep for the use of buoys except in the narrowest channels, and for the same reason there are very few hazards. Where individual rocks occur, usually near groups of small skerries, they are almost always marked by fixed perches mounted permanently on the danger, rather than being indicated by buoys.

Buoys

When following the direction of buoyage, green buoys will be to starboard, and red buoys will be to port. The

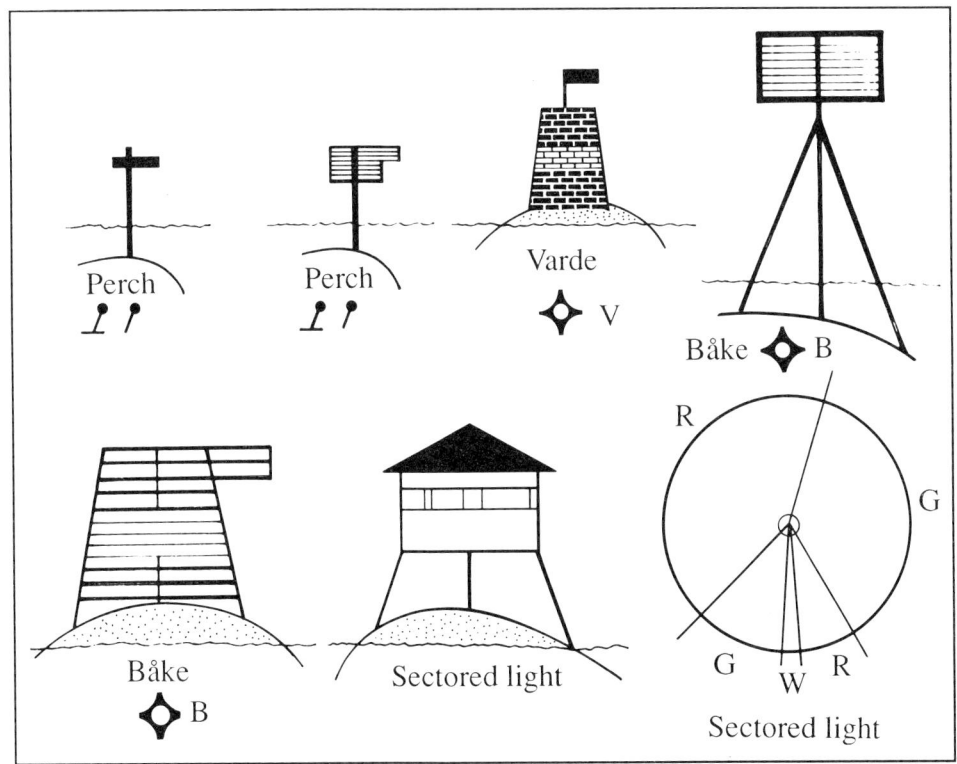

direction of buoyage originates at Norway's S-most point, Lindesnes, and proceeds in two paths. One path follows the coast as it curves to the W, N, NE, E and S, and finally even to the W not far from the Russian border; the other path follows the coast to the E and NE, then splits N towards Oslo and S towards the Swedish border. In interior leads and fjords, the direction of buoyage is inwards from the sea, independent of the compass direction. Around islands, where there can be confusion regarding the direction of buoyage, the chart must be consulted.

Black/yellow N, E, S, W cardinal buoys are also used, often without double triangle topmarks or lights. On the Norwegian charts, green buoys have their outline filled in, while red ones have the inside of the symbol left blank, and so are easy to miss on the chart.

Vardes, båkes and perches

The Norwegian *vardes* – stone towers painted black, often with a white stripe – make up what is probably the oldest system of navigational aids still in use anywhere in the world. They are conspicuous, recognisable individually when known, and clearly marked on the charts with a special four-pointed star and 'V'. The skill of their siting makes navigation of even the narrowest and most complex of channels relatively easy. They often carry topmarks consisting of a short post supporting a single horizontal arm, in which case the varde should be passed on the side towards which the arm is pointing. However, the pointer should not be blindly followed without identifying the varde on the chart, and checking the depth shown. Other vardes may be passed on either side, and they are also used on the coast to act as landmarks, progress marks or leading marks.

Another common type of beacon is the *båke* (*baake*). This is not one unique shape, but most often it is a tripod, or a latticework structure shaped much like a varde. The båke is charted with the same four-point star symbol as the varde, but marked with 'B' rather than 'V'. Both the varde and the båke may be lit.

Perches (steel pipes – *jernstang*) are used in exactly the same way, but at a more local level. Channels through groups of rocks are often marked by numerous perches, while offshore shoals will be marked by perches with outward-facing topmarks. They are clearly marked on the charts, but unlike the vardes they are often visible only at relatively short range, and sometimes only project a short distance above the surface at HW, so it is necessary to keep a sharp lookout. It would be a pity to be sunk by hitting a perch marking a rock over which one could have passed quite safely! Since the pointing arm on a perch may have become twisted, it is wise always to check on the chart as to which side to pass. Many perches have reflecting strips, sometimes red or green; the colour is not necessarily consistent with the buoyage colour scheme, so do not depend absolutely on the colour to indicate on which side of the perch to pass.

Hundreds of small sector lights are placed strategically in the skjærgård, enabling very accurate navigation in these intricate waters during the darkness of winter. These lights are extinguished during the summer, when of course the sectors cannot be used, but the distinctive little cylindrical white houses with orange roofs remain useful reference points for pilotage.

There are 13 400 vardes, båkes and perches along the coast of Norway, some as single isolated beacons, and some clustered densely together. Many channels such as the Blindleia (see p.144–5) are positively alarming when first looked at on the chart, but are in practice perfectly easy to follow as at every point of difficulty there is a perch or a varde to steer for.

MOORING AND ANCHORING

The vast majority of the quays that will be used for mooring have old motor tyres secured along them to act as fenders. This is a great help, but it does render topsides absolutely filthy after a time. It is little use trying to overcome this by the use of ordinary fenders, as these always work their way into the holes in the middle of the tyres, after which they are useless, so owners who are proud of their yacht's good looks will do well to ship a plank to put outside their own fenders against the tyres. On quays for large ships, one needs to be careful that at low tide the yacht does not drop below the lowest tyres; and on old wooden quays the bottoms of some of the pilings may have rotted off, and at low tide the yacht may drift under them and get hooked as the tide rises. This is a mistake that is especially easy to make if berthing near HW. In moderate conditions, an anchor run out from amidships may be sufficient to hold the yacht away from the quay. Sometimes fish farms, surrounded by a maze of buoys located just where one wishes to sail, present a navigational puzzle. Although the mooring ropes to the cages are usually laid out to avoid causing problems for boats passing outside the buoys, it is not unknown for there to be a mooring rope running close beneath the surface between a buoy and the nearby shore.

Many quays are privately owned, and in such cases permission to use the quay should be requested. If in doubt, then always enquire – for permission to moor will usually be granted while failure to ask is considered to be the height of bad manners. Particularly in N Norway, away from the pressures of population density, it is expected that a visiting yacht will moor up to whatever presents itself as suitable: a quay, pontoon, fishing boat, another yacht or a vacant mooring; however, it is also expected that the visitor will not impede other activities. Guest pontoons are often provided in larger towns and cities, frequently with some combination of electricity, water, showers and washing/drying machines; many private boat-club pontoons also have space designated for visitors, or permit the use of members' vacant spaces. There is usually a moderate charge for this guest berthing (in 1994 it ranged from 20 to 50 NKr), often via an honesty box. In the larger harbours there may be an official who will come to collect the fee, and if you are fortunate you may be missed out!

Anchoring can present problems, especially on the W coast. At least 60 m of cable should be carried, as even the small vessel anchorages are often very deep, and I would strongly recommend the shipping of both a CQR-type anchor and a large fisherman one. At various places on MB's 1976 cruise he found bottoms of stiff clay with weed on which his fisherman anchor refused to hold, while the heavier CQR dug in and would have held in a hurricane; conversely, thick kelp on which the CQR clogged up and skidded, the fisherman held on to well. Of the two, the fisherman is by far the more useful, and indeed Norwegian yachts seem most often to carry grapnel-type anchors, whose characteristics are close to those of the fisherman anchor.

In many anchorages there is only a narrow and sloping shelf of favourable anchoring depth. Sometimes this can be used to advantage by dropping an anchor as far inshore as possible (the extremely shallow depth compensating for the unfavourable downsloping angle of the bottom) and dropping a second anchor in deep water offshore from the yacht (the resulting short scope being compensated for by the favourable upsloping angle of the bottom).

Many small anchorages will be found to have mooring bolts: T-shaped metal pickets hammered into the rock. These are marked by target-like rings painted on the surface of the rock around them, as they would otherwise be very difficult to see against the background. Often these bolts will also be found in narrow channels – not, of course, for mooring, but as an aid to sailing vessels, particularly in the past, to warp through. Rings are sometimes used instead of bolts.

Occasionally one can moor between two bolts or rings, but the normal practice is to lie between one of them and an anchor. The anchor may be used from bow or stern and, where possible, the line to the bolt should be carried into the direction of the expected wind. This enables an anchorage to be used safely in heavy weather even where the holding is only moderate, as all the strain comes on the shore line – although of course an anchor watch should be set in such conditions if there is thought to be any danger of a major change in the wind direction. In practice, many of the anchorages are so sheltered that little or no wind reaches them even when it is blowing hard outside, but the opposite may be the case if in the lee of high steep ground. Yet, even though the Norwegians are extremely enthusiastic about taking lines ashore, there are drawbacks. The time and effort to rig and unrig shore lines can be considerable. Side loading by winds on the beam produces very high stress. If the wind comes up, perhaps from an unexpected direction, and one decides to change the mooring arrangement, it may be very difficult to retrieve the shore lines and effect the change. It may often be preferable to lie to two or three anchors, and you may wish to evaluate the situation before assuming that just because the local boatmen use shore lines that you will wish to also.

It should be mentioned here that it is customary in Norway to leave the smaller and more remote anchorages to the first comer, and to move on elsewhere if your first choice proves to be occupied. This is of course subject to time and weather, but if you do anchor in a remote place that is already occupied, it is considered good manners to hail the incumbents and ask if they mind before you drop your hook. This still applies if there are two yachts there, as they are very likely to be cruising in company. The carrying out of this courtesy creates a good impression, and can often result in a jolly good party into the bargain! The tradition only applies, of course, to the quiet and secluded anchorages, and not to those overlooked by villages or where there is traffic.

FOOD, DRINK AND WATER

Both food and drink should be the subject of considerable forward planning. As far as food is concerned, the Norwegians have more English tastes than are to be found elsewhere in Europe, and English brands of food are easily obtainable. Unfortunately, this similarity does not extend to price,

Crowded anchorages are seldom a problem in Spitsbergen, and one rarely has to ask permission to stay. This one in Trinityhamna, Maydelenfjorden, 626 miles from the N Pole, may never before have seen such a crowd of yachts!

which is often double (or occasionally even three times more expensive), so it is worth stocking up heavily with staples before departing for Norway. Excellent bread is available at moderate prices; 'kneippbrød' is a tasty wholegrain bread that keeps well.

The price of beer, wine and spirits simply does not bear thinking about, and the boat should be fully stocked with duty-free supplies before departing for Norway. Any reasonable quantity should cause no problem with customs officials.

There are two delicious and free supplements to your food supply, just waiting to be taken advantage of in Norway. The first, wild blueberries (*blåbær*), are plentiful in August, and one can easily pick enough for daily consumption – and even to preserve if desired. Blueberries growing wild are for the taking, but not so *multer* (cloudberries), which look like a pale orange raspberry; these are a Norwegian delicacy, held almost in reverence by those with the acquired taste for them, and sometimes jealously guarded even when growing wild.

Fish is the second bonus awaiting your pleasure. Even if you have never tried to catch fish from your yacht, or have tried with little success, in Norway, especially along the NW coast, you can easily catch all you can eat, mostly *torsk* (cod) or *sei* (coalfish, saithe, pollack). Cooking your catch just a few hours later makes you realise how *unfresh* most fish is by the time you buy it at market. A good size torsk, nice for filleting, will be well over $1/2$ m long, with typical sei running a bit smaller. Unlike fishing as sport, wherein much of the fun is in the uncertainty, fishing in Norway for food is just a matter of pulling up fish: if you fish in a reasonable place with reasonable gear, you will catch fish quite quickly. For a yacht, the best places are isolated shoals of 5–20 m, or sometimes along a shelving bottom at those depths. If you have not caught fish within five to ten minutes, then try elsewhere. The rising tide is supposed to be better than a falling one, but in many areas it does not seem critical. It is best not to fish near population centres, as the fish may have been feeding on sewage.

For gear, one can buy or make a simple wooden reel with a crank or just a bit of wood with notches on each end (such as is used for a kite string) to hold 30 m of heavy (150 kg test, 1 mm diameter) monofilament. At the bottom of this, tie a weight of around $1/4$ kg, most elegantly but expensively a 'Svenske Pilk' (which is shiny and fish shaped, around 18 cm long, with hooks), and at 1.5–2 m intervals above this weight, tie on a couple of leaders around 10 cm long with medium-sized red plastic tubular 'worms'. It is a good idea to use a leader a bit lighter than the main line, so if the line gets hooked on the bottom, then all is not lost. Stop your yacht over a shoal, watching the echo sounder, and drop the weight to the bottom, pull it up $1/2$ m and jig it up and down slowly, then raise it slowly in $1/2$ m stages, jigging the while. When you feel a fish on the line, pull up smoothly and hoist the fish into the boat, perhaps using a simple gaff if it's a monster torsk. If you pull up a prized orange-coloured *rødfisk* (redfish, ocean perch), be aware of the poisonous spines.

Many local fishermen are happy to instruct visitors regarding how to put together the gear, and in cleaning and filleting techniques, especially if one first of all opens with a request to purchase a freshly caught fish from them! One can section the fish and poach or boil, or fillet and fry or bake – but be careful not to overcook it. No licence is required to fish in salt water for personal consumption. In some areas, mussels and clams are abundant; but sometimes in S Norway there may be times when micro-organisms in the water make it unsafe to eat these shellfish, so it would be wise to ask the local residents before taking the risk.

Eating ashore is definitely not recommended in general. Cafés tend to be self-service, unlicensed, with poor choice and very expensive; an unexceptional stew with potatoes, followed by an ice cream, accompanied by a glass of orangeade, then followed by a cup of coffee, will cost roughly the same as a lunch with half a bottle of wine in a good London restaurant. Much better, then, to spend half the money on something really extravagant and consume it aboard. There are fine restaurants in the larger cities, but they are very expensive.

Returning to alcoholic drink for a moment, it has to be said that in Norway the question of drinking or not drinking seems to be more an issue than elsewhere in Europe. It is good to know someone reasonably well before offering a drink, as it could actually be resented by extreme temperance supporters.

CLEANLINESS

Norway generally has little current and tidal stream to carry away any rubbish thrown over the side, and the beautiful waters of the skjærgård would quickly be ruined were it not for the very high level of discipline displayed by local yachtsmen and other users of the waters. They are spotlessly clean, and so are almost all of the harbours and quays, and they should be kept that way. There are large containers for rubbish in almost all harbours, and if one is spending a day or two in an anchorage, it is far better to take your rubbish to the tip at your next harbour than to throw it in the clear waters, where it will hang around accusingly for the rest of your stay. In any case, one is risking prosecution by throwing refuse overboard within the skjærgård.

The use of marine toilets also requires thought and common sense. It should be avoided inside harbours, particularly the smaller ones, and in some it is specifically against the regulations. In any case, the sheer aesthetics of pumping out into the brilliantly clear water should be enough to put most people off the idea. At sea, though – even in fairly confined areas – there is no great problem with pumping out the marine toilet, owing to the relatively small population.

MISCELLANEOUS

Norwegians are very flag conscious, with a flagstaff on almost every country house. It is therefore important to fly the Norwegian courtesy ensign, and to observe proper flag etiquette. The British Blue Ensign is little understood, and often produces awed enquiries as to whether one has sailed all the way from New Zealand. Naval vessels are usually punctilious in their dipping drill.

Bear in mind that a 'mile' to a non-sailing Norwegian is 10 km, so if you are told that a shop is 1½ miles up the road, do not expect it to be a pleasant half-hour stroll!

Calor gas (propane) is more expensive and less common in Norway than in the UK, and you will have difficulty getting your tanks refilled – except in the larger cities. If you are making an extended stay in Norway you may be able to make use of the aluminium 11 kg Norwegian industrial propane bottle, which uses fittings identical to American ones (nearly the same as UK, but with a slightly smaller diameter thread that will not take the UK fitting, although the Norwegian fitting will work satisfactorily on a UK bottle). After purchasing the Norwegian fitting locally you might be able to use the bottle directly, or you can decant the propane into your own bottle. The bottle can be swapped when empty, and returned for 60 per cent of the purchase price (which, although not cheap, is reasonable for an aluminium bottle). An adaptor for Camping Gaz can be obtained in the UK from most Calor distributors. Camping Gaz is more expensive, but can be bought in most large ports.

Mosquitoes and flies can be a problem to those sensitive to them, and they seem to grow to the size of sparrows by 3 o'clock in the morning! Screens, therefore, are highly recommended.

Severe cold can be experienced in summer, particularly on the coast N of Stavanger if it sets in to blow from the N. In the famous hot summer of 1976, MB experienced temperatures in the cabin falling to 10°C by early morning, which implies outside temperatures in the low single figures. This was in late July, but a fortnight or so later, in the same latitudes in Oslofjorden, the crew wore swim suits or less, and the heat ashore was positively baking. It is therefore important to take a wide variety of clothes.

It is worth mentioning that business hours tend to be early, with factories and workshops starting up at 0700, and shops and businesses opening at 0800. Many shops close at 1600, and one will be unlikely to find anything open after 1630 (especially in small villages) except petrol stations and kiosks, which often stay open until 2100, offering limited provisioning.

Small shops with a good supply of basic groceries are likely to be found in any harbour where there are more than a few houses; these small shops come and go frequently depending on their success, and so no systematic attempt has been made in this *Norwegian Cruising Guide* to document them, although they have been mentioned where noted. Water is available free of charge at most quays, except perhaps at an urban fuel quay where one may be expected to buy fuel also. Diesel fuel ('gasolje', relatively cheap without road tax) is widely available because of the large number of small fishing boats active along the coast, and you may find fuel in surprisingly small harbours. If you are really desperate, you will probably be able to find a fisherman who will manage to give you a few litres. Sometimes showers are available at a restaurant, hotel, youth hostel, campsite or even a fish processing plant, so it pays to ask the local residents where you might find them. Washing machines and dryers are becoming more widely available, and these are indicated in the text simply as 'laundry'.

Norwegians are very proud of their 'county', and perhaps also their local region, and so are extremely pleased when visitors show some awareness and knowledge of the names of these regions – hence this information is included in this book.

Norway is a country of seabirds, with several coastal islands internationally known for large colonies: Runde near Ålesund, Røst in Lofoten, Fuglnyken and Bleiksøya in Vesterålen, and Fugløya in Troms. Nordland, especially in Salten N and S of Bodø, is heavily populated with the magnificent *havørn*, the huge sea eagle. You will probably enjoy being able to identify the many new species of seabirds you will see: *Seabirds,* by Peter Harrison, is a fine worldwide reference book (Christopher Helm, ISBN 0-7136-3510-X).

There are numerous areas in the skjærgård which are designated as Nature Reserves, Bird Reserves, Bird Protection Areas and Landscape Protection Areas. In general, in these areas there is to be no disturbance of the terrain or natural condition of plants, birds or mammals, and no camping or unleashed dogs. In some Nature Reserves motorised travel is prohibited, as is the use of sailboards. More significantly for sailors cruising the skjærgård during the nesting season from 15 April to 15 July (1 August in Rogaland), landing ashore or approach within 50 m (or more than 50 m, as specified) of the tideline in some Bird Reserves is prohibited. In Bird Protection Areas travel is permitted, but not disturbance to birds or their environment. Many of the more stringently protected areas are signposted. S of Sognefjorden there are approximately 250 Bird Reserves, mostly small in area and not easy to identify. *Den Norske Los* gives only a sketchy description of each area, suggesting that local county or community offices be consulted for details. These areas are roughly identified on *Båtsport* charts, but not on the main 100 series charts. The national directory of protected areas is referenced to the 1:50 000 land charts using the UTM grid, rather than sea charts using a lat/long grid, thus making it of little use to the sailor. If exploring the skjærgård off the main leads and away from villages, one should be sensitive to this high degree of seabird protection, and ask local advice regarding areas you propose to visit. N of Sognefjorden it is easier to identify these protected areas,

Approaching Kirkefjorden: JA says the crags resemble those in the Yosemite valley, California.

as there are only approximately twenty Bird Reserves (usually fairly large), and they are mentioned in the harbour descriptions.

Several areas in Norway offer superb mountain, rock and glacier climbing, and there are commercial outfits offering instruction and guidance. Åndalsnes, SE of Molde, is internationally known for rock climbing, and there is a climbing outfit active in Lofoten in the summer (see Bibliography). The Jostedal glacier is the longest in continental Europe, and guided tours on the glacier are offered from several centres that are not too distant from harbours in Sognefjorden and Nordfjorden (local tourist offices can advise on details). It is a short easy walk from a yacht to the beautiful snout of the Svartisen glacier in Holandsfjorden, S of Bodø, and guided tours on the glacier are offered from tourist centres farther inland.

The 24 hours of daylight (or at least twilight) available during the summer in high latitudes adds a delightful flexibility to a cruising itinerary. On passage, more miles can be made in a day without sacrificing scenery, navigation is easier, and there is no need to worry about arriving and mooring in an unknown harbour before dark. Passages and expeditions ashore can be scheduled to take best advantage of good weather, and N of the Arctic Circle the most beautiful part of the day is often the 'wee hours'. With no darkness, many find that less sleep is needed, and a long day seems less fatiguing. The table on p. 18 shows how the midnight sun and hours of twilight vary during the cruising season at different latitudes.

One way to increase the time available to cruise in Norway is to leave your yacht there over the winter, spending more than one season enjoying the coast without the need for a long passage there and back each year. This also facilitates early and late season cruising: July is the traditional time for Norwegians (and many others) to take their holiday, so if you are concerned about crowding

Location	Midnight sun	Number of hours without civil/nautical twilight					
		15 May	15 June	15 July	15 Aug	15 Sept	
Göteborg @ 58° N	–	5:30	3:20	4:40	7:00	9:40	Civil
		2:00	–	–	4:50	8:10	Nautical
Bergen @ 60° N	–	4:50	1:40	3:50	6:40	9:30	Civil
		–	–	–	4:00	7:50	Nautical
Trondheim @ 63° N	–	3:00	–	1:00	5:40	9:20	Civil
		–	–	–	1:00	7:20	Nautical
Bodø @ 67° N	5 June – 9 July	–	MS	–	4:00	8:50	Civil
		–			–	6:30	Nautical
Tromsø @ 70° N	21 May – 23 July	–	MS	–		8:20	Civil
		–			–	5:20	Nautical
Longyearbyen @ 78° N	20 April – 20 August		MS			5:30	Civil
						–	Nautical

MS = midnight sun

in S Norway, this can be minimised. The days are longest early in the season, with probably drier weather than during mid-summer, and in April and May there is still enough snow remaining in the high peaks to enhance the scenery. In September and October the leaves are gold and red, the peaks are dusted with new snow, and although the days are getting short the scenery is at its best. Autumn nights seem to be good times to see the *Polarlys,* the Aurora Borealis. In good years, September and October offer splendid cruising, although in a poor year it can be cold, windy and rainy – even snowy. Hauling and winter storage costs, or in-the-water berthing costs, can be modest compared to many areas in the UK or on the Continent; the harbourmaster in a larger harbour, and local sailors in smaller areas, can usually advise regarding commercial, boat club or private contacts. Except in areas fed heavily with fresh water, harbours on the coast W from Kristiansand (S) are ice-free all winter. If you live aboard your yacht, a winter spent in Norway can be a real treat, with winter mountain scenery all around, and skiing right off your yacht. JA spent the winters of 1993–4 and 1994–5 near Narvik, at 68° 21′ N, and loved it. Even above the Arctic Circle the temperature at sea level is typically around +5° C to –5° C, seldom as low as –10° C. Strong winds are more of a problem, so a secure sheltered berth is essential. Electricity (entirely hydro-power) is cheap in Norway, so electric heating makes life simpler. December is indeed a dark month, but on clear days even above the Arctic Circle there are several hours of blue sky with many hours of twilight, and it is more gloomy as a result of cloudiness than from the sun being below the horizon. Although the winter dark can be enjoyable and exciting rather than depressing, it is none the less a real thrill when the sunlight shines in through the portlights for the first time in the spring.

Under Norwegian law, when a foreign yacht enters Norway, the crew is required to report to an immigration official, usually through the local police station, and get passport stamps that permit touring in Norway for three months. There must be an exit from Norway for six months before getting a new three-month stamp. Norway readily permits a longer stay by residents of EEA (European Economic Area) countries, but not by visitors from other countries. Customs regulations require a foreign yacht to check in and to complete forms of 'general declaration' and 'prior notification' (as for a large ship), which will grant the yacht a stay of six months in Norway; upon request, this will likely be extended for overwintering, but sometimes you may be required to post a large VAT guarantee bond. These are the formal requirements, but many foreign yachtsmen cruising in Norway have found when contacting local officials on arrival that passport stamps and customs papers have been waived. Foreign yachts and crews often do make extended visits, or overwinter unofficially and unnoticed, without great difficulty.

Although Norwegian coastal traffic is generally alert and courteous, sometimes ships fail to give way to sailing yachts, or pass disturbingly closely at high speed, in seeming contradiction to the courtesy and high level of seamanship one usually finds. Sometimes this occurs in relatively open waters, where it would not be difficult for the ship to give way or pass with more clearance. This may be caused by two unusual factors, unlikely to be known to a foreign yacht skipper. There are Norwegian Rules for Navigation in Inland Waters that are slightly more restrictive than the International Rules. In the two Norwegian traffic separation zones (Nord-Jæren and Ytre Oslofjorden), vessels under 20 m or sailing must keep clear of engine-driven boats that are following the lead. Furthermore, pleasure boats and open or sailing craft are required to keep clear of larger ships, ferries on route and other commercial vessels when in narrow routes, in crowded or busy leads and in harbour areas. What is considered 'narrow' or 'crowded' is subject to interpretation, and harbour boundaries can extend miles from the inner harbour. What causes the most trouble is that there is a widespread belief that this rule applies to *all* coastal waters; for example, the *KystGuiden* states that, 'In principle, all pleasure craft shall keep clear of commercial traffic', and a popular boating instructional book states even more baldly, 'Pleasure boats must always keep clear of commercial boats', although there is no such suggestion or requirement in the Inland Rules. This unfortunate misunderstanding of correct procedure sometimes causes confusion between even Norwegian yachts and ships as to which vessel is to hold course and which one is to keep clear, and a foreign yacht is even more likely to be an unwitting victim. Awareness of this situation may help foreign yacht skippers avoid unpleasantly close encounters, and to understand what occasionally seems like boorish behaviour on the part of ship captains.

Before May 1995 all the Norwegian coast N and E of 66° 56′ N to 26° 40′ E (except Lofoten W of Henningsvær), and large areas around Oslo, Kristiansand, Lista, Stavanger, Bergen and Trondheim, were 'Restricted Military Areas' under Royal Decrees of 1968 and 1983, and were marked so on the charts; all foreign vessels were required to obtain permission from the Navy before entering, to provide a daily itinerary, to travel only on the most frequented routes, and to stop only at populated harbours (no wild anchorages). Vessels over 50 tonnes required a pilot.

Most yachts were unaware of these requirements, and cruised in happy ignorance; fortunately, they were seldom noticed. There are still a few small military restricted areas (indicated on the latest charts), some of which may not be entered, and some of which may be transited without anchoring, fishing or diving. Special requirements apply to yachts over 50 tonnes, or 24 m in length; details can be obtained from the Oslo government centre at Tel: 47 22 34 90 90.

Norway has a comprehensive transportation system, and it is possible to arrange for a crew change at almost any populated harbour, since even very small villages are served by the coastal boat service (often a 38 knot catamaran). The Hurtigruten ('express route') ships carry passengers and cargo between Bergen and Kirkenes (an expensive 5 day trip), with a northbound and a southbound ship stopping daily in each of the 35 ports along the route. The fastest (and probably least expensive) transportation is by air, using a major airport such as Stavanger, Oslo, Bergen, Bodø or Tromsø. Three publications that give details of scheduled transportation service are listed in the Bibliography.

The Norwegian language is changing, and one will encounter variation in the spelling of place names. Often the same place will have a different spelling on two different charts depending on the date of issue, yet another spelling in *Den Norske Los*, and perhaps still another version in a tourist guidebook. For example, the oldest spelling indicating an 'island' was just 'ø', the next evolution was 'øy', and most recently 'øya' is used. One will often find a village and its parent island having the same name, but sometimes with a slight variation in spelling.

The official place-namers in Oslo have decided to use the definite form for names unless local usage dictates otherwise, and this book attempts to follow that practice. The English and Norwegian languages indicate the definite form of a noun differently, creating a problem in using Norwegian place names in an English book: in English, one would write 'an island' and 'the island', but in Norwegian one would write 'ei øy' and 'øya', indicating the definite form with a word ending rather than a prefixed article. The Norwegian word 'Lofoten', for example, is shown to be definite with the ending 'en', and when a Norwegian reads in English 'the Lofoten' it is as though an English person were reading 'the the Lofoten'. It seems less awkward to write 'sailing to Lofoten', therefore, than 'sailing to the Lofoten'. To confuse things yet more, in earlier days the last letter of the Norwegian alphabet, 'å', was often written as 'aa'. The 'aa' form is still often used in personal and place names, but is replaced by 'å' in general usage. Similarly, the next to last letter, 'ø', was written until recently as 'ö'.

Since the vast majority of Norwegians speak English, many visiting sailors will learn little Norwegian beyond 'Takk' for 'Thank you', but will probably want to be able to pronounce place names. The biggest problem lies with the vowels, especially those exotic-looking extra ones at the end of the alphabet: 'æ', 'ø' and 'å', which (unfortunately) resemble letters used in English although they have quite different sounds. The letter 'æ' sounds much like the 'a' in 'cat'; 'ø' resembles the 'u' in 'mud'; 'å' is somewhere between the 'o' in 'pole' and the 'a' in 'awl'. Some guidance will be given here, but you will still probably find Norwegians mystified when you talk to them about your favourite harbour, and then after showing them where you mean on the chart, you will be amazed to hear how you should have said it or, even worse, that what you hear sounds exactly like what you thought you said. But at least one can avoid the most blatant mistakes, usually caused from speaking Norwegian as though it were English. And even though one's attempts may not be too successful, they will certainly be appreciated. Here are some place names and their English phonetic pronunciation, with stress shown in **bold**:

Stavanger (stah-**vahng**-er)
Molde (mold-**uh**)
Gjøvik (**yuh**-veek)
Kristiansand (**krihst**-yahn-sahn)
Kjøbenhavn (**hyuh**-ben-hahvn)
Norge (**nawr**-guh)
Myrdal (**meer**-dahl)
Ålesund (**awl**-uh-soon)
Lofoten (**loh**-futen)
Sverige (**svay**-ree-uh)
Trondheim (trohn-**hæ**-eem)
Narvik (nahr-**veek**)
Dovrefjell (daw-vruh-**fyel**)
Oslo (**os**-shloh)
Jotunheimen (yoh-**tuhn**-hæ-eem-en)
Tønsberg (**tuhns**-bairg)
Værøy (vær-**uh**-ee)

Note that 'g' is never soft, and is often suppressed. The letter 's' is often slurred: Norsk (nawr-shk). Especially in Nordland, 'd' is often silent, as in Nordfjord (nor-fee-or). This is also often true of a final 't': Tjelsundet (chel-soon).

Several things need to be said about the sailing wind in Norway. Although the waters are sheltered, the scenery splendid and the people very friendly, the winds are not up to the same standard. You will of course occasionally find fine sailing conditions, but you should expect to use the engine much more than is usual in other cruising grounds. The wind is probably more dependable for sailing in S Norway than in the N. In summer fair weather with inland heating, there is a very reliable afternoon breeze blowing 'against the clock' in a band around the SW, S and SE coasts, becoming quite fresh in Oslofjorden by late afternoon. Terrain has a great effect on the wind, both in deflecting its direction and in causing gusting. If one is fortunate, there may be lovely long spinnaker runs zig-zagging in the leads along the coast with the wind always aft – but it seems more often to happen the other way around, with the wind staying right on the nose no matter how one twists and turns. At a certain distance from the shore in the lee of high steep ground there will be strong turbulent gusting, and you will see little whirlwinds and gusts picking spray up off the water in a most surprising manner. One has to motor or motorsail well reefed down in such conditions, or otherwise risk getting flattened. Anchoring in the lee of high steep ground will often be a poor choice, with extremely gusty winds peaking far in excess of the average.

PART 2

From Sognefjorden to the Russian Border

1 Sognefjorden to Kristiansund

Counties: Sogn og Fjordane, Møre og Romsdal

This area has fine coastal scenery, including the famous Hornelen that towers nearly vertically overhead as one sails by. Nordfjorden and Geirangerfjorden are two of Norway's best known scenic fjords, offering access to inland mountains and glaciers. Ålesund is one of Norway's most beautiful towns, and Ona and Grip are famous historic out-island harbours.

CHARTS

Charts 307 and 308 provide the 1:350 000 overview; charts 208 and 209 at 1:150 000 might be a nice luxury: the recommended detailed coverage is provided by charts 25 to 33 at 1:50 000. Nordfjorden is covered by chart 253 at 1:80 000. The following charts at 1:50 000 are recommended as appropriate: 126 for Hjørundfjorden, 127 for Geirangerfjorden, 125 for the fjords E of Stattlandet, and 34 for the fjords SE of Molde. Harbour charts are available for Florø (479), Ålesund (456), Molde (484), and Kristiansund (454).

TIDES AND STREAMS

The greatest spring tides in the area are 1.5–2 m. HW at Ålesund is 15 minutes after Bergen. Tidal streams are moderate except in a few constricted passages, with the direction depending on local topography.

PASSAGE

This area is divided by the notorious headland Stattlandet, one of the few places along the coast where a sheltered 'inside route' is not available. The tidal stream off Stattlandet, although not great by UK standards, tends to make it relatively rough for Norwegian waters. On a reasonable day, the passage is straightforward, but in some conditions of wind and tide it will be uncomfortable and even dangerous. A tunnel is planned to bypass Stattlandet, even for large ships. There is an unmarked but charted 1 m rock *Skjerbøen*, said to be the graveyard of many ships, only 100 m out of the white sector a couple of miles

S of Buholmen Light at the W extremity of Stattlandet.

Another area lacking a good 'inside route' is the Stoplane and Haugesundet Leia section of the coast, NE of Bud (chart 35; 62° 58' N, 7° 00' E); this area is known as Hustadvika and has an evil reputation among Norwegian mariners. The inner channel (*leia*) makes a very interesting exercise in intricate navigation, but only on a fairly settled day; especially just S of Kvitholmen Light, it may seem as though there is no way through, but the way does unfold just in time. Naïvely accepting local advice that it would provide shelter in a westerly Force 6, I (JA) entered at the SW end and soon found myself in a nasty mess, with breakers on all sides and a maze of stakes and rocks to thread between. It was with enormous relief that I exited at the first opportunity to the clear passage 3–4 miles offshore.

A very pretty detour for the 15 miles W of Kristiansund goes under the 23 m bridge at 63° 01' N, 7° 21.5' E (chart 35), circling around Averøya and approaching Kristiansund from the S. There is also a sheltered and quite beautiful intricate inner route just N of Averøya, with two 16 m bridges.

HARBOURS AND ANCHORAGES

Trovåg (SE Ytre Sula)
Chart 24   61° 00' N, 4° 44' E
A small fairly scenic and well sheltered harbour with quays inside a mole, inhabited by the families of five fishermen. There are larger harbours with fuel nearby, Nåra 1.5 miles NxE, and Kolgrov 1.5 WNW.

Kjerringvågen (NW Nesøya)*
Charts 24, 25   61° 04.5' N, 4° 52' E
A wild enclosed cove with good anchorage around a deep central pool; enter either side of the islet near the 3 m and 5 m soundings.

Listraumen (E Risnesøya)*
Chart 251 inset   61° 08.4' N, 5° 12.2' E
Good anchorage in a sheltered location, with an easy entry; some kelp.

Sildevågen (NW Risnesøya)
Chart 251 inset   61° 08.7' N, 5° 10.6' E
A beautiful sheltered anchorage in 3 m sand in a tiny cove S of Risnestraumen; strong stream, probably requiring lines ashore.

Søndre Ospesund (S Ospa)*
Chart 25   61° 12.1' N, 4° 45.8' E
A complex sheltered bay, entered from the W via Djupsundet, turning N just after the 5 m sounding, and continuing E to anchor in the N or NNW parts of the bay.

Bulandet
Chart 25   61° 17.5' N, 4° 37.7' E
A well sheltered scenic harbour at the outer edge of the skerries NW of Sognefjorden, the local 'Venice'. There is a pontoon and quays, historic park and museum, shop, café, fuel, showers, laundry and nice walking paths. After entry via the clear lead from the S, the fuel quay is to port on Nikøyna ('N' on the chart), the café is farther NNW on Jelsa, and the guest harbour is even farther N on Jelsa.

Aldevågen (S Alden)
Chart 25   61° 19' N, 4° 46' E
A small well sheltered harbour, with four inhabitants. The N quay is for the ferry; one can berth alongside a fishing boat, or anchor with a line ashore. There is a nice trail to the mountain-top with good views.

Askvoll
Charts 25, 26, 27   61° 21' N, 5° 05' E
On the mainland E of Atløya. There is a

SOGNEFJORDEN TO KRISTIANSUND 25

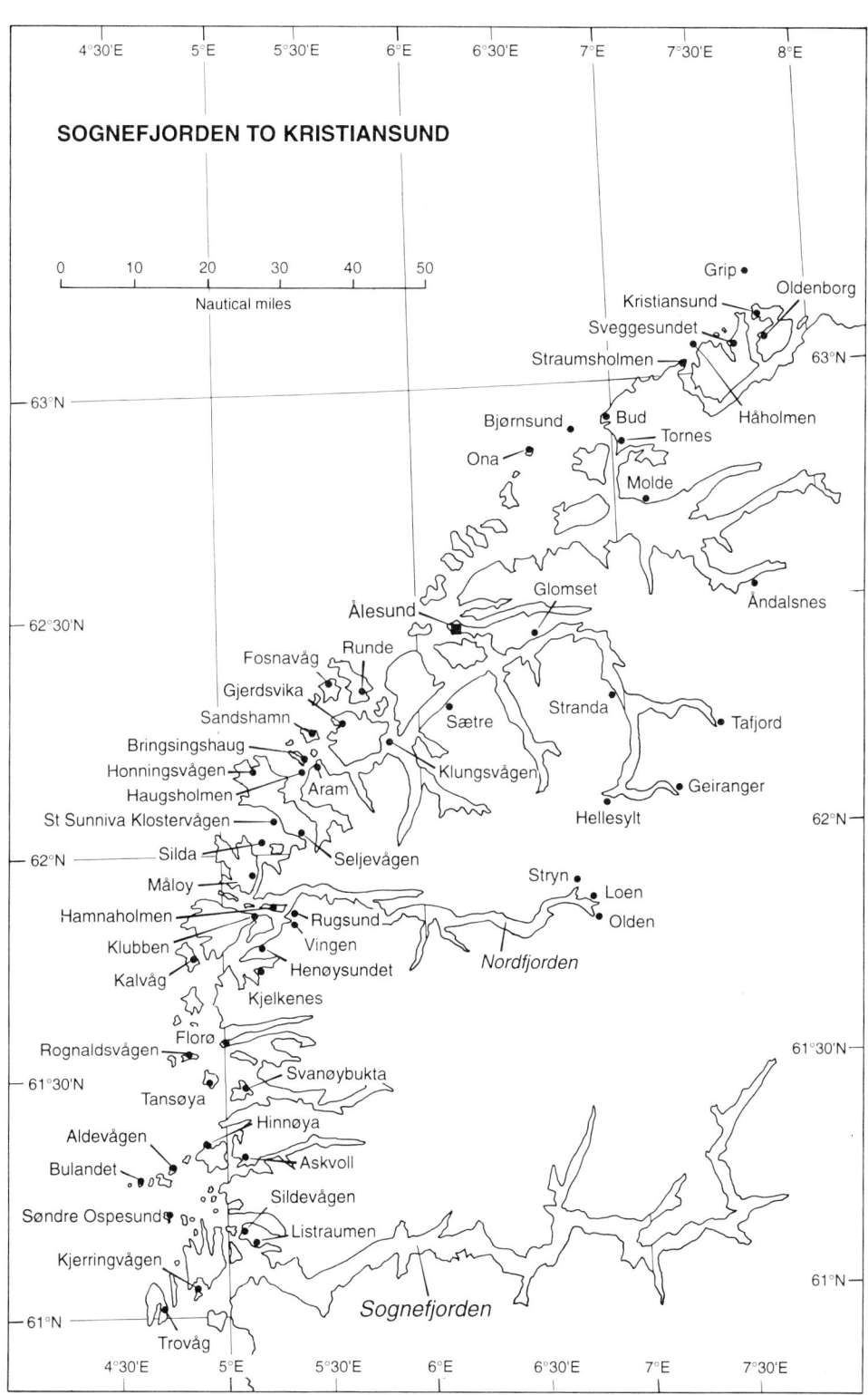

small mole harbour just E of the village, with guest pontoons (moderate charge). The fuel quay is sometimes subject to severe wash from passing boats.

Hinnøya (NW of Atløya)
Charts 25, 26   61° 22′ N, 4° 53′ E
A delightful anchorage with good holding in 10 m, in the pool as charted NE of the attractive island Hinnøya. Herland, 1 mile S, is a well sheltered mole harbour, with a rough quay to starboard on entry, and a pontoon inside a tyre-barrage. Pleasant walks on shore.

Svanøybukta (NE Svanøya)
Charts 26, 27   61° 29.8′ N, 5° 07.8′ E
Svanøybukta is a well sheltered harbour with pontoons, car ferry, PO, shop, boatyard, and museum with a mansion. **Kvalstadbukta (S Svanøya)**, 61° 28.6′ N, 5° 05.7′ E, is a good anchorage in beautiful surroundings, with a small quay, good walks and scenic views. **Slettvik (N Svanøya)**, 61° 30′ N, 5° 06′ E, is a fine natural cove with anchorage and a quay. Svanøya was once a hunting preserve, and is now a Nature Reserve with deer and birds (brochure available from Svanøy Stiftelse avd Kvalstad, N-6965 Svanøybukt, Norway).

Tansøya (SW Askroven)
Charts 26, 27   61° 30′ N, 4° 58′ E
An anchorage in rural surroundings, with good holding and shelter available from all wind directions. The lift-bridge to the E is usually open; the S entrance has an overhead cable 19 m; the NW entrance is unrestricted.

Rognaldsvågen (NW Reksta)
Chart 26   61° 34′ N, 4° 48′ E
A very charming and sheltered harbour facing Kinn. Tie to the workboat; nice scrambles up the hills for fine views. Dinghy, or take the ferry, to Kinn to see the eleventh-century wooden church.

Florø
Charts 26, 27   61° 36′ N, 5° 02′ E
This sizeable town has various quays, and guest pontoons at the E by the 'Rimi 1000' sign. The plethora of lights and marks just to the W can be confusing from a distance, even with the help of the 1:25 000 inset on chart 26; it may help to know that Stabben Light resembles a very large white house, and Græsskjær Light is a typical small sector light. There is a fine maritime museum, showers and laundry. One can give Florø Radio a call to see about visiting their facility.

Kalvåg (SE Frøya)
Chart 28   61° 46′ N, 4° 53′ E
Use a quay, for the pontoon is rolly; this harbour is less sheltered than one would expect from looking at the chart. There is a coastal museum, fuel, showers and laundry.

Kjelkenes (in Midtgulen)
Chart 28   61° 44.5′ N, 5° 09′ E
This small fairly well sheltered cove is near the centre of a triple-armed fjord system SE of Frøysjøen. One can berth at the stone quay NE of the red spar buoy, but the tyres are a problem at low tide. There are attractive views of fjords with snowy mountains and farms along the water's edge.

Henøysundet (in Frøysjøen)*
Chart 28   61° 49′ N, 5° 13′ E
A small sheltered sound S of small Hænøya, with anchorage and lines ashore if desired, and possibly berthing at small quays to the E.

Vingen (in Frøysjøen)
Chart 28   61° 50′ N, 5° 20′ E
Vingen, at the far E of Frøysjøen, is the stopping point to see the hundreds of prehistoric rock carvings. Superb views of Hornelen. One can berth at a tourist-

boat quay, but it is poorly sheltered in W winds.

Hamnaholmen (SW Rugsundøya)
Chart 28 inset   61° 52.6′ N, 5° 13.3′ E
A quiet and pleasant anchorage, just N of the little island, with a small traditional community (a planned tunnel could result in this being a less attractive anchorage).

Klubben / Honskår / Skatestraumen
Chart 28 inset   61° 52.3′ N, 5° 13′ E
A small mole harbour at the NE tip of Bremangerlandet, and base for the nine-hour climb of the spectacular Hornelen (859 m), Norway's highest cliff measured directly above the water. (With less exertion, one can navigate alongside Hornelen, nearly touching the wall; beware sudden blasts in this vicinity, though, if there are high winds aloft, and expect some tidal stream.) If you don't find satisfactory shelter at Klubben, consider a dinghy ride across from Hamnaholmen.

Rugsund
Chart 28   61° 53′ N, 5° 20′ E
A small sixteenth-century mercantile village NE of Rugsundøya, with some restored buildings and no cars – a very pleasant visit. Quays and a pontoon for berthing, showers, and possibly a laundry. Watch the bridge and overhead cable heights, and the currents in the sounds.

Nordfjorden
Charts 253, 308   61° 50′ N, 6° 55′ E
Nordfjorden is one of Norway's major fjords, but seldom visited by yachts. The main attraction is the mountain and glacier scenery concentrated near the major inland tourist areas at the end of the fjord, **Stryn, Loen** and **Olden**. The huge Jostedal glacier is accessible, with guided explorations available, as well as the Jostedalsbreen National Park Centre. There is summer glacier skiing, hiking, trekking on horseback, folk dancing and museums. Olden has several large cruiseship quays; one can call ahead (47 57 87 34 15) to determine availability. There are also quays at Stryn, and at the Hotel Alexander in Loen. It is also possible to anchor on the river deposits at Stryn and Loen.

Måløy (SE Vågsøya)
Charts 28, 29 inset   61° 56′ N, 5° 07′ E
A sizeable town harbour, with pontoons to the SW and many quays. A major fishing boat town, with all major services. Diesel fuel is available 24 hours a day, on production of a credit card. However, it may be difficult to find a berth free from wash from passing traffic.

Silda (E)
Chart 29   62° 01′ N, 5° 12′ E
An especially fine harbour, well sheltered inside a mole, with a pontoon (moderate fee). There is a shop, and showers available in the school. A very nice restaurant sits on stilts ¼ mile S, and there are pleasant walks on the island – a good place to wait for reasonable weather to round Stattlandet. Osmundsvåg, 2 miles S, is an alternative very small well sheltered harbour; follow the stakes exactly, and berth at the outer concrete quay to the N, anchor in the outer harbour, or tie to a fishing boat in the inner harbour. No supplies.

St Sunniva Klostervågen (NW Selje)
Chart 29   62° 03′ N, 5° 18′ E
There is a pontoon (watch depth) and quay in the tight little harbour at the ancient monastery ruins – a very worthwhile stop. The entrance requires care, and the harbour is not suitable for bad weather, when it would be better to berth at the quay at the E of the island

and walk across to the ruins. There is a nice view from the top of the hill, and good walking.

Seljevågen / Seljehamna (E of Selje)
Chart 29   62° 03′ N, 5° 21′ E
A useful supply stop, with convenient shopping. Use the more northern harbour; the quays and pontoons are exposed to the W. Showers and laundry are available, and guided tours of St Sunniva Kloster. The long beach to the N helps to attract tourists to the area.

Honningsvågen / Stattvågen (NW Stattlandet)
Chart 29 inset   62° 12′ N, 5° 12′ E
A sheltered and scenic harbour right at the tip of Stattlandet, surrounded by high cliffs and mountains (which can cause violent gusting in some winds). The entrance looks formidable, but is well marked: it breaks dangerously in strong NW weather. Good anchorage with swinging room, a small quay, and fuel and shopping available.

The cluster of the next five harbours provide stopping points soon after rounding Stattlandet; only Bringsinghaug had a pontoon in 1994. On the S shore of Sandøya is a Nature Reserve, and the area S of Sandøya to Kvamsøya to Åram is a Bird Protection Area.

Haugsholmen (S of Kvamsøya)
Charts 29, 30   62° 10.5′ N, 5° 24′ E

Bringsinghaug (SE Kvamsøya)
Charts 29, 30   62° 12′ N, 5° 25′ E

Åram
Charts 29, 30   62° 12′ N, 5° 30′ E

Sandsham (E Sandøya)
Charts 29, 30   62° 15′ N, 5° 29′ E

Gjerdsvika (W Gurskøya)
Chart 30   62° 15.5′ N, 5° 34′ E

Klungsvågen (N Eikøya)
Chart 30   62° 14.7′ N, 5° 53.4′ E
A small, pretty, sheltered cove, with a mooring marked 'guest'. There is also anchorage in the tiny cove 1 mile ENE, at the S of Selvågholmen, the island SE of Selvåg. The complex channels to the NW, known as the 'Green Passage', make a very interesting route towards Runde, 12 miles NW, with many anchoring and berthing possibilities along the way.

Fosnavåg (N Bergsøya)
Chart 30 inset   62° 21′ N, 5° 38′ E
A large sheltered harbour, with fishing boats at quays for berthing alongside, and a pontoon. Kvalsund*, a mile W, and Kvalsvik*, 3 miles NW, have good anchoring room inside the moles, but most of the pontoons are too shoal for a yacht. Rimøy*, 1 mile NE, has pontoons with sufficient depth. Eggesbønes*, 1 mile SE, is another large harbour, with pontoons behind the northern point.

Runde (E)
Chart 30 inset   62° 24′ N, 5° 40′ E
This steep high island is noted for seabirds, with tens of thousands teeming on the SW cliffs. From the W side of Runde to the NE of Grasøyane to the NE is a Bird Protection Area. The mole harbour offers good shelter, but barely adequate berthing. The pontoons are private and often not made available to visitors. In front of the information office the quay has tyres that can be used with fender-boards. In front of the ladder on the fish processing building, there is a dangerous concrete projection below the surface which one may not see if the tide is up. In front of the white building farther N, there is an overhead projection likely to foul the rigging; an anchor off the beam might solve this problem. Berthing alongside a moored large boat might be a possibility, but

only by agreement with the owner if one is likely to be absent for several hours while hiking to see the birds and views from the high ground. There is a café and shop. There are many paths that traverse the high ground of the island, and little maps are available showing the system. The paths rise gradually on the N of the island, and steeply at the SE. The views are superb. To see the birds best one must descend the very steep trails at the SW (a considerable exertion after already having ascended to the ridge), or bring the yacht close inshore at the SW cliffs in calm conditions.

Sætre (SE Vartdalsfjorden)
Chart 30   62° 18' N, 6° 06' E
This small mole harbour provides a stopping point in the long and beautiful Vartdalsfjorden. Farther en route towards Ålesund, the large mole harbour at **Hareid***, 4.4 miles NNW, offers anchorage and berthing at a quay or pontoon. Liavågen, SE of Hareid, is a narrow desolate cove open to the NE, with heavy commercial docks, light pontoons and anchorage in 18 m.

Geirangerfjorden is one of the most famous and most photographed fjords in Norway, and the journey down its length in a yacht is very impressive and beautiful. And with luck, one might even sail all the way in and all the way back out with a fair wind.

Glomset
Chart 126   62° 28' N, 6° 38' E
On the port hand SE of Ålesund, heading into Geirangerfjorden. A very pleasant and sheltered anchorage with good holding in 14 m in the centre of the pool; watch for sunken rocks on entry. The owner of the brown boathouse in the NE corner can provide a map of the area, and has a dinghy landing area.

Stranda / Hagevika (Geirangerfjorden)
Chart 127   62° 18.1' N, 6° 57.6' E
Just S of the small town of Stranda is a mole harbour with pontoons (moderate fee), and shops nearby. The scar on the other side of the fjord is said to be from an enormous rockfall that some 200 years ago swept forty farms into the fjord, causing a tidal wave.

Hellesylt (Geirangerfjorden)
Chart 127   62° 05' N, 6° 53' E
The small town Hellesylt has a pontoon at a campsite, well fendered and railed (of uncertain availability during the busy season). One can anchor in 15 m. The fjord is open to the NE, so could get rough, in which case Geiranger might offer better shelter. Inbound for Geiranger, it might be worthwhile to detour into Hellesylt for a look around, in order to know the alternatives upon arrival at Geiranger.

Geiranger (Geirangerfjorden)
Chart 127   62° 06' N, 7° 12' E
Sited near the great waterfalls and steepest walls – a major tourist attraction, with extensive facilities. Seaplane sightseeing flights are available. The quay is busy in the season, and probably not available nor desirable for berthing. There is a shelf for anchoring; beware for it shoals extremely suddenly, especially near the stream outflow. Open to the NW, and in strong winds one might have to leave for Hellesylt or stand on up the fjord. The renowned Prekestolen ('pulpit') can be climbed by a path leading up from its SW, and local advice might suggest how to reach the starting point.

Tafjord (SE Tafjorden)
Chart 127   62° 14' N, 7° 25' E
A quiet small-boat harbour in an arm of Geirangerfjorden, with PO, shop, bank and café.

Ålesund

Charts 30, 31, 456   62° 28' N, 6° 09' E

Perhaps the most handsome of Norway's coastal towns. Much of the town was destroyed by fire in about 1920 and rebuilt in a very distinctive 'Jugend' (Art Nouveau) style. Ålesund has an aquarium, a museum and notable churches. Climb the 418 steps to the restaurant at the top of the cliff for great views, including one's own yacht far below. The sounds to the SE (note chart 31 inset) make a pleasant alternative route to Geirangerfjorden or S towards Stattlandet; the bridge at the W end of Ålesund is 17 m. Berthing is primarily at guest pontoons at the S end of the central inner harbour (moderate harbour dues), reached through the entrance between the moles at the N. Showers, toilets and washer/dryer are available, for additional fees. The 1994 opening of a disco adjacent to the guest pontoons has reduced the attractiveness of this berth; the N pontoons will be the least noisy and busy, and one may do even better to berth elsewhere in the inner harbour at a suitable spot where permission can be obtained. Another option is to berth at the Ålesund Seilforening pontoons 1.5 miles ExS, N of Hundsvær and E of Vollsdalsnesset. There are also pontoons available at Gåseide(vika), 2.9 miles ExS from the inner harbour, approached from the N (frequent bus service to the centre, running past the yacht club as well), and also inside the longest mole 4 cables WSW of the inner harbour. At these three alternative berths, one will need to borrow a key to the pontoon access gates. Departing Ålesund N, one passes numerous undistinguished and easy to find small mole harbours situated on the large islands lying to port; these are shown on the chart and described in *Den Norske Los*. In addition, Brattvåg, on chart 33 at 62° 36' N, 6° 27' E,

Ålesund, perhaps Norway's most attractive city. (Photo: George Earle)

which offers sheltered pontoons and all services.

Molde (in Romdalsfjorden)
Charts 33, 34, 484   62° 44′ N, 7° 09′ E
An attractive large town, sited on the N side of beautiful Romdalsfjorden. There is a guest pontoon by the light (moderate fee). Fuel is available a mile or two farther E at the boat-club harbour. Try the laser video disc display in the lobby of the Hotel Alexander for some good glimpses of inland mountain scenery that one won't see from a yacht. Molde has an annual summer jazz festival, attracting internationally renowned musicians.

Åndalsnes
Chart 34   62° 33′ N, 7° 40′ E
Twenty miles SE of Molde, a mountain-climbing and tourist centre in spectacular surroundings, with quays adequate for berthing (small-boat harbour under construction – enquire locally). One can hitchhike or take the train or bus up to the famous Trollstigveien switch-back mountain road and Stigfossen waterfall.

Ona (NE Husøya)
Charts 33, 32   62° 52′ N, 6° 33′ E
A famous and very good example of a well preserved traditional fishing village. Well sheltered quays and a pontoon, small shops, handicrafts and fuel. Follow the leading lights from the SE. **Sandøy**, 2.6 miles SxE, is another well sheltered harbour with a pontoon, but not so picturesque as Ona.

Bjørnsund
Charts 32, 35   62° 53.5′ N, 6° 49′ E
A beautiful and sheltered group of harbours, with many quays for berthing. In 1970 the population was over 700, but then the inhabitants were subsidised to move to the mainland and now there are only summer residents. The three principal islands are Nordre, Midtre and Søre Hammarøya, and the main settlements lie along the sounds between the islands; approach heading towards the sector light Hammarøyskjeret from the NW, SE or SxE.

Bud
Charts 32, 35   62° 54′ N, 6° 54′ E
At the W tip of the mainland peninsula N of the island of Gossa, a mole harbour with a guest pontoon immediately to port upon entry (moderate harbour dues). The small boat harbour to the E is not suitable for yachts. There is a large Second World War fort and museum on the island, a restaurant, and fuel is available. Gossa has a Nature Reserve on the NW side of the island, and Bird Protection Areas on the NW and SE sides. If one is sailing N, Bud is the last harbour before the Hustadvika area mentioned in the Passage section. At **Tornes***, 5.5 miles SE, Nesabukta is an alternative small mole harbour, with pontoons (chart 33).

Straumsholmen (W of Averøya)
Chart 35   63° 00.6′ N, 7° 18.8′ E
A small Scuba diving centre, with instruction, equipment to hire, bottle filling service, and guided diving in the area. There is a quay for berthing, and a restaurant. Approached via the 23 m bridge that is 1.3 miles ENE. There is a Nature Reserve on NW Averøya.

Håholmen (W Averøya)
Chart 35   63° 01.8′ N, 7° 23.8′ E
The home of Ragnar Thorseth, a notable Norwegian adventurer and sailor, author of *Saga Siglar*, which describes his circumnavigation via Greenland, Chicago and Fiji aboard a replica Viking boat. The boat sank off Spain in 1992, and the wreckage is displayed in a museum. Ragnar's wife and children accompanied

him part of the way around the world, and also wintered in Spitsbergen's Kongsfjorden in 1988. Håholmen is a holiday centre, with conference hotel, restaurant with bar, and showers. The facilities, quays and pontoons are on the SE of the tiny island, which is identified on the chart as 'H'. The 1992 edition of *Den Norske Los,* volume 4, features Håholmen as the cover photograph.

Sveggsundet (N Averøya)
Chart 35   63° 06.4′ N, 7° 36′ E
An attractive and sheltered harbour just S of the 16 m bridge, with a pontoon, shop and fuel.

Oldenborg (W Frei)
Chart 35   63° 03.6′ N, 7° 43′ E
An outstation of the Kristiansund Seilforening, with pontoons in an attractive and sheltered cove just a few miles S of the city. There is a fine clubhouse, and no access by road.

Kristiansund
Charts 35, 36, 454   63° 07′ N, 7° 44′ E
'Kristiansund N', not to be confused with 'Kristiansand S', is an attractive small city with a large harbour area in the shape of a cross with the N arm closed. The W and E entrances are under bridges of 32 m and 28 m respectively, and the S entrance is unrestricted. At the W of the open centre of the cross is a guest pontoon for stops shorter than overnight, but off-season one might be able to lie there overnight; the inside of the pontoon is less affected by wash. To port halfway up the N arm of the cross there is a large guest pontoon with moorings for bows-on overnight berthing, and limited berthing alongside (moderate fee). Past this guest pontoon are the Kristiansund Seilforening pontoons, where berthing might be arranged. Next is the very interesting wooden boat workshop, with extensive facilities for owner repair of old wooden boats (contact Sverre Joan Svendsun, museum director), and there are often several large wooden boats berthed at quays – and the possibility of berthing alongside, provided one is always ready to move if necessary. Still farther along are the pontoons of the local boat club, where berthing might be arranged on request. The hardware shop on the waterfront sells nearly everything.

Grip
Chart 36   63° 15′ N, 7° 36′ E
Grip is a small lighthouse island off Kristiansund, famous for its unique historic flavour. The entry to the fine mole harbour, from the SE, is shown on the chart.

2 Kristiansund to Rørvik

Counties: Møre og Romsdal, Sør-Trøndelag and Nord-Trøndelag

Although parts of this area are quite scenic, most yachts are likely to be in transit to Lofoten, Nordkapp or Svalbard. There are many possibilities for routes more interesting than just following the main lead, as suggested below in the Passage section.

CHARTS

Charts 308 and 309 provide the 1:350 000 overview; chart 218 at 1:100 000 might be a nice luxury: the recommended detailed coverage at 1:50 000 is provided for the more inshore route along the coast by charts 36 to 38, 43 to 46 and 48. For exploring the outer islands of Smøla, Hitra and Frøya, one will need charts 40 and 41, and perhaps chart 42. To sail to Trondheim, charts 39 and 130 are recommended, although chart 309 is probably sufficient, and chart 131 for the inner reaches of Trondheimsfjorden. The following charts at 1:50 000 are for areas less likely to be visited: chart 47 for Namsenfjorden; charts 128 and 129 for Sundalsfjorden and Halsafjorden. Harbour charts are available for Kristiansund (454), and Trondheim (458).

TIDES AND STREAMS

The greatest spring tides in the area are 2–2.5 m. HW at Kristiansund is 25 minutes after Bergen, and at Rørvik it is 55 minutes after Bergen. Tidal streams are moderate except in a few constricted passages, with the direction depending on local topography.

PASSAGE

A beautiful detour bypassing the relatively less scenic Trondheimsleia E of Kristiansund is via Årsundfjorden, Auresundet, Torsetsundet, and Dromnessundet, and back on to the main route in Trondheimsleia. Departing Kristiansund to the S and then turning E, one must pass under an 18 m bridge. Without chart 129, between charts 308 and 37 one will have the unusual experience of sailing in Norwegian waters with no chart coverage except perhaps a tourist road map, but there are no hidden dangers and the way is clear. There is a bridge 16 m in Torsetsundet at 63° 19′ N, 8° 37′ E, with shoal depth except under the small light on the bridge (chart 37); there are several anchorages and quays along the route. Alternatives for an earlier exit from the detour are Soleimsundet with 18 m bridge clearance (note a new overhead cable 21 m, and 28 m cable lowered to 21 m, in the S part of the sound), and Imarsundet.

The coasts of the large islands of Smøla, Hitra and Frøya offer an unusual cruising ground, another alternative to the Trondheimsleia. Don't be put off by the first glance at the chart; it is nearly covered in blue, indicating depths less than 10 m and seemingly nothing but a maze of skerries that no sane sailor would go anywhere near. There are innumerable well marked channels easily navigated in reasonable weather, and many secure harbours, often with tiny fishing villages existing in an edge-of-the-world atmosphere. The fishing seems to be especially good in this area, and the local residents may be able to tell you where to see old whale bones. The harbour at Halten lighthouse is the outermost point in this area.

Farther N, at Buholmråsa Light, 64° 24′ N, 10° 27′ E outside Sætervika, one has a choice between the rather dull direct route 'outside' and a complex interesting route 'inside'. The inside route has several variations marked on the chart, winding among many small islands and skerries with anchoring possibilities; *Den Norske Los* includes large scale chartlets of this area, which are useful although not necessary.

HARBOURS AND ANCHORAGES

For **Kristiansund** (chart 35) see the end of the previous section.

Ringholmen (S)
Chart 36   63° 12.2′ N, 7° 57.6′ E
In about 1990, an air traffic controller called Øyvind Jünge made a bid to purchase an old fishing centre on a small island 8 miles NE of Kristiansund, and much to his astonishment his bid was accepted. He and his wife have transformed this centre into a unique and unusual restaurant serving superb cuisine (at reasonable prices) in a most intriguing and pleasing setting. Several new cottages have also been added. There is a pontoon for overnight berthing, quite well sheltered for ordinary summer weather. There are additional pontoons in the lagoon to the N, with just enough depth to be usable with sufficient tide and local pilotage. Ringholmen (unnamed on recent charts) is the small island with the varde 1.5 cables SxW of Hammersund Light; the varde is incorporated into the roof structure of the large building. One may approach from the N from Ytrefjorden, or in settled weather from the SW through the leads as charted. If anchoring across from the pontoon, beware the charted cable. Øyvind can also advise about cruising areas nearby.

Bårdsetøya (in Skålvikfjorden)
Chart 128   63° 06.5′ N, 8° 16.5′ E
The likelihood of balmy inland weather makes this a favourite weekend rendezvous with sailors from Kristiansund. At the SE side of the island Bårdsetøya there are several pontoons, a barbecue, children's play area, and many berries in season. If one is on this 'inside route', note that there are especially good anchoring possibilities near Valsøya, 7 miles ENE, around 63° 09′ N, 8° 33′ E.

Mjosund*
Chart 37   63° 13.5′ N, 8° 30.4′ E
A large pontoon system in attractive surroundings, well sheltered. The approach from Aursundet is via a tiny lead with the sounding 2.5 m.

Eidestranda / Nordre Eidsbukta
Chart 37   63° 18.2′ N, 8° 32.3′ E
An attractive sheltered harbour with moderately priced marina pontoons, showers, shop and fuel. Enter from N, E of Eidsholmen. Note the 16 m bridge 2 miles ENE, with shoaling except under the small light on the bridge that marks the channel. Note also the 15 m bridge

KRISTIANSUND TO RØRVIK

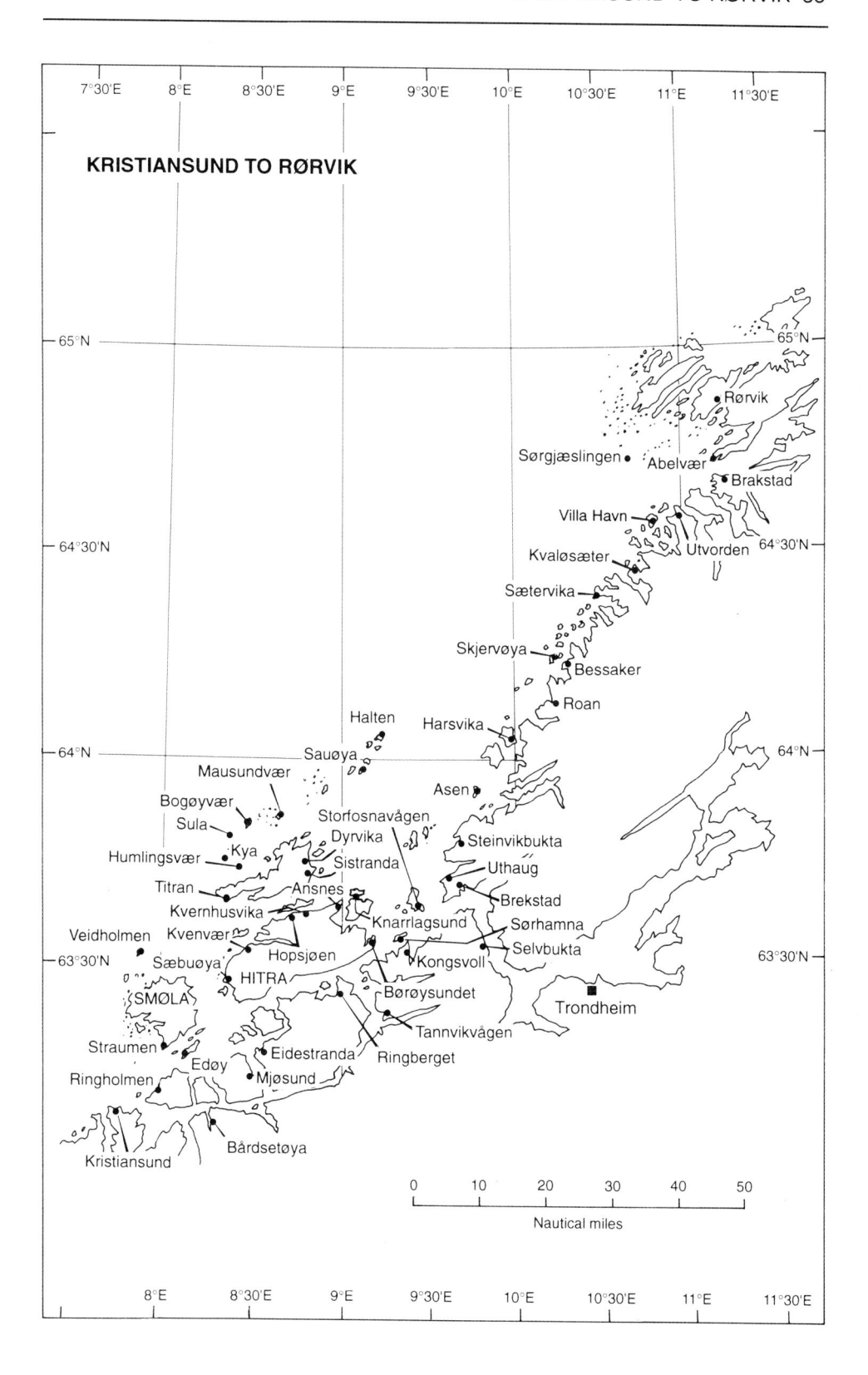

2.5 miles NW at Akvik, should one be inclined towards that route.

Edøy (SW Edøya)
Chart 37, 40   63° 17′ N, 8° 08′ E
The old church is the site of an unusual outdoor Viking saga that is presented each summer. The quay inside the mole is rather rolly from passing boats, and makes a better day stop than an overnight one. Ringholmen is only a few miles SW, offering a more comfortable overnight berth.

Straumen (S Smøla)
Chart 40 inset   63° 20′ N, 8° 05′ E
A very well sheltered harbour with several hundred inhabitants, with a pontoon, quays, shops, PO, bank, doctor and fuel. The SW side of Smøla is a General Animal Protection Area.

Veidholmen (NW of Smøla)
Chart 40 inset   63° 31.2′ N, 7° 57.5′ E
A very well sheltered harbour, with quays, shops, PO, bank and fuel. Veidholmen is at the end of an impressive island-hopping road that makes an interesting walk; frequent bus service can bring one back, or even enable a day trip to be made from Kristiansund.

Titran / Innervågen (SW Frøya)
Chart 41   63° 40′ N, 8° 19′ E
A sheltered harbour with quays, shops and fuel; the main harbour is S of the church. A guide is available for the Second World War fort. There is a monument that is a memorial to the 140 fishermen lost on the night of 13/14 October 1899 – 100 of them from Titran alone, which then had a population of around 600. One may possibly be met by schoolmaster Lasse Skauge, who often befriends visiting yachts.

Sæbuøya / Rørøya (W of Hitra)
Chart 37   63° 30′ N, 8° 16.3′ E
The sound between these two islands offers several sheltered anchoring places, and one especially recommended is in the mouth of the first cove to the W after entry from the S, between the two small quays. There are several quays where one can berth, with permission, and an old shop. *Note that the charted overhead cables 14 and 16 m just N are now 11 m.*

Kvenvær (W Hitra)
Chart 37   63° 32′ N, 8° 23.5′ E
In the lead between Hitra and Helsøya, a sheltered mole fishing harbour with showers, fuel, restaurant, bank, shop and PO. *Note that the overhead cable 2 miles SW charted as 19 m is now 18 m.*

Hopsjøen (N Hitra)
Charts 37, 41   63° 37.5′ N, 8° 43′ E
In the narrow lead between Hitra and Dolmøya, an attractive sheltered harbour with pontoons, hotel and restaurant – but no fuel; the historic old shop is also a museum. Hopsjøen once operated an enforced monopoly controlling all trade between Lofoten and Bergen. There is a 16 m bridge 1.5 miles to the E, and 5 cables E of the bridge lies the shipbuilding centre Kvernhusvika, with a pontoon, and fuel.

Kvernhusvika (N Hitra)
Chart 41   63° 38.2′ N, 8° 48′ E
Also in the narrow lead between Hitra and Dolmøya, 5 cables E of the 16 m bridge. There are quays and pontoon, a hotel, café and fuel.

Knarrlagsund (S Uljvøya)
Charts 38, 41   63° 40′ N, 9° 05′ E
In the narrow lead between Fjellværøya and Ulvøya, W of a 17 m bridge. There are pontoons at both sides, public to the N and private to the S, with a shop and fuel.

Ansnes (NE Hitra)
Charts 38, 41   63° 38.3′ N, 9° 00′ E
A mole harbour, with shops, and fuel; just SW of a 16 m bridge.

Børøysundet (SE Hitra)
Chart 38 63° 34.3′ N, 9° 12′ E
The mole nearly closing the N end of this sound makes a good sheltered harbour with several pontoons and quays, just N of an industrialised centre.

Kya (N of Frøya)
Chart 41 63° 46.5′ N, 8° 19′ E
An interesting abandoned mole harbour, entered from the SE, probably untenable in strong southerly winds.

Humlingsvær (N of Frøya)
Chart 41 63° 45.4′ N, 8° 25′ E
A sheltered abandoned harbour. Enter holding far to port; anchor, with lines ashore.

Sula (N of Frøya)
Chart 41 63° 50.7′ N, 8° 27.7′ E
One of the larger harbours in this area, Sula is also a tourist centre, with around 300 residents. There are guided tours describing the local culture and which go up to the lighthouse that offers fine views. There is a large pontoon, quays, PO, bank, shop and fuel. Enter from the N; the channel is well marked.

Bogøyvær (N of Frøya)
Chart 41 63° 52.3′ N, 8° 33.2′ E
A sheltered harbour with a few dozen inhabitants, and a pontoon, PO, shop and fuel. Old whale bones are to be found. Enter from the N.

Mausundvær (N of Frøya)
Chart 41 63° 52.2′ N, 8° 40′ E
A bustling fishing harbour, with a quieter smaller harbour 1 cable SW, and pontoons 4½ cables NW×W (at the 17 m sounding). Bridge 13.5 m to SW. Repairs, PO, shop and fuel.

Sistranda (E Frøya)
Chart 41 63° 44′ N, 8° 50′ E
The waters just E of Frøya are somewhat sheltered by Inntian and Uttian, and in the right weather can be a pleasant sailing area. The small mole harbour has pontoons and quays, PO, museum, bank, hotel, dentist and fuel.

Dyrvika (E Frøya)
Chart 41 63° 46′ N, 8° 49′ E
A small mole harbour with quays and anchorage, just S of a 16 m bridge.

Sauøya (NE of Frøya)
Chart 42 64° 00′ N, 9° 11′ E
An isolated, sheltered fishing harbour (population 6) with a handsome church. There are small quays; severe kelp may prevent anchoring. There is a shop, showers, and fuel. Approach from N or SE. The skerries between Mausundvær and Halten are Nature and Animal Protection Reserves.

Halten
Charts 42, 44 64° 10.5′ N, 9° 24′ E
The most northerly of the islands stretching out from Frøya, a small 'outpost' island community at the Halten lighthouse, with anchorage sheltered by a mole, quays, and possibly fuel. Enter from the SE.

Ringberget (SE of Hitra)
Chart 38 63° 27′ N, 9° 00′ E
This harbour is not particularly scenic, but makes a useful passage stopover. There is a large concrete fish-factory pontoon for berthing, in the E bay. Somewhat exposed to the SW. There is also good anchorage to the W off Magerøya, a state recreation area.

Tannvikvågen (Hemnefjorden)
Chart 38 63° 23′ N, 9° 14′ E
An attractive anchorage just short of the overhead cable. Pleasant walks by the lakes NE.

Sørhamna (S Sørleksa)
Chart 38 63° 34′ N, 9° 20′ E
A tiny well sheltered and very attractive mole harbour, E of Hitra, quiet and

peaceful. The entrance is well hidden till one is very close. The first quay is for the ferry, so one should use the second quay, or possibly the quay to starboard of the ferry quay, or tie to a fishing boat. The pontoons are too small for a yacht.

Kongsvoll (SE of Sørleksa)
Chart 38   63° 33.2′ N, 9° 24.5′ E
Marina pontoons are available for an overnight stay in this pleasant sheltered cove (moderate fee). Showers, laundry and fuel available.

Storfosnavågen (S Storfosna)
Charts 38, 43   63° 39′ N, 9° 24′ E
An attractive bay with excellent anchorage, and sheltered guest pontoons near the ferry quay at the N. Note that Kråkvågøya 2 miles W is a prohibited military area, and that Tarva/Husøya to the N is a firing range, with activity announced on Ch 16. The area between Storfosna and Kråkvågøya is a Bird Protection Area. Note that Kråkvågøya, 2 miles W, is a prohibited military area, and that Tarva/Husøya to the N is a firing range, with activity announced on Ch 16. The area between Storfosna and Kråkvågøya is a Bird Protection Area.

Selvbukta (NW Trondheimsfjorden)
Charts 39, 43   63° 37′ N, 9° 44′ E
A pretty bay, with good anchorage as charted.

Brekstad
Chart 43   63° 41′ N, 9° 40′ E
A mole harbour just N of Trondheimsfjorden, with guest pontoons (unprotected from ferry wash and E winds). Shopping, fuel, laundry, and showers available. One can give Ørlandet Radio a call to ask about a visit to their nearby facility. **Austrått**, 2 miles ENE, is an attractive mole harbour with a guest pontoon, showers, and fuel; one can tour an attractive historic manor house, and an impressive WWII battleship turret emplaced as coastal artillery.

Trondheim
Charts 39, 130, 458
63° 26′ N, 10° 22.5′ E
Norway's attractive third largest city, once the capital, offers cathedrals, churches, palaces, and several museums, including an unusual and attractive museum of classical music. There are several berthing possibilities: one of the best is in Kanal Havna, surprisingly quiet and convenient to the centre of the city. Enter between the W-most moles at the position given above, heading SE, to pass under the Skansen Railway Lift Bridge, which monitors VHF Ch 74 most hours and whose VHF aerial provides extended coverage. The canal is 5 cables long and ½ a cable wide, with many private quays that are usually available with permission. There are also several private pontoons, so, if space is available and one is able to borrow a gate key, these are another possibility. The other option is the guest pontoon to starboard inside the Nidelva Bridge, in the Nidelva river at the junction with the E end of the canal; the Nidelva Bridge will open by arrangement at all hours except traffic rush hours, but the arrangement must be made during working hours 0800–1500 via the harbourmaster (Ch 14) or via the Skansen Bridge operator. The Port Public Guest House is very near these guest pontoons, with showers and washer/dryer; the key is available for a visitor at any berth, from the nearby Royal Garden Hotel. There is another small-boat harbour with guest pontoons W of the Skansen Bridge, but it is poorly sheltered and less convenient to the city centre. Located at this harbour

is the clubhouse of the Trondheim Seilforening (yacht club), whose pontoon is central in the canal, with kitchen facilities and a washer/dryer, and where visitors are welcome. Contact the helpful harbourmaster (Ch 14) to arrange for fuel delivery via barge.

Uthaug (Bjungfjorden)
Chart 43   63° 44′ N, 9° 35′ E
A large mole harbour with many quays and anchoring room; laundry. There are Bird Protection Areas SW and E of Uthaug.

Steinvikbukta (Valsfjorden)*
Chart 43   63° 49′ N, 9° 39′ E
A useful passage anchorage; there are three additional anchorages charted nearby NE.

Asen / Vågsøya (E of Asenleia)*
Charts 43, 44   63° 56.4′ N, 9° 46.1′ E
A sheltered anchorage with beaches, charted 2 m.

Harsvika / Stokksund (SE Stokkøya)
Chart 44   64° 03′ N, 10° 01′ E
In an interesting and pretty area, Harsvika has a quay with a fuel pump by the grocery shop, with reasonable berthing alongside. The small mole harbour 7 cables SW offers more shelter, with berthing alongside a moored fishing boat. **Stokksund,** 1 mile SE, has pontoons near the yacht clubhouse in Kuringvågen, the small circular cove at 64° 02.4′ N, 10° 03.8′ E (not named on the chart), with a shop, fuel, PO and bank; enter the cove heading S, E of the small island, to avoid a shoal SW of the island.

Roan (NE Bergfjorden)*
Chart 44   64° 11′ N, 10° 13′ E
A sheltered mole harbour with pontoons, PO, bank and medical centre.

Bessaker
Chart 45   64° 15′ N, 10° 19′ E
A fairly well sheltered cove SE of Børøya, with quays and moored fishing boats, a shop and laundry. There are several anchorages charted nearby. Good walking area.

Skjervøya (NE)
Chart 45   64° 18′ N, 10° 18′ E
One can berth at a well sheltered quay or tie to a fishing boat in the attractive sound between Ytre and Indre Skjervøya.

Sætervika / Sætervågen
Chart 45   64° 24′ N, 10° 29′ E
A scenic mole harbour at the SW tip of a large mainland peninsula. There is a quay just to starboard after entry, a fuelling quay farther in, and a pontoon in the centre of the harbour. A short walk to the top of the rocky hill, or towards the lighthouse, provides fine views. Vingsand, a sheltered mole harbour with pontoons, shop and fuel, 3 miles SxW, and Sandvikberget, a large mole harbour 5 miles SxW, are alternative harbours (photo p. 40).

Kvaløsæter
Chart 46   64° 28.5′ N, 10° 42′ E
A small mole harbour on the 'inside route', a pretty spot. Berth alongside a fishing boat or use an available mooring. Note that the area SW of Heiskjær Light (64° 27′ N, 10° 31′ E) may break dangerously when a swell is running.

Villa Havn (E Villa)
Chart 46   64° 33′ N, 10° 42′ E
A lovely small harbour on the 'inside route', with good swinging room for anchoring. There are two quays in the interesting little sound. This is the site of the oldest coal-burning lighthouse in Norway, now disused. There are pleasant walks on the island.

Sætervika: a typical mole harbour in attractive scenery. (Photo: George Earle)

Utvorden*
Chart 46   64° 35.65′ N, 10° 57′ E
A small mole harbour at the NE end of the 'inside route', with fuel available.

Brakstad (NW Jøen)
Chart 47   64° 40′ N, 11° 12′ E
There is an experienced sailmaker in the village of Brakstad, should one need repairs. Good anchorage in the cove with the 10 m sounding, at the position given above, ¼ mile W of the village. Supplies are available at Fosnes, 1½ miles away.

Abelvær (SW Kalvøya)
Charts 47, 48   64° 44′ N, 11° 11′ E
At the SW tip of a long string of islands from the mainland, between Lille and Store Kalvøya. A sheltered town quay is available. Some yachts have found this an attractive stop although others have not.

Sørgjæslingan
Charts 46, 49   64° 44.5′ N, 10° 46.7′ E
A very interesting out-island historic harbour, once important in cod fishing and with 6000 residents – now there are only 20 inhabitants. The old PO and shop, known as 'Woxengs samlinger', is open under the aegis of the Rørvik museum. Enter as charted to the ferry quay area N of Heunværet Light, and then either seek local advice or use the 1:5000 chartlet in *Den Norske Los* for pilotage into the quieter little bays formed by moles to the W. One could ask locally about the notorious grounding (in 1962) not too far away of a Hurtigruten ship, from an unexplained gross navigational error.

Rørvik (SE Vikna/Vikten)
Chart 48   64° 52′ N, 11° 14′ E
A few cables N of the high bridge, turn NW into the substantial mole harbour. Berth at the ends of the pontoons (modest fee). A laundry and showers are available at the clubhouse. There is an interesting museum, with an enthusiastic director who can describe interesting areas nearby. There are Nature and Bird Reserves at Tjørnsøyvågen, SW Vikna, Borgann and Frelsøya, NW of Vikna, and Kvaløya and Raudøya, N of Vikna.

3 Rørvik to Bodø

Counties: Nord-Trøndelag and Nordland;
Regions: Helgeland, Sør-Salten

The most northerly and southerly parts of this area are likely to be used in transit by yachts bound for Lofoten, Nordkapp or Svalbard. The central part, near the Arctic Circle, is especially attractive and worth spending more time in; one can visit the Svartisen glacier in Holandsfjorden, the monolithic offshore islands of Lovund and Træna, the outlying lighthouse harbours of Sklinna, Bremsteinen and Myken, as well as other exceptionally fine anchorages and harbours as described below.

CHARTS

Charts 310 and 311 provide the 1:350 000 overview; chart 319 at 1:200 000 might be a nice luxury: the recommended detailed coverage is provided by charts 48, 51 and 53 to 59, and charts 61 to 65 at 1:50 000. The following charts are recommended should one wish to sail unusually far inland: chart 60 at 1:50 000 for Mo i Rana and inner Ranafjorden, chart 224 at 1:100 000 for the inland area N of 65°, and chart 227 at 1:100 000 for the area E and NE of Bodø. If one wishes to sail W of Rørvik and Leka, charts 49 and 50 (needed for Sklinna) at 1:50 000 are recommended. Harbour charts are available for Brønnøysund (488), Mo i Rana (463), and Bodø (476).

TIDES AND STREAMS

The greatest spring tides in the area are 2.5–2.8 m. HW at Rørvik is 55 minutes after Bergen, and at Bodø it is 1 hour 45 minutes after Bergen.

Tidal streams are generally moderate, flowing N with the flood, but the stream reaches 2–3 knots at Brønnøysund, and 4–5 knots off Strømøya (5 miles N of Brønnøysund).

An exceptional tidal stream is Saltstraumen near Bodø, which flows at 8 knots according to *Den Norske Los*, and at 28 knots according to the Nordland tourist brochure. It is an impressive sight at full flow when viewed from the shore or the bridge overhead, with many whirlpools and rips, and an occasional fisherman riding through nonchalantly in a small outboard. *Den Norske Los* gives the N-going stream as beginning $1^1/_2$ hours after HW Bodø.

PASSAGE

Note that these perches were reported missing in 1994: Stabben, chart 63, 66° 44.7′ N, 12° 44.5′ E; Vågsholmtaren, chart 61, 66° 32.5′ N, 12° 12.3′ E; Seiholmflua, chart 61, 66° 36′ N, 12° 31′ E; and Kirkgrunnen, chart 65, 67° 15.6′ N, 14° 14′ E.

42 FROM SOGNEFJORDEN TO THE RUSSIAN BORDER

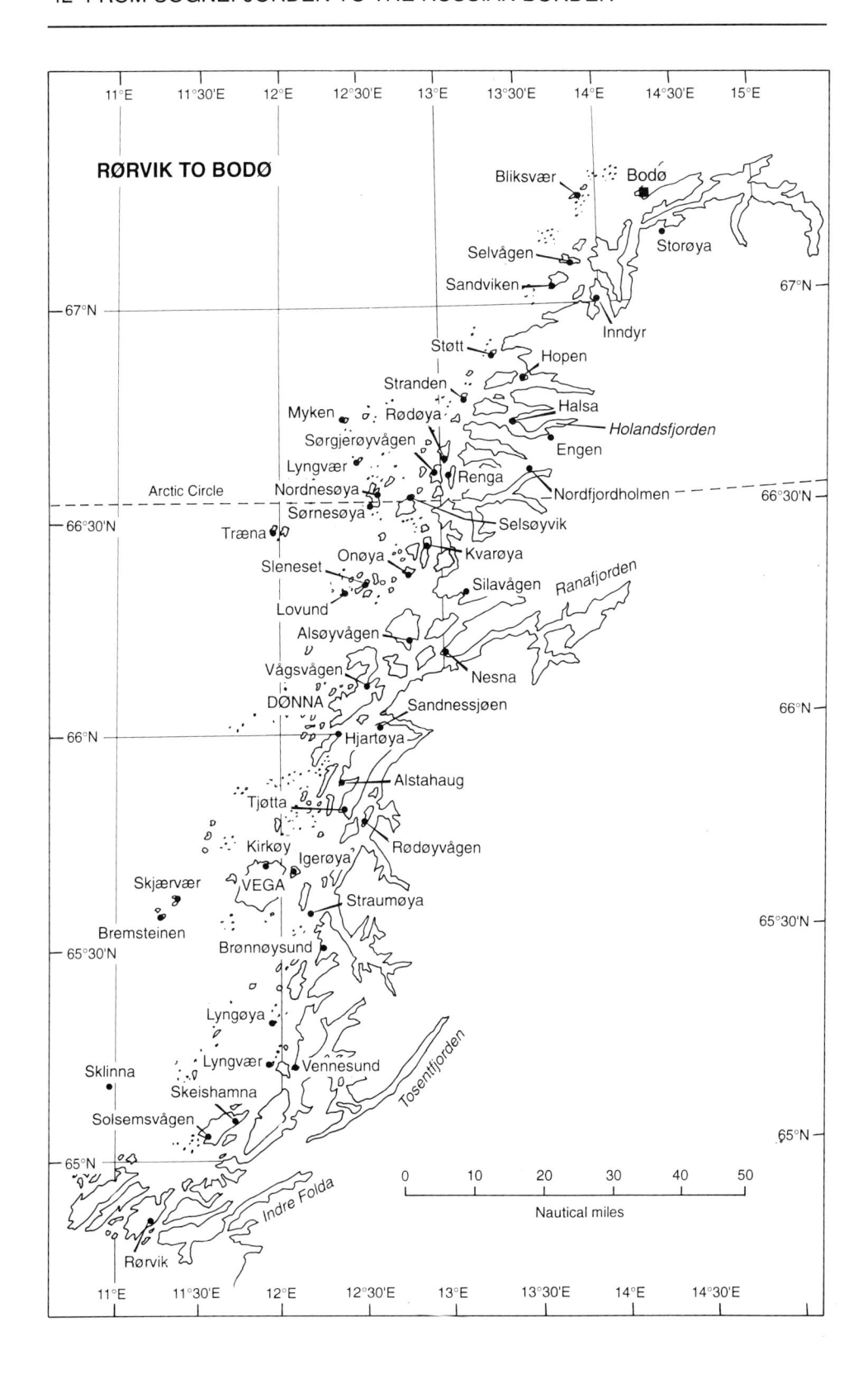

RØRVIK TO BODØ

HARBOURS AND ANCHORAGES

Rørvik (chart 48) see the end of the previous section.

Solsemsvågen (S Leka)
Chart 51   65° 03' N, 11° 33' E
A good anchorage except in S winds. It is an interesting expedition to visit Solsemhola, the ancient (although rather modest) cave drawings nearby: walk about ½ mile up the road to a small sign to starboard near a food kiosk, ask at the house adjacent for the key to the electric light in the cave and sign the guest register (a very small donation is requested), then walk for around 20 minutes up an attractive rocky path ending at the electric poles. The director of the museum in Rørvik can provide more information about the drawings. There is a Nature Reserve and Bird Protection Area on the N side of Leka.

Skeishamna (E Leka)
Chart 51   65° 05' N, 11° 44' E
There are pontoons in a small mole harbour with a well marked entry. Leka is formed of an unusual type of rock, which was brought to the surface by the collision of the continental plates; this mantle rock is found only here, and in Cyprus and New Zealand. The Leka church has a notable sixteenth-century Dutch carved altarpiece. Each July, a week-long festival culminates in an outdoor Viking drama. The island provides fine walking, and is of great geological, archaeological and biological interest.

Sklinna*
Chart 50   65° 12' N, 11° 00' E
An interesting stop outside the usual cruising routes, a minimal outpost island community (population two) at the Sklinna lighthouse, with anchorage and quays. A mole at the NE closes the harbour, which is entered from the SW.

Vennesund*
Chart 51   65° 13' N, 11° 02.5' E
A sheltered small-boat harbour, with laundry, showers, kiosk and café. Enter via the buoyed channel from the S. Nearby is the historic cave Olavskilden.

Lyngvær / Vågøen
Chart 51   65° 15.4' N, 11° 58.8' E
An exceptionally fine wild anchorage with good shelter and holding. Anchor as charted along Bukholmen, or a bit farther NE along Steinøen.

Lyngøya / Sandværøya
Chart 53   65° 20.6' N, 11° 59.4' E
A secure and scenic anchorage, with nice views of Torghatten. Use two anchors, or a line ashore, either W or E of Lyngøya.

Brønnøysund
Chart 53 inset, 488   65° 28' N, 12° 12' E
An attractive large town straddling many islands, with guest pontoons (moderate charge) inside a mole N of the fuel quay. The small-boat harbour just S is not suitable for yachts. There is an excellent serve-yourself lunch available at the Yacht Harbour building. A walk up to the high bridge provides a splendid view. Torghatten, 5 miles SW, is a well known landmark because of the hole piercing the mountain; one can climb up to the hole, from the anchorage Moihavn charted NE of the peak (S of the 10 m cable), or better, at the head of Vestvågen N of the peak.

Straumøya
Charts 53, 55   65° 33.3' N, 12° 14.6' E
Said to be the most popular out-harbour in the area, and likely to be crowded at weekends (20 boats!). Enter heading NE, just E of Strømøerne Light, to the pontoon at the charted 11 m anchor symbol. Note the two additional anchorages charted just NE, entered via the next lead to the E.

Igerøya (E)*
Chart 55   65° 40.5' N, 12° 07.9' E
A new mole extending SW from Årboholmen encloses guest pontoons. There is a shop, and bicycle rental. There is a local history museum 4 miles W at Gladstad church (Vega). At the NE side of Ylvingen, a couple of miles SE, are bunkers and cannons from the Second World War.

Kirkøy (N Vega)*
Charts 54, 55   65° 42.5' N, 11° 54.4' E
A pleasant and sheltered harbour with a quay for berthing, shop and fuel. There is a Nature Reserve and Bird Protection Area at Holandsosen, near Kirkøy. There is also anchorage inside **Havnøya** at the SW corner of Vega, not far from the recently discovered ancient ruins a couple of miles inland NE. As from 1995, a new small-boat harbour is being developed at **Sjøvika**, SW Vega, at 65° 36' N, 11° 52' E. Vistenfjorden, to the E of Vega, is said to be very scenic.

Bremsteinen*
Chart 54   65° 37.4' N, 11° 23' E
Outside the usual cruising routes, a small 'outpost' island community at the Bremsteinen lighthouse, with a small mole, anchorage and quays. Enter from the SW or NE. Nearby is Europe's largest colony of black guillemots.

Skjærvær*
Chart 54   65° 46.5' N, 11° 35' E
Another small 'outpost' island community outside the usual cruising routes, with a mole to the SE, anchorage and quays. Enter as charted through the widespread skerries.

Rødøyvågen (W Rødøya)
Chart 55   65° 48' N, 12° 33' E
The anchorage in the attractive three-armed bay on this red island may be obstructed by fish farms, in which case berth at the quay or alongside a fishing boat. An ancient rock carving shows the world's first recorded skier. Note that the Rødøya 50 miles to the N is the better known Rødøya.

Tjøtta (SE)
Chart 55   65° 49' N, 12° 26' E
A mooring in this small mole harbour may be used as a passage stopover. Fuel, showers, shop and PO.

Alstahaug (SW Alsten)
Charts 56, 57   65° 53.4' N, 12° 23.6' E
This deep pretty little bay at the tip of Alsten is the site of poet Peter Dass's home and a lovely little church (see the text under the entry for 'Røst' for the origin of the altar-board), and makes a very pleasant stop. There is good holding ground mixed with less good, and the S bay is preferable; strong SW winds would probably be uncomfortable.

Hjartøya (S of Donna)
Chart 57   66° 00' N, 12° 24' E
A superbly sheltered and scenic wild anchorage, with an eagle nesting in a tree, abandoned fruit trees and Viking burial sites.

Sandnessjøen (NW Alsten)
Chart 57   66° 01' N, 12° 38' E
Sandnessjøen is a busy port and a pleasant town. Alsten is capped by the spires of the 'Syv Søstre' (the Seven Sisters) (1000 m), and whether one takes the direct route to the W or the detour to the E of the island, the views are splendid. There are guest pontoons to the SE in the main harbour, just E of the ambulance and pilot boats, with fuel to the NW; the Sandnessjøen Båtforening small-boat harbour lies ½ a mile SW of the main port, with pontoons, showers, laundry and fuel. Bjørn, 4 miles NNW, offers a less populated anchoring stop, with shopping.

Vågsvågen (E Dønna)
Chart 59 66° 09′ N, 12° 36′ E
The anchorages in this attractive bay are a bit stony. **Dalsvågen's** scenic inner pool, just SE, offers anchorage on a sandy shelf near the waterfall.

Nesna
Chart 59 66° 12′ N, 13° 02′ E
On the tip of a mainland peninsula just W of Hugla, the sizeable town of Nesna has a small town mole harbour with a pontoon to starboard on entry (four-hour stay, for shopping), and guest berths (moderate fee, electricity) on the ends of the pontoons to port, and also at the far end of the harbour (1.5 m depth passing the narrow passage leading to the guest pontoons). Showers and a kitchen at the fine clubhouse, a club slipway if one needs to haul out, and laundry nearby.

Alsøyvågen (SE Tomma)
Chart 59 66° 13.7′ N, 12° 49.5′ E
The charted anchorage between Alsøya and Tomma, at the position given above, is rocky without swinging room, but there is an old quay. Note the overhead cable 20 m. The mole harbour 7 cables NE of this anchorage is very industrialised. Fine alternative anchorages are charted at SW and N Tomma.

Silavågen (N of Handnesøya)
Chart 59 66° 19′ N, 13° 08′ E
A large landlocked bay with spectacular mountains and waterfalls. Anchor outside small-boat moorings to the N. Note that, in easterly winds, the sound Sjona just to the S is notorious for being extremely rough. Stokvågen, 3 miles NW, is being developed as an attractive small-boat harbour, with a museum and Second World War forts nearby.

Sleneset (E Straumøya)*
Chart 59 66° 22′ N, 12° 37′ E
A small fishing village with quays and pontoons in a sheltered and attractive cove. Entry is from S through a narrow opening, or from N under a 15 m wire. SW 3½ cables is a small mole harbour with guest pontoons. Shops, P.O., and fuel. There are many anchorages in the skerries nearby, especially around Åsvær 10 miles SW, Svenningen just NW, and Buøya just SW.

Lovund (NE Lovunden)
Chart 59 66° 22′ N, 12° 22′ E
Lovunden is a very dramatic offshore island, with a well sheltered mole harbour, Lovund, between Naustholmen and the NE corner of Lovunden. Enter from the E, then head S, following the perches under the 25 m cable to a pontoon (permission required). There is also a pleasant new small-boat harbour with pontoons (moderate fee, electricity) operated by a guest house that serves as a tourist centre (Lovund Turistheim, 8764 Lovund, Norway, Tel: (47) 75 09 45 32), 5 cables W of the main harbour entrance: follow the charted depths of 8, 6 and 4 m. There is one of the world's largest colonies of puffin, and prehistoric ruins, just half an hour's walk away, and marked trails with viewpoints (details and aerial photograph available at the guest house).

Træna (Husøya and Sanna)
Chart 61 66° 30′ N, 12° 06′ E
The dramatic jagged spires of Sanna, dominated by Trænstaven, with the village of Træna in the foreground, are featured on the cover of *Den Norske Los*, volume 5. 'Træna' refers to an entire archipelago, and there is no island of that name. The village, on Husøya, is an historic and interesting out-island community, with several quays, and boats moored in the sound S of the church. The cove by the church is shallow. At the entrance to the small cove

behind the ferry quay, by the Arctic Circle globe monument, is a pontoon (with some ferry wash) with shops, bank, and PO nearby. On Sanna there is a small mole harbour at the NE; the quay must be vacated for the coastal boat once or twice a day, and the pontoon is exclusively for the use of the military. There is good anchorage in sand 3–4 m near the quay, or you may be able to borrow a mooring. There are no supplies. Sanna has several impressive caves, and excavations show Kirkehellaren to have been occupied from around 6000 BC. An interesting walk through a 700 m unlighted tunnel (flashlight necessary) leads to dramatic views from the ridge far above the harbour. **Selvær,** 7 miles NNE, is a large sheltered harbour with many quays and a small guest pontoon. The octogenarian 'King of Dørvær' is the sole resident of **Dørvær,** 4 miles NE. Note that the perch Vågsholmtaren, 3 miles NE of Træna, was reported missing in 1994.

Onøya (N)
Chart 59   66° 24′ N, 12° 51′ E
There is a small fishing village with quays here, S of Sjåhlneset, and especially pleasant walks ashore. Note that in transiting to the E of this area, it is possible to pass between Lurøya and Stigen if motoring or with the wind aft.

Kvarøya (NE)
Chart 62   66° 29′ N, 12° 58.5′ E
There is a pleasant mole harbour at the NE of Indre Kvarøya. The small island Vikingen, which is 2.5 miles to the N and 1 mile S of the Arctic Circle, is the site for a handsome *Polarsirkel* monument. The peak Hestmanden (the horseman), 4 miles NW, is well known for its remarkable appearance as a mounted horseman when viewed from the S.

Nordfjordholmen (in Nordfjorden off Melfjorden)
Chart 62   66° 36′ N, 13° 32′ E
A beautiful wild cove tucked in behind the small island at the N of the fjord. There is good swinging room but the holding is not good; there are two moorings said to be secure in summer weather. This fjord, overhung by several tongues of the Svartisen glacier, is one of the most spectacularly beautiful in Norway.

Nordnesøya (NE Nesøya)
Charts 61, 62   66° 35.5′ N, 12° 40′ E
Sørnesøya (SW Nesøya)*
Chart 61   66° 34.3′ N, 12° 38′ E
Nordnesøya is a pleasantly scenic and well sheltered harbour, with a guest pontoon to starboard well inside; shopping. Sørnesøya has several quays, PO, and possibly a shop.

Lyngvær (W Lyngværøya)*
Chart 61   66° 40′ N, 12° 33′ E
This is a most pleasant anchorage immediately to the W of the centre of Lyngværøya.

Myken
Chart 63   66° 46′ N, 12° 29′ E
Outside the usual cruising routes, a small 'outpost' island community of a few dozen people at the Myken lighthouse, with well sheltered anchorage and quays. The lighthouse building is now a tourist facility, with lodging, fishing gear, sailboard, diving tank compressor and local guidance (Myyken Fyr Holiday, Gro Bygdevoll/Helge Eriksen, N-8199 Myken, Norway). Enter from the SW or NE. **Valvær** to the ENE is an attractive and interesting harbour, abandoned except for two summer-use houses; good shelter but open to SW, with moorings available.

Kyrah *lying outside a fisherman at Engen in Holandsfjorden below the Svartisen glacier.*

Selsøyvik
Chart 62   66° 34.5′ N, 12° 58.8′ E
Between Sundøya and Rangsundøya, Selsøyvik is a pleasant community dating back to the 18th century, where excellent smoked salmon is prepared. The harbour is not sheltered in N winds, but there is a sheltered visitors' pontoon (the rough pontoon requires extra fendering), fuel, shop, PO and showers.

Renga (SW)
Chart 62   66° 36′ N, 13° 06′ E
This superb anchorage inside Hansøya is particularly scenic and is a favourite of eagles. Good walking and scrambling ashore. A few cables NW, the varde Lamandskjær is likely to have an eagle perched, and if one pulls up fish from the nearby rock charted 12 m and tosses the fish to the eagle, there may be a rare opportunity to see an eagle manoeuvring only a few metres from the boat.

Sørgjerøyvågen (W Gjerøya)*
Chart 62   66° 37′ N, 13° 00′ E
A small pretty fjord with a quay, and possibly a small shop. Note the charted 16 m overhead cable.

Rødøya (S)
Chart 62   66° 39′ N, 13° 05′ E
There is a small pontoon (probably to be expanded in 1995) at the S of Rødøya, near the centre of the village (showers, fuel, shop, bank and medical clinic). There may be strong gusting here in ENE winds. There are boat-club pontoons in the sheltered cove NW of the village, with guest space. Walk around the cove and climb the opposite rocky hill to take a postcard-style photograph of this idyllic bay, and if one is fortunate there may be eagles circling below. There is a trail to walk up the mountain Rødøyløven. There is also good anchorage, with a line ashore, to

the NE between Ytre and Indre Rodøya. Note that there is a less well known Rødøya 50 miles to the S.

Engen / Holandsfjorden
Charts 62, 63   66° 42.5' N, 13° 43' E
The large Svartisen glacier tumbles down almost to the sea in Holandsfjorden. A beautiful stroll of less than an hour from the berth at Engen brings one to the spectacular and beautiful blue ice snout of the glacier; this walk is probably most enjoyable in the evening after the tourist boat has departed. There is also an unusually beautiful little forest between the moraine lake and the sea. There is a restaurant that owns a long pontoon with depth 2–4 m (beware the mooring ropes); permission should be obtained. If unusually strong winds rise, one would need to move alongside a larger boat in the fjord, pick up one of the guest moorings (security uncertain), or leave the fjord (photo p. 47).

Halsa
Chart 63   66° 44.6' N 13° 33.0' E
A pleasant sheltered small-boat harbour, with pontoons, laundry, showers, fuel, shop and PO. Enter from the N into the W arm of the bay; the 10 m overhead cable has been removed, and there is sufficient water for a yacht. This is a good spot if the weather is bad, and one is waiting to visit Holandsfjorden.

Stranden (SE Bolga)*
Chart 63   66° 48' N, 13° 14' E
A useful mole passage harbour, with shop and PO; fuel is just to the N.

Hopen (E Mesøya)
Chart 63   66° 51' N, 13° 40' E
A rather pretty tiny cove, with just room to anchor in moderate weather. The mole harbour at Ørnes, 1 mile NE, offers shelter if needed, and has pontoons, boatyards, shopping, a bank and fuel. Fore, 3.5 miles NNW, is another alternative mole harbour. Note that Glomen to the SE is very industrialised and Glomfjorden is not especially attractive.

Støtt
Chart 63   66° 56' N, 13° 27' E
Lying off the headland of Kunna, Støttvær is a landmark frequently heard mentioned in the weather forecast. A mole connecting Indre Støtt and Svenningen creates a pleasant well sheltered harbour, with many quays. The buoyed channel is charted at minimum depth 2.1 m just SW of the 20 m overhead cable; carry on almost to the mole and turn 180° to port, as indicated by perches, to approach the inner quays and pontoons (moderate fee, electricity). There is a shop, PO and fuel. Between Støtt and Fugløya, it is best in southerly winds to hold to the W to avoid severe gusting from the high ground.

Inndyr
Chart 64   67° 02' N, 14° 02' E
At the W of a mainland peninsula, Inndyr is a pleasant harbour with a guest pontoon; shopping, bank, PO and fuel. Approach can be made through the pretty sound 3 miles SW (the charted 8 m overhead cable has been removed) near Forstranda, where there is a cave, Brosteinshola.

Sandviken / Sørfugløy (SW Fugløya)
Chart 64   67° 03' N, 13° 47' E
This is an unusually pretty and interesting harbour, very pleasing. Moles give good shelter, there is a guest pontoon to port. The harbour contains several small white sandy beaches, and across the neck is an impressively long beach. There are several attractive summer homes and a farm. The island is noted for large numbers of puffin. A rudimentary and interesting path, not easy to locate, climbs around large boulders

and up alongside the small stream tumbling down the cliff behind the houses, and leads into a beautiful hanging valley (rich in blueberries) with superb views and an opportunity to scramble to the top of the mountains. Note that in the skerries SW there are recent soundings under 2 m either not charted, or charted deeper on the 1988 edition of chart 64.

Selvågen (S Fleina)*
Chart 64 67° 06' N, 13° 52' E
A fine anchorage. The harbour Sørarnøy, 3 miles NE, is said to be noisy and crowded.

Storøya (by Saltstraumen)*
Chart 65 67° 12' N, 14° 28' E
Said to be a good anchorage, near Saltstraumen.

Bliksvær*
Chart 65 67° 16.6' N, 14° 00' E
A small old fishing community in one of Bodø's offlying skerries, now mostly deserted. The settlement is around Kvernsteinen to the NE. A 10 m overhead cable between Kvitvardholmen and Bliksvær closes the NE end of the small sound, but the lead charted just SW of the light is clear. The N quay is used by a ferry; the next quay is rough but usable with fender boards. The S quays are not suitable. One can also anchor or tie alongside a fishing boat. Vestervågen offers alternative anchorage. There are likely to be seals about. Bliksvær, Kjværvær to the S and Terra to the NE are Nature and Bird Reserves, with a Protection Area for birds extended out to 2 km; landing is permitted at any time. Givær, WNW, is said to offer good anchorage.

Bodø
Charts 65, 476 67° 17' N, 14° 23' E
Bodø is a major transportation hub and a city offering extensive services. After entering, one may berth alongside the outside of the extensive pontoon system to starboard, but there is considerable wash from passing boats. After passing the pontoon system, the visitors' pontoons are farther in and slightly to starboard. There are moderate harbour dues, with electricity included. In the summer months, a harbour hostess with a car is available to assist visiting yachts with gas, laundry, etc. (Ch 12 VHF). Luxurious showers at the SAS hotel. UK/US propane tanks can be filled by Nor-Rek A/S, Tel: (75) 58 00 50. Fuel can be obtained via automatic credit-card machine (no cash) at the pontoon which is to starboard as one enters the harbour, or from the Shell dock or fuel tug to the N. Lowold's chandlery is extensive. There is an excellent dental clinic at Storgt 12. To find the laundry, walk up the hill and turn left at the Skagen Hotel, and the Renseri Vaskei will soon be on the right. Enquire about new (post-1994) self-service laundry availability. The new national aeronautical museum is very comprehensive. It might be worthwhile calling Bodø Radio to see about a visit to their handsome facility just a short distance to the W of the guest pontoon. The harbourmaster (Ch 12) is very helpful concerning any problems one might have.

Note that the perch marking Kirkgrunnen, 4 miles SW of Bodø and 3 cables SW of Svartoksen Light, was missing in 1994.

4 Bodø to Narvik

County: Nordland; Regions: Lofoten, Vesterålen, Ofoten, and Nord-Salten

This area, comprising the northern third of the county of Nordland, offers what must surely be one of the highest concentrations of splendid scenery, wild anchorages and village harbours of great character to be found anywhere in the world. The nearly peninsular line of Lofoten Islands shelters the area from the Atlantic, and stuns the eye with scenery that seems scarcely believable, with jagged crags rising precipitously above tiny fishing harbours. Farther inland, narrow fjords penetrate deeply into the snow-capped mountains, with spectacular remote anchorages where eagles are one's only companions.

Vestfjorden, partitioned from the Atlantic by Lofoten, is the world's richest cod ground, and this determines a great deal of the character of the area. Lofotfisket, with hundreds of moderate-sized fishing boats following the cod as they leave the Barent Sea to spawn in Vestfjorden from January to April, is a major economic force as well as a cultural and social one. The outer villages have a rich history and unique character shaped by this means of existence, which was until recently a very harsh one. And during the summer months, the fishing is at a low level, leaving plenty of berthing room for cruising yachts. On sailing into these waters, you are entering a world almost totally oriented to the sea. You may encounter some bewilderment over the bizarre choice of voyaging on the sea for pleasure, but as a mariner one is understood and welcomed.

A SPECIMEN CRUISE

My midnight landfall at the outermost tip of Lofoten, with the sun just peeking over a low cloud bank and the islands rising higher and higher in the distance, is a sight I will never forget; I cannot think of a better introduction to Lofoten. Skomvær lighthouse makes a fine landfall for a yacht crossing from the mainland near the Arctic Circle, perhaps from Myken, Træna, Lovund or Holandsfjorden.

A logical plan for cruising the area is to continue NE along the 'inside' Lofoten coast, visiting fishing village harbours as time allows, and making forays to the Atlantic 'outside' if so inclined. Just E of Svolvær, Raftsundet provides a near-mandatory detour to Trollfjorden, and one might wish to continue a bit further N into the area dominated by the peak Møysalen; this will take one temporarily out of Lofoten and into Vesterålen. This would also be a likely route N if bound for Nordkapp or Svalbard. The return from farther N can be made nicely via Tjelsundet and into Ofotfjorden at Lødingen. After returning from Raftsundet, continuing ENE into Ofoten gives access to the splendid wild anchorages in Øksfjorden and many-armed Tysfjorden, fully as deserving of attention as the more famous Lofoten. The circuit can then be completed by heading SW down the mainland coast to the large island of Hamarøya with its notable spires and lovely anchorages, and thence down the coast towards Bodø; or alternatively, from Hamarøya one could cross back to Lofoten and reverse the inbound route.

CHARTS

Chart 311 provides the 1:350 000 overview; chart 320 at 1:200 000 and charts 227 and 229 at 1:100 000 might be a nice luxury: the recommended detailed coverage is provided by charts 66 to 75 at 1:50 000 and chart 230 at 1:80 000. Harbour charts are available for Bodø (476), Svolvær (462), and Narvik (461).

PASSAGE

Note that these perches were reported missing in 1994: Kjeipbøen, 1.7 miles NNE of Landegode, 67° 28′ N, 14° 26′ E (charts 65 and 66), and Moholmsundet Søre, on the N side of Moskenesøya, 68° 06.8′ N, 13° 07.8′ E (chart 72).

Note also that the shoal SW of Store Kallsøya, 1 mile E of Fløtningsviken on the route between Svolvær and Trollfjorden, has been found to have only 1 m depth just SE of Kallsøboen.

TIDES AND STREAMS

The greatest spring tides in this area range just over 3 m. HW is 1½ hours after Bergen.

Tidal streams in Nappstraumen, Gimsøystraumen and Raftsundet peak at 4 knots, flowing northerly between 2½ hours before HW and 3½ hours after HW. In the narrows of the Raftsundet, the N-flowing stream can reach 7 knots with a strong S wind. As with tide-races more common in UK waters, Moskenstraumen (the inspiration for Jules Verne's *Mælstrom*) can be dangerous with strong wind against the tide, and it is a good idea to avoid the lumpiness in the area between Røst and Værøy by staying a bit to the SE. The rock-strewn N approaches of the Gimsøystraumen are notoriously dangerous with a strong northerly wind against the tide.

HARBOURS AND ANCHORAGES

As suggested above, the harbours and anchorages are listed below starting at the outer Lofoten and moving clockwise. To assist in planning, here is a list of those considered most outstanding:

Røst
Reine
Kirkefjord
Henningsvær
Trollfjorden and Grundfjorden
Straumshamn on Hamarøya
Gullvika on Store Molla
Vestpollen in Øksfjorden
Stefjordbotn
Sildpollen in Stefjorden

Skomvær
Chart 70   67° 24′ N, 11° 52′ E
The small, low island of Skomvær is at the very tip of the 120 mile long Lofoten chain, where the mountain ridge forming the islands finally sinks entirely under the sea. Surrounded by numerous outlying skerries, Skomvær offers only a very marginal anchorage charted close

52 FROM SOGNEFJORDEN TO THE RUSSIAN BORDER

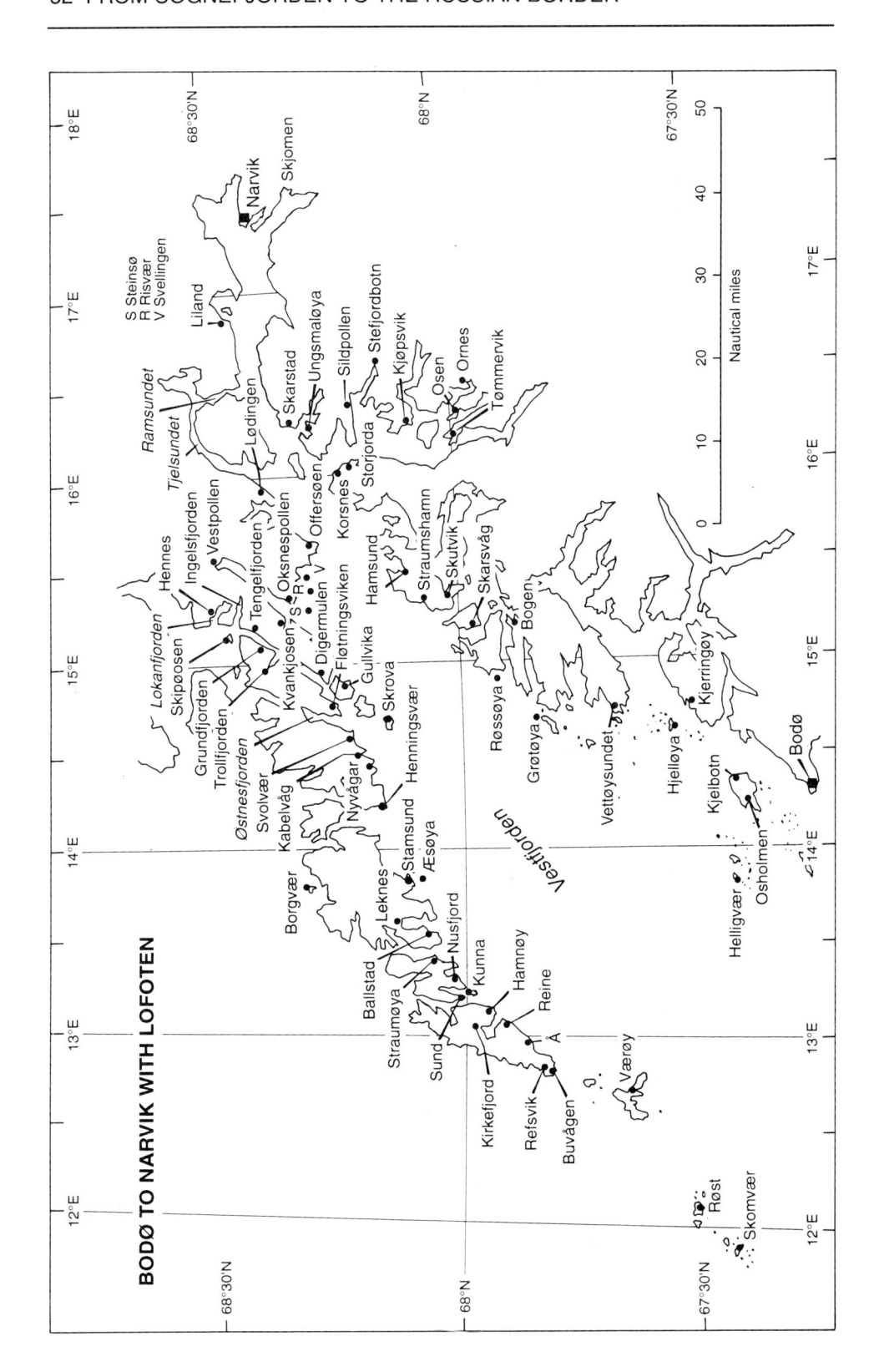

to the S. As Skomvær is passed, there will be several large grotesquely shaped islands close by to port as one progresses towards the high snowy peaks of the inner Lofoten just visible over the horizon. On triple-peaked Trenyken, a deep cavern has recently been discovered that contains a Stone Age painting.

Røst (SE Røstøya)
Chart 70   67° 30.5' N, 12° 04' E

Low-lying Røstøya, the outermost inhabited island in Lofoten, offers an unusual atmosphere of remoteness. The main harbour, Røst, lies between the two narrow peninsulas with roads opening SW, and there are numerous additional berthing and anchoring possibilities nearby. The charted entrance route from the NNW via Skarvhl, and the route from the ENE just S of the main island, are shoal in places, except at high tide, and are better avoided in favour of the other charted routes. These look complicated on the chart, but in reasonable weather will not be found difficult. In heavy weather, approaching an unfamiliar Røst would be dangerous.

The church altar-screen is an unexpected art treasure donated to Røst in 1520 by the Netherlands Princess Elisabeth 'in heartfelt thanks for surviving a stormy voyage', a sentiment that will no doubt find sympathy in the heart of the modern cruising mariner. The control tower at the small airport makes an interesting visit. There is a great profusion of seabirds between dramatically precipitous Vedøya and Storfjell, and a possibility to moor in very calm weather in a tiny crack at the SE extremity of Vedøya. Tens of thousands of kittiwakes nest on Vedøya, some in a sizeable cave at the N, off which one can anchor in a very calm sea. The owners of Ellefsnyken, Hernyken, Trenyken, Valvær, Eflateskjer, Storfjell and Stavøya (and their associated skerries) prohibit any interference with seabirds during their nesting season from 15 April to 15 August. On Storfjell are remnants of a thirteenth-century settlement. At the centre of Sandøya is the Querini monument to the Italians shipwrecked there in 1472 who, after wintering with a sheep farmer from Røst who found them in December, wrote a remarkable description of Røst that is still in the Vatican archives.

Værøy
Chart 71   67° 39' N, 12° 43' E

This spectacular high island has a coastal plain to the SE with two long peninsulas; between them is a large harbour with anchoring room or berthing alongside the rather rough W wall; the E peninsula is split at its tip by a fishing harbour lined with quays. Entrance to these harbours is possible in any usual summer weather. There is a pleasant museum on the N coast. One may anchor in fine weather off a popular beach just W of Sørland, or off the abandoned village Måstad to the W, from which a scramble to the top of Måhornet (445 m) provides superb views. A dramatic inner channel lies close off the SW tip of the island, teeming with nesting birds early in the season, and culminating in a minuscule cove (immediately S of Elsneset lighthouse) that can be entered in very calm weather.

Refsvik (SW Moskenesøya)
Charts 71, 72   67° 51' N, 12° 51' E

On the Atlantic side just around the SW tip of Moskenesøya, Refsvik is an especially attractive fair weather anchorage, with small beaches beneath towering cliffs (likely to give severe gusting in strong E winds). During the early part of the approach, the set from Moskenstraumen may require substantial compensation; the inner part of the approach is well marked but does require care. Refsvikhule, a moderately interesting cave on the coast 1 km SW from the anchorage, is reached by a pleasant trail or a short dinghy trip; there are said to be drawings 3000 years old on the cave walls, and strong torches would be useful in searching for them.

Buvågen (S Moskenesøya)*
Charts 71, 72   67° 50′ N, 12° 49′ E
Just S of Refsvik (see above); it is said to be a good harbour with several large mooring buoys placed by fishing boats. Strong gusts in winds from the E. There is a very steep trail with a fixed-rope over the ridge-top and down to the cave by Refsvik.

Å (SE Moskenesøya)
Charts 71, 72   67° 53′ N, 12° 59′ E
This tiny ex-fishing harbour is at the end of the road near the end of the island, and is named after the end letter of the Norwegian alphabet. This notoriety, and the comprehensive museum, attract numerous tourists who arrive in caravans and buses. Berthing is very limited, but one can probably lie alongside a tourist boat of the quay in front of the museum; it would be essential to check before leaving the yacht unattended. It is not very well sheltered in strong winds between the E and S. Nearby are the small scenic fishing harbours of **Tind**, **Sørvågen** and **Moskenes.**

Reine (SE Moskenesøya)
Chart 72   67° 56′ N, 13° 05′ E
Voted by the Norwegians themselves as Norway's most beautiful scenic area, the harbour of Reine is surrounded by looming spires and cliffs. Unfortunately, the village itself is touristy and unimpressive. There is a steep but safe trail to the top of Reinebringen, towering 615 m overhead to the SW, from which there are breathtaking views. There are also various trails to the nearby lakes and valleys. A guest pontoon will be found by bearing to port after passing the inner entrance buoys. Strong W winds buffeting over the crags can kick up an uncomfortable chop in the rather large harbour, and the pontoon has two offlying moorings to share some of the strain. In severe weather, nearby Hamnøy (inside an 18 m bridge) is better sheltered.

Hamnøy / **Havnøy** (SE Moskenesøya)
Chart 72   67° 57′ N, 13° 08′ E
A sister village to Reine (also spectacular), with numerous quays and a doll museum. The road between the two villages makes a pleasant walk. Hamnøy lies inside an 18 m bridge, and the final perch in the narrow harbour entrance must be left to starboard in spite of any red reflecting tape on it. Fuel available.

Kirkefjord (SE Moskenesøya)
Chart 72   67° 59.5′ N, 13° 01′ E
Inside Reine and Hamnøy (and an 18 m bridge), the island of Moskenesøya is cut nearly in two by a triple-pronged fjord, with the N arm Kirkefjorden being exceptionally beautiful. There is a good quay at the very end, with a short dredged channel; either drop a kedge short of the quay, or be prepared to row one out if the wind comes up hard from the S. There is a fine walk NNW on a path over the saddle to an enormous Atlantic beach at Horseid.

Selfjorden (between **Moskenesøya** and **Flakstadøya**)
Chart 72   68° 02′ N, 13° 06′ E
This area is on the backside of the

spectacular scenery in Kirkefjorden, but a detour via Sundstraumen (bridge 16 m) will likely prove disappointing.

Sund (SW Flakstadøya)
Chart 72   68° 00′ N, 13° 13′ E
An attractive well sheltered harbour at the E side of Sundstraumen between Moskenesøya and Flakstadøya; the best quays for berthing are well inside on the port hand (but watch for fresh creosote on the decking).

The well known artistic blacksmith Hans Gjertsen has founded a fine museum here, where one can stand at the elbow of his protégé Torvgerd Mørkved as he forges a lump of red-hot iron into a beautiful statue of a cormorant; there are also historic 'tonka-tonka' marine semi-diesels that one can watch being hand-started. The charted 15 m overhead cable has been removed.

Kunna (off S Flakstadøya)
Chart 72   68° 00.3′ N, 13° 14.3′ E
A pleasant wild anchorage with good views of the mountains. The cove is open to the NE, with anchorage in sand 9 m.

Nusfjord (SE Flakstadøya)
Chart 72   68° 02′ N, 13° 21′ E
This picturesque, compact and well sheltered harbour with an easy entrance is noted for restored *rorbuer* (fishermen's huts, rented to holidaymakers). There are numerous quays for berthing. Some SW swell may roll in. There is an old-fashioned shop and PO, café, showers and laundry.

Straumøya (SE Flakstadøya)
Chart 72   68° 04′ N, 13° 24′ E
An attractive wild anchorage, with an extensive area of 10 m sand and bolts on shore; there are also a couple of small coves (one containing the wreck

The Anvil of the Gods (1396 m), Stetind, seen from Stefjorden, Tysfjorden, 68° N.

of a large wooden boat) that may have suitable depth.

Ballstad (SW Vestvågøya)
Chart 72 68° 04.5′ N, 13° 32′ E
A scenic complex and busy fishing harbour, with a chandlery, shipyard (adorned by Norway's largest wall painting), shops and fuel.

Leknes (SW Vestvågøya)
Charts 72 inset, 74 68° 08′ N, 13° 37′ E
One can berth here at a quay or anchor for access to the nearby small airport. This airport is said to be less likely to be fogged in than the airport at Svolvær.

Borgvær (NW of Vestvågøya)
Chart 75 68° 20′ N, 13° 48′ E
This is an attractive anchorage on the Atlantic side of Vestvågøya, with an abandoned farm in an atmosphere of remoteness. Local sailors and fishermen often comment on how fine it is on 'the other side', but few yachts venture over; this anchorage might be a good starting point. One can anchor in 2.5 m sand in the cove to the E, with a line ashore.

Æsøya (SE of Vestvågøya)
Charts 72, 73 68° 06.2′ N, 13° 48.3′ E
An unusual anchorage in a tiny cove, in 2–3 m sand, with bolts on shore. Isolated, wild and beautiful.

Stamsund (SE Vestvågøya)
Chart 73 inset 68° 08′ N, 13° 52′ E
Stamsund is a large old whaling harbour with many quays for berthing. Although not notably attractive or scenic, there is an interesting puppet shop and theatre.

Henningsvær (SW Østvågøya)
Chart 73 68° 09′ N, 14° 12′ E
Perhaps the best known of Lofoten fishing harbours, Henningsvær is a gem. A group of small islands connected together by moles at the SW tip of Østvågøya forms the harbour, situated at the foot of high craggy mountains. Entrance from the W is under an 18 m bridge; from the E there is no height restriction. There seem to be miles of quays at which to berth; seeing Henningsvær in the summer, one would hardly imagine that in the winter fishing season it's likely to be filled wall to wall with hundreds of fishing boats. There is a guest pontoon at the closed S end of the harbour, and the restaurant pontoon is free for patrons. Moderate harbour dues may be collected sporadically. The *Galleri Karl Erik Harr* painting and photography museum is excellent. A walk up to the Nordland boat monument by the bridge, or on to the bridge itself, provides superb views, as does a walk out to the lighthouses on the cliffs to the S.

Nyvågar (SE Østvågøya)
Chart 73 68° 12.53′ N, 14° 27.00′ E
A quality tourist development, with many modern *rorbuer* cabins, a restaurant and conference hall, an aquarium and Lofotfisken museum. In the *Galleri Espolin*, life in earlier days in Lofoten is compellingly depicted in the works of notable artist Kåre Espolin Johnson. Nyvågar is tucked in a small channel on SE Østvågøya, with entrance between Sagøya and Reksteinen and then NE up the channel shown by perches. Harbour dues, a bit higher than usual for the region, include berthing at a quay or pontoon, sauna and shower (be early to have it hot!); fuel and laundry are available but expensive. The quay at the restaurant deck is shallow as well as very public, and a few of the pontoon berths are shallow; the management can provide an aerial photograph with the depths shown at all the berths. Severe swell enters in strong SW winds, and in winter SW storms the tide has been known to cover the restaurant floor!

Kabelvåg (SE Østvågøya)
Chart 73   68° 13′ N, 14° 29′ E

This very old fishing village has a pleasant market square, but the quays are unattractive and the outer ones are poorly sheltered; pontoons can be reached near HW. Best visited by walking from Nyvågar (see previous page).

Svolvær (SE Østvågøya)
Charts 73, 462   68° 14′ N, 14° 34.18′ E

This is the 'big city' of Lofoten, with museums, art centres, a fine old church, city shopping, boatworks, fine quays (apt to be busy) and guest pontoons with electricity. Go past the large quays on the port hand when entering from the S (modest harbour dues). (A new and expanded guest harbour arrangement is expected, post-1994, in the centre of the harbour on the N side of Lamholmen, just NE of the older guest pontoons.) The Marinepollen boat-club pontoons in the NW part of the harbour are quieter and more scenic, but less central, with a low berthing fee and coin-metered electricity; if your vessel has a tall mast, the 14.8 m bridge on the way to the Marinepollen must be bypassed. The fuelling point close NE of the bridge is said to be unusually inexpensive; there is another fuelling point past the Marinepollen boat-club pontoons. Fuel is also available at Osan not far to the W, but perhaps not in the small nozzle size and pressures best for most yachts. It may be possible to leave laundry at the Youth Hostel for a reasonable fee, and showers are available at the Havly Hotel. There is a very scenic but steep and strenuous path that climbs to the base of *Svolværgeita* (Svolvær goat), 569 m, the twin-summited rock spire overlooking the city. There is a small airport nearby, and often seaplane sightseeing flights can be arranged from the harbour.

Skrova
Chart 73   68° 10′ N, 14° 40′ E

A large old whaling harbour 5 miles SE from Svolvær, with many quays and a pontoon, entered from the SW.

Østnesfjorden (SE Østvågøya)
Chart 73   68° 19′ N, 14° 44′ E

A pretty fjord just E of Svolvær, with very fine views of the high peaks towards Trollfjorden. There is possible anchorage at Langstrand, and better at Sildpollen, or just outside Sildpollen use a mooring buoy and bolt, or the good quay by the church. On the E shore near a stream there are ruined stone quays (with marginal depth) that make a very pleasant day stop. There is a 16 m overhead cable across Østpollen. The head of the fjord has many houses pleasantly situated, with anchoring possibilities, and a 3 km walk to 'the other side' where fishermen used to haul their small boats across on the snow.

Fløtningsviken (E Østvågøya)
Chart 73   68° 16′ N, 14° 46′ E

A very pretty anchorage N of Storøya – a good place to wait for the tide in Raftsundet. Note that the shoal SW of Store Kallsøya, 1 mile E of Fløtningsviken, has been found to have only 1 m depth just SE of Kallsøboen.

Trollfjorden (E Østvågøya)
Chart 69   68° 22′ N, 14° 56′ E

This famous tourist attraction is an impressively narrow and deep fjord surrounded by snowy peaks. There is a useful quay at the end, from which one can walk up along, and in places on to, the hydroelectric pipeline, then bear left across a scree slope to a very spectacular 'alpine' lake with superb views that are well worth the strenuous effort of getting there. The attempts to vandalise the fjord by painting boat-names along the walls have been only partly successful.

The scenery in Øyhellesundet and Raftsundet during the approach to Trollfjorden is exceptional. Djuphavn, 5 cables S of the entrance to Trollfjorden, is a tiny 'crack in the wall', where one can tie between the N and S walls in a real micro-harbour – but beware the overhead cable.

Grundfjorden (E Østvågøya)
Chart 69   68° 23′ N, 15° 00′ E
An exceptionally beautiful wild anchorage just NE of Trollfjorden, with a lake and a small herd of elk. At mid-tide there is a uniform 2 m over the shoal at the entry; it would be prudent to proceed dead slow and on the rising tide unless near HW. Once past the shoal there is good depth, with shoal areas as charted. One can moor very near the cascades at the N (in heavy rain the outflow creates a 5 knot side current), in the tiny cove straight ahead of the entrance channel, or at the S, in all cases using shore lines and anchors. With gusting from the mountains, and limited room to manoeuvre in, this fjord is not the best place to be in strong winds.

Tengelfjord (SW Hinnøya)
Chart 69   68° 25.4′ N, 15° 09′ E
A small enclosed cove in NE Raftsundet, with PO and shop; enter with great care and extremely close N of the perch to stay in the best depth. One can anchor or use a vacant mooring, with permission. There is a nice walk to the lake.

Ingelsfjorden (SW Hinnøya)
Chart 69   68° 28′ N, 15° 24′ E
At the NE of Raftsundet, this wild and scenic fjord offers a fine walk E on an elk path to Øksfjorden. Note the 21.5 m overhead cable; there is a fine anchorage charted just outside the overhead cable S of Nesøya. One can anchor at the end of the fjord, possibly with a line ashore also, but be sure the anchor is into the bottom and not the extensive weed. Just S of the entrance to the fjord is the tiny island Gunnar-skjåen, mentioned in the Viking sagas as a strategic lookout point against potential enemies approaching in Raftsundet.

Skipøosen (E Brotøya)
Chart 69   68° 29′ N, 15° 12′ E
A scenic and convenient anchorage, quite well sheltered, with good swinging room in 8 m sand. The island is very fine for walking, and there is a notable home bakery in one of the farms at Brotøen at the W of the island. A mile SW lies a larger but less idyllic anchorage, S of Hanøya.

Lonkanfjorden (SW Hinnøya)
Chart 76   68° 30′ N, 15° 22′ E
Just N of Ingelsfjorden, Lonkanfjorden is wild and attractive, with fine views of Møysalen and the surrounding high peaks. There is good holding in 3–4 m at Sørbotn. The 15 m overhead cable charted on the way into the fjord has been removed.

Hennes (SW Hinnøya)
Chart 76   68° 32′ N, 15° 14′ E
A small sheltered harbour with a pontoon; the departure point for reasonably priced weekend guided group climbs of Møysalen, which, at 1266 m, is the highest peak in Lofoten/Vesterålen.

Digermulen (SW Hinnøya)
Chart 69   68° 19′ N, 15° 00′ E
This small harbour has quays, a small pontoon and shop. There is a well marked and maintained path to the top of Keiservarden (388 m), which provides spectacular panoramic views (and plaques commemorating the ascents made by the German Kaiser Wilhelm II in 1889 and 1903). In N winds, anchor

SSE to the E of Bukkholmen, or 5 miles SSW at Gullvika.

Gullvika (SE Store Molla)
Chart 69   68° 15′ N, 14° 54′ E
This is an exceptionally attractive and scenic anchorage, with good swinging room in the E cove in 4–9 m sand, and numerous mooring bolts around the edges of the cove. There are good crops of blueberries on the NW side of the W cove, but it may be best to row over as the shoal between the coves needs half-tide or better for passage. There are walks along the old road, now a trail, to lakes to the N, and to the settlement of Brettesnes to the S (which has a quay not particularly well suited for a yacht). There are several alternative anchorages nearby, but none so fine as Gullvika: Mollgavlen, 4 miles NNE, is a sheltered and pleasant anchorage, with the entrance probably needing half-tide; Ulvågen, a couple of miles NNE, is a small fjord worth a short detour for the splendid views upon entry, but the inner part of the fjord tends to be deep for anchoring (there are several quays near the entrance, in sheltered and pleasant surroundings); Krabvågen, 1.5 miles SSW, is a charming tiny cove with a sandy bottom in 3 m and a small beach, somewhat exposed to the S (photo p. 79).

Kvankjosen (SW Øksfjorden–SW Hinnøya)
Chart 69   68° 22′ N, 15° 11′ E
Near the entrance to the fjord on the port hand, one can meander into this pretty, interesting and complex group of little coves and islets surrounded by wooded hills, ideal for shore-side expeditions (especially for cruising children). Some ingenuity with anchors and shore lines might be required to feel secure in a heavy blow, but the area is extremely well sheltered.

Øksnespollen (SE Øksfjorden – SW Hinnøya)
Chart 69   68° 22′ N, 15° 22′ E
A wild and moderately pretty anchorage to starboard near the mouth of the fjord, with good swinging room on an uncharted 1.2 m rocky and sandy shoal just inside the entrance to the two narrow bays running N and S, immediately NE of the 12 m sounding. There is also an uncharted 0.8 m rock 3.7 cables NW of this shoal, just NW of the 32 m sounding.

Vestpollen (NW Øksfjorden–SW Hinnøya)
Chart 69 inset   68° 31′ N, 15° 34′ E
At the NW head of a very scenic fjord, this is an exceptionally beautiful and wild anchorage, with the summit of Møysalen soaring 1266 m up from the end of the fjord. One can anchor on the charted 3 m rocky and sandy shoal with good swinging room just E of Tyvhellarneset, or on the rather narrow sandy shelf at the end of the fjord. The cave Tyvhellar ('thieves' cave') at the N side of Tyvhellarneset (S of the 21 m sounding) is mentioned in the Viking sagas as the overwinter refuge of Sigund Slembe, who mistakenly entered Øksfjorden thinking it was Raftsundet when fleeing his enemies. Note that there is a 15 m overhead cable three-quarters of the way up the fjord.

The next few harbours lie in the archipelago of small islands and intricate channels S of Hinnøya, skerries that are unusual in Lofoten. Traversing this archipelago on a moderate day is interesting, and sailing inside it with a southerly wind is easy and pleasantly sheltered.

Steinsø
Chart 69   68° 15.7′ N, 15° 04.1′ E
There is a charming and well sheltered

sandy-bottom anchorage at the 4 m sounding E of Store Steinsøya. The channel to the NE has more than the charted 2 m depth, but that to the S has less than the charted 2 m.

Risvær
Chart 69   68° 16′ N, 15° 07.5′ E
Risvær was once a major Lofoten fishing port, but now only a few families live in this unique and interesting tiny community lining the narrow sound between Bortero and Hjemøya. The least depth 1.8 m is not far inside the N entrance. Fuel is available at the large outside quay. The best quay for berthing is hard to port immediately after entering the sound from the N, at the SW tip of the quay. The pontoon at the N end of the sound has insufficient depth for a yacht, but there are several new private pontoons serving holiday cottages that may be available with permission.

Svellingen
Chart 69   68° 17.3′ N, 15° 20.3′ E
Svellingen, a bit farther E in the archipelago, has several anchorages. In the most attractive, almost a lagoon, one can tie between the heart-shaped (or skull-shaped) island 1 cable in diameter (lying E of the centre of Lille Svellingen) and the tiny islet NW, at the position given above; entry is in good depth by heading SW from Lysøya Light, then turning N with Lille Svellingen to port and the heart-shaped island to starboard. Another fine anchorage lies 7.5 cables due N of the one just described, E of a charted rock awash, entered heading ENE, at 68° 18.07′ N, 15° 20.2′ E. Another anchorage, at the W side of Store Svellingen, is well sheltered even in strong SW winds; but although it offers beautiful distant views, the anchorage itself is less attractive. Proceed S along the W side of Store Svellingen, leaving the 3 m sounding and tiny islet to starboard, then turn E between the two larger islands lying just W of Store Svellingen, then turn N into the diminishing channel; there is a small quay to port with 3.5 m depth, and lines can be taken to bolts on both shores. The anchorage charted SE of the NE-most point on Store Svellingen is frequently rocked by heavy wash from the 38 knot catamaran coastal express that transits just 1.5 cables N; the effect can be minimised by pulling well in towards the bolt.

Offersøen (S Hinnøya)
Chart 69   68° 18.5′ N, 15° 38.6′ E
A moderately pleasant harbour with pontoons, likely to be bustling with campers and tourists at the small hotel. May be rolly in SW winds. Entrance is heading due N between islets, leaving a single perch to port.

Lødingen (S Hinnøya)
Charts 230, 69   68° 25′ N, 16° 00′ E
Lødingen is a pleasant town with a fine mole small-boat harbour (Melkebukta) at the E edge of town. The harbour is entered from the N between two lighted perches. The least depth in the neck of the entrance, near the third lighted perch, is given in *Den Norske Los* as 1.9 m, but 1.5–1.7 m is more likely, and caution should be used when the tide is low. Berthing is available at the pontoon ends, with a modest guest donation requested. Fuel is available near the pilot boat; there may be insufficient depth at LW for fuelling. The marine supply shop adjacent to the harbour has a good stock of general boating gear. The 15 m overhead cable that once crossed the harbour entrance has now been removed. There are fine mountain walks nearby.

Tjelsundet and Ramsundet
Charts 230, 77   68° 30' N, 16° 20' E
These sounds, separating Tjeldøya from Hinnøya, are quite interesting and pleasant. Tjelsundet is a major route between Lofoten/Ofoten and areas to the N. In Ramsundet, at the 19 m bridge, the leading marks (both ahead and behind) must be followed accurately in spite of the strong tidal streams. There is no stopping in the military area just S of this bridge.

Liland
Chart 230   68° 28.5' N, 16° 53' E
On the N central shore of Ofoten, Liland is in a pretty farming area offering a soft contrast to the crags of Lofoten. There are excellent guest pontoons, a small clubhouse grill, barbecue, picnic tables and showers. Bogen, 3 miles NE, has an old wooden quay at which it is possible to dry on the tide for scrubbing; this will greatly excite the local residents as this operation is virtually unknown in Norway.

Narvik
Charts 230, 461   68° 26' N, 17° 25' E
An attractive small city at the E end of Ofoten, with two mole harbours, both with guest pontoons and fuel: the one at the N of the city is handy, but less quiet and secure; the one at **Ankenes** just to the SW is very quiet and secure, with friendly cruising sailors and a sailing dinghy programme. Watch the depth entering Ankenes at LW. The fuel pontoon in the northern Narvik harbour is quite shoal, so watch the tide. Showers and laundry are planned for Ankenes, and buses pass several times each hour for the 15 minute ride to Narvik. There is an excellent museum in Narvik depicting the fierce naval and land battles that occurred in 1940; the chart shows numerous large-wreck symbols where huge warships still lie, and one can be seen even at the surface in Rombakfjorden. The rock carving at Vassvik is very near the N Narvik harbour. The day-return rail trip from Narvik through the mountains to the Swedish border is an inexpensive and very scenic excursion; at Riksgrensen, one can visit Sven Hörnell's *Subartisk* photographic gallery. Skjomen, just W of Narvik, is especially attractive; one can anchor below the Frostisen glacier as charted or at the bottom of the fjord. Beware that in strong SE and ESE winds, Skjomen often sends unexpectedly heavy blasts several miles out into Ofotfjorden.

Skarstad
Chart 230   68° 21.9' N, 16° 16.7' E
A small pleasant mole harbour, well sheltered, with a quay, pontoon (small fee) and shop. The pontoon space next to the ramp will just accommodate a 39 foot yacht.

Ungsmaløya (NW Æfjorden)
Chart 230   68° 19' N, 16° 15' E
Æfjorden cuts deeply S into the mountains at the W end of Ofoten. On the starboard hand at the mouth of the fjord, Ungsmaløya is a lovely anchorage with fine views, around to the N of the little island or S, depending on the wind direction; there are three helpful uncharted perches at the N entry to the bay. The remainder of Æfjorden is quite scenic, with reasonable fair weather anchorage at the end. There is also pleasant scenic anchorage in 15 m 2–3 cables W of the 25 m overhead cable between Straumøya and Hestneset, at 68° 20' N, 16° 14' E.

At the E end of Vestfjorden, the six fingers of Tysfjorden penetrate far into rugged mountains almost to Sweden. All of the branches would be considered scenic by anyone's standards, and several are outstanding – even in this area of superlatives. All of the islands and river outlets in Tysfjorden are part of the Bekkensholmen National Park.

Korsnes (NW Tysfjorden)
Charts 69, 230   68° 15' N, 16° 04' E
To the W at the entrance to Tysfjorden, Korsnes is a small very sheltered mole harbour with several pontoons and quays (use the S pontoon; there is an overhead cable at the N); 1 km S is a short trail leading to one of Norway's notable areas of rock carvings.

Storjorda (NW Bessfjorden)
Charts 69, 230   68° 12' N, 16° 04' E
A pleasant harbour with access to the remainder of Tysfjorden. There are pontoons, a shop handy, and bigger shops with phone and PO 2 km W. There are leading marks in the approach to the harbour. Anchoring is possible farther into the bay. In late October, outer Tysfjorden and Ofotfjorden are visited by hundreds of *spekkhogge* (orca – killer whales) that follow the herring in from the Atlantic.

Sildpollen (NE Stefjorden)
Chart 230   68° 14' N, 16° 29' E
A superlatively beautiful wild anchorage surrounded on three sides by huge granite walls, with forests, a stream and a sandy bottom in 8–10 m.

Stefjordbotn (SE Stefjorden)
Chart 230   68° 11' N, 16° 36' E
This exceptionally spectacular anchorage is at the foot of the NW face of Stetind (1396 m), 'The Anvil of the Gods', a beautiful chisel-shaped peak visible from many miles away; the summit appears to loom overhead at 70°, although the actual elevation is only 43°. There are a dozen houses at the end of the fjord, with anchoring in sand in 10–15 m (photo p. 55).

Kjøpsvik (central Tysfjorden)
Chart 230   68° 06' N, 16° 22' E
A pretty village on a handsome wooded slope, with shops and fuel. During the approach, the ambiance is marred by the nearby huge cement plant; however, once one is ashore the industry is invisible behind a hill. The harbour has several quays and large pontoons as well as finger-pontoons; in a strong southerly, one would want to be on the inside of the pontoons. Sørfjorden and Holmen offer pleasant and moderately scenic (but rather deep) anchorage in Indre Tysfjorden to the E.

Ørnes (SE Mannfjorden)
Chart 230 inset   67° 58.5' N, 16° 31' E
A protected very pretty cove anchorage in sand, with good views of the high mountains; a base for a steep hike up the S shoulder of the handsome granite peak Multind, which rises 853 m overhead.

Osen (NE Grunnfjorden)
Chart 230 inset   68° 00' N, 16° 20' E
This is a pleasant anchorage in 6 m sand with swinging room, somewhat open to the NW. Eidvik, just to the SW, is a very well sheltered anchorage, but requires anchoring in 25 m. The remainder of the fjord is pleasantly scenic; anchoring at Grunnfjordbotn would be in 20 m.

Tømmervik (NE Hellemofjorden)
Chart 230 inset   67° 59' N, 16° 17' E
A pretty anchorage in 10 m sand, open to the NW. The mountain scenery around Indre Musken at 67° 53' N, 16° 13' E is superb but there is no protected anchorage. The remainder of the fjord is pleasantly scenic, with a couple of dozen buildings at Hellemobotn and a quay and anchoring/tie-off possibility, only 5 horizontal km from Sweden. On the NE wall inward from Kidbukta, at 67° 50' N, 16° 27' E, there are extensive

unusual glacial melt-water scouring patterns in the granite walls of the fjord.

Note that although Hamarøya is named as an island and is usually called an island, it is actually a peninsula.

Hamsund (N Hamarøya)
Chart 68   68° 07′ N, 15° 31′ E
Anchorage in a pretty inland bay with an interesting entrance between islets, which enables you to visit the home and museum of Nordland's notable novelist Knut Hamsun (Nobel Prize Winner, 1920). One can anchor in the 5 m pool near the end of the bay, row ashore, and it is then just a short walk to the museum.

Straumshamn (NW Hamarøya)
Chart 68   68° 06.5′ N, 15° 23′ E
Nestled in a small fjord at the foot of Hamarøya's crags are three picture-book anchorages, each unique. Passing through the narrow entrance, keep to port to avoid the charted 2 m rock that will probably be visible in the clear water. These delightful choices unfold:

1 To starboard just inside the narrow entrance lies a tiny cove edged with a white sandy beach, with not quite sufficient depth to allow sheltering as deeply into the cove as one might like, but sufficient for most summer weather, using shore lines and an anchor.

2 A bit farther into the fjord there is a fine anchorage between a tiny rocky island and the nearby shore, with mooring bolts on each and a sandy shoal area nearby for an anchor if desired.

3 Continuing farther in at well over half-tide and sounding carefully, crossing the sandy shoal brings one into a small deep pool ideal for an anchor on the shoal and lines ashore to trees. A small cascade empties into this pool, and a short

Kyrah in Straumshamn, NW Hamarøya, lying to two anchors and a shore line in the first of the three anchorages described. The other two are visible in the background.

portage with the dinghy allows it to be launched on the beautiful freshwater lake at the foot of the mountains.

Dalsvær, the rather complex little bay just S, is sheltered by islands and offers several attractive spots to anchor in sand, but it is rather overshadowed by Straumshamn.

Skutvik (SW Hamarøya)
Chart 68 68° 01′ N, 15° 21′ E
Skutvik is a major ferry port. There is a pontoon inside the mole harbour, with a short walk to the bustling tourist centre.

Skarsvåg (SW Lundøya)
Chart 68 67° 58′ N, 15° 13′ E
A quiet and very pleasant wild anchorage in 7 m sand, well sheltered; two anchors, or lines ashore, might be required with changing wind direction. Beware the 12 m overhead cable at the head of the anchorage. The cove charted as an anchorage S of Alsvikskjær, 0.8 miles WNW, is an attractive wild anchorage in 5–10 m sand, well sheltered except from the SSW.

Bogen
Chart 68 67° 54′ N, 15° 11.6′ E
A small cove SE of the bridge with pontoons, fuel (200 m), PO and shop.

Røssøya (W Røssøya)*
Charts 67, 68 67° 55.3′ N, 14° 56.6′ E
A small harbour in the skerries off Steigen kirke, with guest berthing and fuel. In fair weather it is pleasant to anchor between Flatøya and L Flatøya, 3.7 miles to the W, and explore the abandoned lighthouse facility.

Grøtøya
Chart 67 inset 67° 50′ N, 14° 47′ E
The island of Grøtøya nestles in an archipelago below dramatic peaks, on a complex but well marked channel that is much easier than it looks on the chart. At the SE side of Naustholmen lies a notable historic trading centre with a museum. There are fine views from the hilltop path, and nature walks. There may be sufficient depth at one edge of the pontoon, and there is also a smoothly faced quay with 2.5 m depth; there is wash from ferries and the tidal stream runs quite strongly. A half mile across the sound to the SE, the small bay off the village Nordskot provides an excellent scenic anchorage, sheltered except from the N; it is probably more pleasant to anchor in the bay and row to Naustholmen. The Shell fuel quay provides a free guest mooring; it's the one to the E festooned with old fenders. Nordskot has several fishing boat quays, a café, showers and shops. There are several pleasant tiny sandy channels for anchorage S of Grøtøya, notably near Andersøya at 67° 49′ N, 14° 44′ E (photo p. 85).

Vettøysundet (E Vettøya)
Chart 66 67° 40.6′ N, 14° 43.7′ E
An especially scenic wild anchorage in Indre Vettøysundet, well sheltered, with wooded hills and eagles. There is good swinging room in 4–5 m sand off the S-most beach. There are also quays and pontoons 3.3 miles NNE at Helnessund (fuel, shop, showers and laundry).

Hjelløya (in Karlsøver)
Chart 66 67° 32.8′ N, 14° 39.6′ E
Lying off Kjerringøy, a small, pretty, secluded channel with sandy bottom; use two anchors. All Karlsøvær and Slovær, just to the N, is a Bird and Nature Reserve, with a Bird Protection Area extended out to 2 km; between 15 April and 15 July one may approach the shore, but not land.

Kjerringøy
Chart 66 67° 31′ N, 14° 46′ E
A notable historic trading port, the grounds serving as a tourist museum,

with café, shop and fuel. Enter from the N to the pontoon; in N winds, anchor to the S for shelter.

Kjelbotn (NE Landegode)
Chart 65 67° 25' N, 14° 24' E
This anchorage is often used, but is also said to be sometimes unsafe because of gusts and uncertain holding; there are other options around the island. The three high peaks of Landegode serve as a landmark that can be seen from anywhere in Vestfjorden.

Note that the perch marking Kjeipbøen, 1.7 miles NNE of Landegode near 67° 28' N, 14° 26' E, was missing in 1994.

Osholmen (SW Landegode)
Chart 65; 67° 24' N, 14°16' E
This wild and beautiful anchorage has several beaches, and many eagles – we once counted 12 in an hour. Entry is from the W or N through small islets, and it is worth exploring a bit before deciding where to drop the hook.

Helligvær (SE Vokkøya)
Chart 65 67° 25.5' N, 13° 59' E
A small isolated village in one of Bodø's outlying skerries, with quays and pontoons. There are also nearby anchoring possibilities charted in the channels between the islets, and a quay at NW Sørværøya, with fuel, PO and shop. Note several overhead cables – some charted, and some added since chart publication.

See also **Bodø** (chart 65) at the end of the previous section.

5 Narvik to Tromsø and Torsvåg

Counties: Nordland and Troms

Most voyagers are likely to traverse this area en route to Nordkapp, Murmansk or Svalbard (Spitsbergen), rather than seeking it as a primary cruising goal. However, anyone cruising in the Lofoten/Ofoten area with time to venture farther N will find many rewarding harbours and anchorages. Indeed, this area is often favoured by Norwegian sailors from the Lofoten/Ofoten area who have grown blasé about their own spectacular home waters. The outer Atlantic side of Langøya offers especially scenic and interesting cruising.

Hinnøya, Norway's largest island, splits the S half of the region, and it is possible to transit one side of the island N-bound and the other S-bound; the routes described below are arranged with this in mind.

Those looking for a pioneering venture might cruise the seldom visited deep fjords and bold headlands on the W side of the large island Senja, which is often mentioned by local sailors as a spectacularly interesting coast to cruise, and one held somewhat in awe. This coast is open to the Atlantic, and especially to the NW there are offlying areas that break unexpectedly if there is a swell running. This coastline can serve as an alternative route to Tromsø and points farther N.

A less daunting venture off the beaten track is the W side of Kvaløya, which offers an interesting and quite well protected alternative route W of Tromsø; a cruise here could be further extended along the W side of Ringvassøya to the NE.

CHARTS

Chart 311 at 1:350 000 and chart 321 at 1:200 000 provide the overview; the recommended detailed coverage is provided from charts 75 to 92 at 1:50 000, selected to fit one's itinerary. Harbour charts are available for Harstad (487), and Tromsø (466).

TIDES AND STREAMS

The greatest spring tides run a bit over 3 m. In the S part of the region, HW is 1½ hours after Bergen; at Tromsø, HW is 2½ hours after Bergen.

The stream in Tjelsundet, NE of Lødingen, peaks most strongly off Sandtorg (4 miles S of the bridge) at 4 knots, flowing northerly 3 hours either side of HW.

The stream in the Risøyrennen between Andøya and Hinnøya peaks at 3 knots, and flows SW with the flood.

The spring tidal stream exceeds 6 knots in the Rystraumen (7 miles SW of Tromsø), turning northeasterly 6 hours before HW Tromsø, and turning southwesterly 30 minutes before HW. At

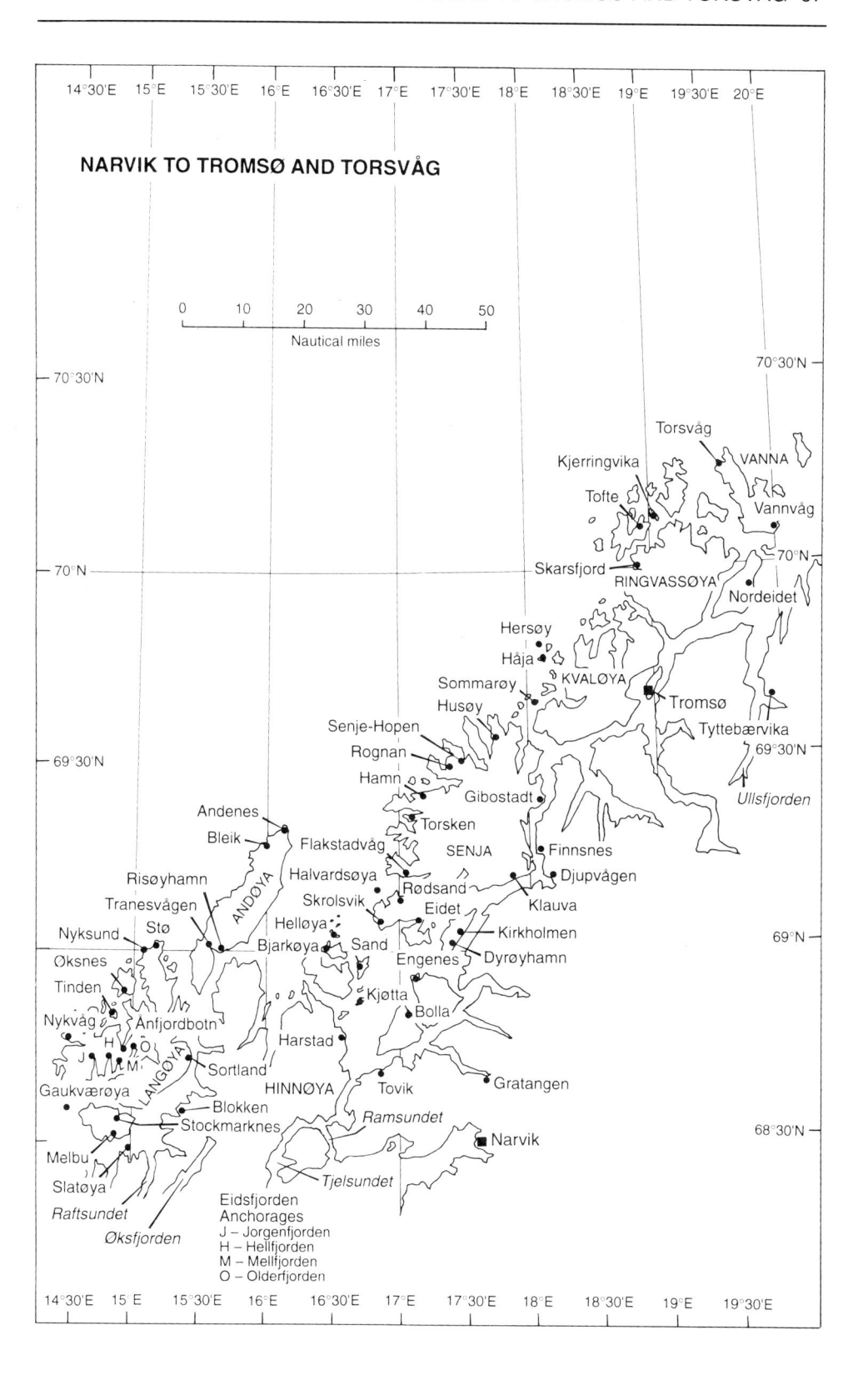

NARVIK TO TROMSØ AND TORSVÅG

peak flow there is a good deal of swirling about that requires a quick hand on the helm. Note that Ryøya, which compresses the stream in the Rystraumen, is populated with Canadian musk oxen, and landing is not permitted.

The stream peaks at 3 knots off Tromsø, flowing SW between 2½ hours before HW Tromsø and 3½ hours after HW.

All of these streams are greatly influenced by strong N or S winds.

PASSAGE

Note that these perches were reported missing in 1994: Store Skjærboen at NW Senja, 69° 29′ N, 17° 37′ E (chart 85), and a perch in Børøysundet, 1 mile E of Tinden, 68° 50.4′ N, 14° 50.6′ E (chart 78).

HARBOURS AND ANCHORAGES

The harbours and anchorages are grouped below in four sections:

1 A N-bound passage from Raftsundet in Lofoten, W of Hinøya and E of Andøya, direct to Tromsø and Torsvåg
2 N-bound along the W side of Senja and Kvaløya, SW of Tromsø
3 S-bound from Dyrøya (a day S of Tromsø), E of Hinøya into Ofoten/Lofoten via Tjelsundet
4 N-bound through the outer Vesterålen to Andenes, clockwise from Raftsundet around Langøya and Andøya

1 *Raftsundet to Torsvåg (N-bound)*

Stockmarknes (NE Hadseløya)
Charts 75, 76 inset   68° 34′ N, 14° 55′ E
This sizeable town has a guest pontoon (a bit noisy from the nearby traffic; moderate fee) just NW of the 15 m bridge; with a tall mast, one will need to pass under the 30 m bridge and then approach from the N. Here one can visit the national museum for the Hurtigruten coastal cargo and passenger service. There is a tourist development with pontoons on the W of Børøya, but there may be insufficient depth for sailing yachts, and a key must be borrowed for shore access.

Blokken (W Hinøya)
Chart 76   68° 36′ N, 15° 23′ E
A beautiful small fishing harbour at the SE side of Sortlandfjorden, well known for the repair of fishing boats.

Sortland (W Hinøya)
Chart 76;   68° 42′ N, 15° 25′ E
A guest pontoon is available at the S end of the town, and a pontoon near the shops for a quick stop.

Tranesvågen (SE Andøya)
Chart 78   69° 00′ N, 15° 34′ E
A pleasant wild anchorage, overlooking pretty wooded valleys between mountains. A good place to wait for the tide through Risøyrennen.

Risøyhamn (SE Andøya)
Charts 79, 78   68° 58′ N, 15° 39′ E
This small harbour on the NW side of Risøysundet is an adequate passage stopover, with a small museum, PO and shop. There is a buoyed channel to the harbour, N of the Hurtigruten quay.

Bjarkøya
Charts 79, 80   69° 00′ N, 16° 32′ E
Bjarkøy was a major Viking centre, to which at one time even the king would send his sons to learn how to become proper Viking kings. A major attraction now is a taxidermist at the W-side anchorage of S Leirvågen, with the largest private collection of birds in N Europe, as well as many other animals.

The nearby anchorage at N Leirvågen is probably a bit better sheltered in W winds. There is a mole harbour with good pontoons in the bight of the large bay on the E side of the island (5 km to S Leirvåg).

Helløya (SW)
Chart 79 69° 01.5′ N, 16° 31′ E
The enclosed cove at the SW corner of the island is a very scenic, pleasant and secure wild anchorage; a couple of free moorings are available, and the holding is said to be poor for anchoring. Enter in good depth through the most S entrance. There is a large colony of kittiwakes on the steep S side of the island, which one can approach closely. Note that Kvøttøya and the archipelago stretching a few miles N is a military prohibited area.

Sand (W Sandsøya)
Charts 79, 80 68° 57′ N, 16° 40′ E
A beautiful anchorage in sand, with good walking ashore and a handsome church. Note the military prohibited area at NE Sandsøya: Hallevika and the area just SE of Dalsneset.

Skrolsvik (SW Senja)*
Charts 79, 80 69° 04′ N, 16° 49′ E
A pleasant fishing village mole harbour, with guest pontoon, and a museum exhibiting *kveite* (halibut) of more than 300 kg. Showers are available within a walk of a couple of kilometres.

Engenes (NW Andørja)
Chart 80 68° 56′ N, 17° 08′ E
A pleasant well sheltered harbour, but with the large quay marked 'Private', there is limited space alongside the remaining smaller fishing boat quay. It might also be possible to tie to a ring on the mole, with a stern anchor.

Eidet / Eidevågen (S Senja)
Chart 80 69° 05′ N, 17° 11′ E

A small pleasant mole harbour with a pontoon, and good walks ashore.

Dyrøyhamn (SE Dyrøya)
Chart 80 69° 01′ N, 17° 26′ E
A small, pretty harbour with quays, a detached pontoon and moorings; open to the NE. Ask at the shop about showering at the fish processing building. Langhamn, a couple of miles N, is another small mole harbour, with an adequate quay and fuel; it is also open to the NE. There is a new 18 m bridge at the NE tip of Dyrøya.

Kirkholmen (E Dyrøya)
Chart 80 69° 02′ N, 17° 29′ E
A charming anchorage in farming country, tucked inside the island just below the churchyard, open to the S and E. You can anchor in 3–6 m sand on the steep shelf, with probably a second anchor in 8–10 m.

Klauva (E Senja)
Chart 83 69° 11.5′ N, 18° 00′ E
An attractive wild anchorage, open to the SE. Anchor in 8 m sand, with good swinging room, or closer to shore using one of the three mooring bolts. Ashore is an abandoned house, interesting older stone foundations, and nice forested walks.

Djupvågen
Chart 83 69° 10′ N, 18° 07′ E
A very pleasant and secure harbour with extensive pontoons (moderate fee), on the mainland at the E end of Solbergfjorden. Although open to the S, a tyre barrage offers good shelter. Home of the very hospitable Senja Sailing Club. Shops are several kilometres to the S.

Finnsnes
Chart 83 69° 13.8′ N, 17° 59′ E
In the centre of Finnsnes, there is a guest pontoon very near shops, useful for a

quick re-supply, but the harbour is very busy and one may get little sleep if staying there overnight. Much quieter are the pontoons at the 'Refa Marina', just SE of the bridge, also with excellent provisioning, fuel and a chandlery. There is also a new (1994) harbour with pontoons just NE of the bridge.

Gibostadt (E Senja)*
Chart 83   69° 21′ N, 18° 05′ E
This harbour at the N end of Gisundet is reported to be heavily washed by passing traffic. Gibostadtsundet is a military area, with no anchoring, diving or bottom-fishing permitted. There is good anchorage just to the N, behind the wildlife reserve Hestøya, which provides shelter from the wake of passing ships. It is reported that if one anchors at Vang to the N (69° 28′ N, 18° 01′ E), there may be coral mixed with the clay clinging to the anchor when it is pulled up, a reminder that the land-mass of Norway was once at the Equator. There are a couple of anchorages charted in W Gisundet around 69° 19′ N, 17° 55′ E that might be worth exploring, and another a couple of miles farther S at Grasmyr.

Tromsø
Charts 87, 466   69° 39′ N, 18° 58′ E
Attractive Tromsø is the world's most northern university city, and offers extensive services. To find the guest pontoons at 'Kai #11', turn W next to the mole immediately S of the bridge; harbour dues are moderate. Fuel is available by telephone request just N of the guest harbour (beware of the overhead crane), or at three locations to the W immediately N of the bridge. Guest berthing is often available at the Tromsø Seilforening (showers, washing machine, and interesting sailors to talk to) just N of the guest harbour, quieter than at Kai #11. A laundrette can be reached by the No 21 bus to the Bleivika Industrial Estate, and the AGA propane outlet is farther along the same route. The 'Army shop' has heavy wool clothing at very reasonable prices. There are showers, jacuzzi, sauna, CNN TV news and beer available at the 'relaxing room' in the nearby Worth Hotel. The Meteorological Office for N Norway is a ten minute walk up the hill, and one can view weather charts and have a personal discussion of the five-day forecast if heading for Svalbard; this is also available by telephoning 77 68 40 44. If one wishes to take away copies of charts, there is likely to be a substantial fee. Those with weatherfax capability on the yacht may find Tromsø so electromagnetically noisy that no weather charts will be received. There is an excellent polar museum, and the modern cathedral boasts Europe's tallest stained glass windows. There is also a mountain cable tramway E of the bridge.

Tyttebærvika (Kjosenfjorden)
Chart 90   69° 35′ N, 19° 58′ E
Kjosenfjorden cuts deeply into the spectacular Lyngen Alps, and at Tyttebærvika (Whortleberry Cove) there is a small quay at a sand quarry. There is good hiking, and Dutch physiotherapist Gooi de Vries, who lives approximately 3 km W, can offer detailed information about the area.

Nordeidet (E Reinøya)
Chart 91   69° 55′ N, 19° 47′ E
A small pleasant and scenic mole harbour, with good holding and swinging room. Lenangsøyra, 8 miles SE, and Nordlenangen, 8 miles E, are alternative harbours.

Vannvåg (SE Vannøya)
Charts 91, 92, 93   70° 04′ N, 20° 00′ E
A busy mole harbour, with several quays and many moored boats. One

might wish to top up with fuel here before departing N to Svalbard. Around Litle Skorøya, 3 miles N, there are several berthing and anchorage possibilities as charted. Note that there is a Landscape and Animal Protection Area in Skipsfjorden, in the N centre of Vanøya, S of a line running 230° from Skotallneset.

Torsvåg (NW Vannøya)
Chart 92   70° 14' N, 19° 30' E
At the NW tip of Vannøya, this harbour is often used as a departure point for Svalbard, since sailing farther ENE does almost nothing to shorten the offshore distance. A last phone check can be made with the Tromsø Met Office. There are numerous quays, and room for anchoring in 3–5 m sand (watch the charted cables). Showers and some supplies may be available, but no fuel. If departing N, beware the offlying skerries. Fugløya to the E teems with birds early in the season; the island is a Bird Reserve, with a Bird Protection Area extended N and W of the island out to 2 km.

2 *North-bound along the W side of Senja and Kvaløya*

This makes a fine alternative route to Tromsø or Torsvåg, as well as an interesting cruising ground per se.

Halvardsøya (NW)*
Chart 82   69° 09.5' N, 16° 52' E
Den Norske Los reports an anchorage in 3 m, in the sheltered bight NW of the tower.

Rødsand (in Selfjorden, SW Senja)*
Chart 82   69° 08' N, 17° 02' E
A small mole harbour in a S bay of Selfjorden.

Flakstadvåg (in Selfjorden, SW Senja)*
Chart 82   69° 11' N, 17° 02' E
A small mole harbour at N Selfjorden.

Torsken (in Torskenfjorden–W Senja)*
Chart 82   69° 20' N, 17° 05' E
A pleasant open cove, with a pontoon. Gryllefjord, a couple of miles N, is a village with many quays, mainly of historic interest.

Hamn (W Senja)
Charts 82, 85 inset   69° 25' N, 17° 10' E
A very pleasant compact fishing village mole harbour on W Senja, with a guest pontoon. There is a café and sauna, but no shopping. This remote village is said to have had the second electrical generating plant in the world!

Rognan (in Ersfjorden, NW Senja)
Chart 85   69° 29' N, 17° 24' E
A small mole harbour at the end of the beautiful Ersfjorden. If one chooses to enter the harbour at Rognan rather than anchor nearby, watch for shoals close S of the NW mole, and in the SE half of the harbour.

Senje-Hopen (in Melfjorden, NW Senja)*
Chart 85   69° 30' N, 17° 30' E
A small and pleasant enclosed bay halfway down the SW coast of Melfjorden, with a buoyed channel and quays. Note that the perch Store Skjærboen, a couple of miles ESE at 69° 29' N, 17° 37' E, was reported missing in 1994. An alternative is Melfjordvær, a small mole harbour to starboard a mile before Senje-Hopen.

Husøy (in Øyfjorden, N Senja)*
Chart 85   69° 32.7' N, 17° 40' E
A substantial and pretty mole harbour, entered from the S, halfway down the E coast of Øyfjorden.

Sommarøy (W of Kvaløya)
Charts 84, 86   69° 38' N, 18° 01' E
At the S side of the W end of Sommarøya, SW of Kvaløya, an interesting area to visit. One can berth at one

of the many quays. If this location seems too busy, there is a very fine anchorage just S of the island marked 'litle' on the chart, at 69° 37′ N, 18° 01′ E; a pretty island with nice beaches.

Håja (W of Kvaløya)*
Chart 86   69° 44′ N, 18° 06′ E
A fine anchorage E of this small island, open to the SE.

Hersøy (W of Kvaløya)*
Chart 86   69° 46′ N, 18° 07′ E
A fine anchorage between Hersøya and Bjørnøya, open to the SE.

Skarsfjord (W Ringvassøya)*
Chart 88   69° 57.5′ N, 18° 50′ E
In a pretty little fjord, with nice walks and mountains; there is a quay on the SW shore, and several anchorages.

Kjerringvika (SE Hersøya)*
Chart 88   70° 05′ N, 19° 00′ E

Tofte (NE Ribbenesøya)*
Chart 88   70° 05′ N, 18° 56′ E
Natural anchorages.

3 Dyrøya to Lødingen via Tjelsundet (Southbound)

This route, to the E of Hinnøya, provides passage between Tromsø and the S via Ofoten and Eastern Lofoten, a good complement to Raftsundet passage W of Hinnøya reported above.

Engenes (NW Andøra) (see above)
Chart 80   68° 56′ N, 17° 08′ E

Bolla (NE Rolla)
Chart 80   68° 50′ N, 17° 05′ E
A sheltered mole harbour, with anchoring in 4 m sand, or berthing at the end of the pontoon is available or at the rather rough quays.

Tovik (S of Rolla)
Chart 77   68° 41′ N, 16° 53′ E
A very small mole harbour with exceptionally friendly people.

Gratangen (Gratangenfjorden)
Chart 77 inset   68° 41′ N, 16° 27′ E
Gratangen was at one time among the busiest fishing ports in Norway, but became completely inactive some years ago. The village has bounced back, and is now a thriving museum of old wooden boats, with weekend boat-oriented activities scheduled frequently during the summer months. At Foldvik, halfway into the fjord to starboard, there are restored old buildings, a restaurant and quays for the larger in-water boats from the museum. The museum, with 15–20 boats on display and around 50 in storage, is located at Gratangsbotn; if one's mast is too tall to pass under the 17 m bridge, local transportation will be organised. Showers and laundry are available. It is best to phone ahead before a visit, to be sure that everyone has not gone off to an old-boat gathering, and to let the organisers know to expect visitors: Tel: (47) 76 92 03 70 or (47) 76 92 15 08. One can write for more information: Gratangen Boat Museum, N-9470 Gratangen, Norway.

Kjøtta (NE of Hinnøya)
Chart 80   68° 52.5′ N, 15° 42.5′ E
There are two scenic, wild and sheltered anchorages between Kjøtta and Kjøttakalven, entered respectively either from the E or W, with pleasant walking ashore.

Harstad (E Hinnøya)
Charts 77, 79, 80, 487
68° 48′ N, 16° 33′ E
This sizeable city has a central guest pontoon that can be noisy during summer nights (moderate fee; washer, dryer and showers). It is also poorly sheltered from the E and NE; should it get unpleasantly rough, one can move 5 miles around the N headland to a pontoon in the Hagan small-boat harbour

at Nygård. One might also find shelter in the inner harbour to the S. At Trondenes, 1.5 km ExN from Hagen, there is a handsome Romanesque mid-thirteenth-century church, and in fair weather one can anchor off and row ashore to visit it. Just to the N of the church a military installation offers guided tours of 'King Adolph', a giant siege cannon from the Second World War. Harstad has a small maritime museum, and there is a notable arts festival in late June.

4 Northbound, clockwise from Raftsundet through the outer Vesterålen, around Langøya to Andenes

Only harbours and anchorages of known special interest are listed; there are many other fishing harbours and isolated anchorages.

Slåtøya (N of Østvågøya)
Chart 69   68° 28' N, 14° 59' E
This small island is particularly pleasant to walk on; there is fair-weather anchorage to the E and SE.

Melbu (S Hadseløya)
Charts 69, 75, 76   68° 30' N, 14° 49' E
At the S side of Hadseløya, Melbu is noted for its Sommermelbu arts festival in July; concerts using huge disused metal tanks as sounding chambers are a special hallmark. Also part of the festival is a guided group hike up Strøna (907 m), across the sound to the S. There is a museum for the fishing industry. Swing to starboard upon entering to find the pontoons sheltered by tyre-barrages; fuel delivery by truck can be arranged from the petrol station. One might also find a berth at a pontoon in the N bight. The walk up an unsurfaced road to the TV tower on the peak 5 km NE passes through a pleasant wooded area, and offers outstanding views of the midnight sun and the mountains and fjords of Langøya.

Eidsfjorden (SW Langøya)
Chart 76   68° 39' N, 14° 48' E
This large fjord, which had a population of 10 000 late in the last century, has several subsidiary fjords with small islands lying below high peaks, offering unusually scenic anchoring possibilities. **Uvågen,** on the port hand inside the entrance to Jørgenfjorden at 68° 40.0' N, 14° 40.2' E, is probably the best sheltered all-weather harbour in this area, with good holding and swinging room. Another very fine anchorage is near **Hellfjord,** at 68° 40.6' N, 14° 48.5' E, to starboard at the entrance to Hellfjorden at the 13 m sounding, with good shelter and swinging room. One can also anchor at the N-most bend in Hellfjorden, in a scenic but somewhat open location. Most of the anchorages in the adjacent Melfjorden have cabins and small pontoons, detracting from the wild surroundings. Olderfjorden abounds in anchoring opportunities (with lines ashore) for those who enjoy intricate navigation, and there is a nice walk by a lake to Ånfjordbotn on the other side of Langøya. **Vottesnes,** S of Melfjorden, is also said to be a fine natural anchorage.

Gaukværøya (SW of Langøya)
Chart 76   68° 37.2' N, 14° 20.2' E
This smallish high island is an especially interesting, but now deserted, outpost that can be visited in settled weather. The last settlers departed in 1952, taking their houses with them, leaving only extensive stoneworks as a legacy of the 300 fisherfolk once resident (600 in winter). There are four charted anchorages on the W side. Skjæringstad has a tiny mole and is said to offer the best shelter, but it is very small; it is entered from the S between two perches. The anchorage E of the 7 m sounding is in

9 m, with less swinging room than the anchorage farther N in 6 m; the latter has a small pontoon used to deliver tourists; these anchorages are both entered from the SW, not from Skjæringstad. An old path, now used by sheep, runs along the W of the island and makes an interesting walk, and the views from the top of the cliffs are superb.

In 1994, the W-most perch marking the 1 m rock at Husleia, SW of the anchorages, was missing.

Nykvåg (W Langøya)
Chart 76   68° 47' N, 14° 28' E
This attractive and pleasant fishing harbour has good anchorage and quays, and the cliffs above the harbour swarm with thousands of kittiwakes. Nearby Fuglnyken is noted for its great population of seabirds and nearby eagles, and the kittiwake colony on the E face of Votten (just S of Fuglnyken) can be approached very near to. The harbour **Hovden** (chart 76 inset, chart 78), 4 miles NE, also offers good shelter.

In 1994, the perch marking the dangerous Lofotbøen SE of Fuglnyken was missing.

Tinden (W Tindsøya)
Chart 78   68° 50.5' N, 14° 45.5' E
Tinden is an attractive trading post preserved from the last century, still operated by its 80-year-old owner as a general store and informal museum. One can browse among a fascinating assortment of miscellany, especially in the upstairs loft, and imagine a bit what it was like in olden times. Note that a perch in Børøysundet, 1 mile E of Tinden, 68° 50.4' N, 14° 50.6' E, was reported missing in 1994.

Nyksund on N Langøya in Vesterålen. This small fishing village is once again almost abandoned.

Ånfjordbotn (NW Langøya)
Chart 76   68° 44.6' N, 14° 53.7' E
A sheltered anchorage surrounded by high peaks, with good hiking SE by a lake to Olderfjorden. Even though partly skirted by a road, it's a wild and beautiful scene. Enter holding to starboard in 2–3 m with a lookout for rocks, and beware an uncharted shoal and rock that just covers at HW, located close NE of the 4 m sounding; once past this rock, there is good swinging room in 4–5 m. The various sounds between this anchorage and Tinden make a pleasant sheltered diversion; one can even see a pretty pink sister of the Copenhagen mermaid overlooking Perneset at SE Nærøya.

Øksnes (S Skogsøya)
Chart 78   68° 53' N, 14° 58' E
The small cove W of the church can be entered with caution at HW in calm weather, keeping extremely close to the channel perches. There is an interesting camp where children come from the state school system to learn about traditional coastal crafts. The camp usually has a free mooring. **Myhre** to the NE is a large harbour with shelter, shops and fuel.

Nyksund (N Langøya)
Chart 78   69° 00' N, 15° 01' E
Nyksund is a small fishing harbour in very attractive surroundings, which was completely abandoned in about 1950, recently resurrected for a few years as an international student centre, and now once again is very nearly abandoned. It's a real ghost town, somewhat depressing, but interesting. Superb views from the hills above the town.

Stø (N Langøya)
Chart 78   69° 01' N, 15° 08' E
Stø is a pleasant small fishing harbour, the site of the new Whale Watch Centre and Museum founded in 1994. One can get advice at the museum or by VHF to the Whale Watch boat as to where to find the whales that frequent the waters upwelling to the NW. Gisløya and Grunnfjorden, 4 miles SE, are Landscape and Bird Protection Areas.

Bleik (NW Andøya)*
Chart 81   69° 16' N, 15° 57' E
Bleiksøya is a noted bird island, and the owner prohibits landing during the nesting season. The harbour of Bleik, a couple of miles E, is a sizeable fishing harbour with many moorings and a small pontoon. There are several miles of fine white beach N and S of Bleik. There is a rocket range between Bleik and Andenes that is used mostly in the winter for auroral research; in the unlikely event of summer use, it *should* be patrolled, and Bodø Radio will be able to advise on any activity.

Andenes (N Andøya)
Charts 81 inset 82   69° 19.5' N, 16° 08' E
Andenes has a large complex mole harbour with many intricate shoals (both in the harbour and surrounding), not especially attractive or accommodating for yachts; the best berth is inside the SE mole, free of shoals, alongside a fishing boat, or alongside the rescue boat (with permission – also a fuelling point). In heavy weather or poor visibility, the most prudent approach from the W is by passing to the E of Andenes with 2 miles offing, and then entering from the E. There is a small Polar Museum founded by Svalbard trapper Hilmar Nois, of particular interest to those bound for Svalbard. The climb to the top of the lighthouse is interesting, and the view from the top is excellent. The Whaling Centre museum offers Whale Safaris to see the large number of sperm and humpback whales frequenting the waters upwelling NW, and one can call

the Whale Safari boat on the yacht's VHF for advice on the current location of the whales. An extraordinary and unexplained ramming of the Safari ship occurred in 1993, leaving a large dent in the side of the ship; one is advised to leave the engine running to be more obvious to the whales, on the presumption that they do wish to avoid a collision!

6 Torsvåg to Nordkapp

Counties: Troms and Finnmark

The mountains and islands of this coast are on a large scale, cut by numerous fjords and sounds offering sheltered scenic passages. The people are fewer, and the miles seem longer. 'Nordkapp' has an alluringly remote ring, and one may sail for several weeks without seeing another yacht.

CHARTS

Charts 322 and 323 at 1:200 000 provide the overview; the recommended detailed coverage is provided by charts 92 to 104 at 1:50 000, selected to fit one's itinerary. A harbour chart is available for Hammerfest (489).

TIDES AND STREAMS

The greatest spring tides range slightly over 3 m at Torsvåg. HW there is 2½ hours after Bergen; at Nordkapp, HW is 3 hours 20 minutes after Bergen. Tidal streams in sounds are generally moderate, but peak at 4 knots in Magerøysundet S of Magerøya (S of Nordkapp) and Kvalsundet S of Kvaløya; the tidal stream flows north-easterly from 3½ hours before HW to 2½ hours after HW.

PASSAGE

Note that these perches were reported missing in 1994: Bortrefallet (charts 94, 95), 70° 04′ N, 20° 15′ E, and Langskjær (chart 94), 70° 01.3′ N, 20° 18.6′ E.

HARBOURS AND ANCHORAGES

See **Torsvåg** (chart 92) and **Vannvåg** (charts 91, 92, 93) shown on pages 70 to 71.

Kristoffervalen (E Vannøya)*
Charts 91, 92, 93   70° 08′ N, 20° 00′ E
An enclosed harbour with several quays, with entry via a buoyed channel open to the E.

Årviksand (NW Arnøya)*
Chart 93   70° 12′ N, 20° 31′ E
A substantial mole harbour with several quays, entered from the W.

Skjervøy (E Skjervøya)
Charts 93, 94   70° 02′ N, 21° 00′ E
This large and busy harbour has an extensive boat-club pontoon system; the quays and guest pontoon (immediately to starboard on entry) may be heavily washed by ferry wakes. Note that Store Follesøya, 10 miles SW, is a Special Bird Reserve, and Lille Follesøya is a Bird Protection Area.

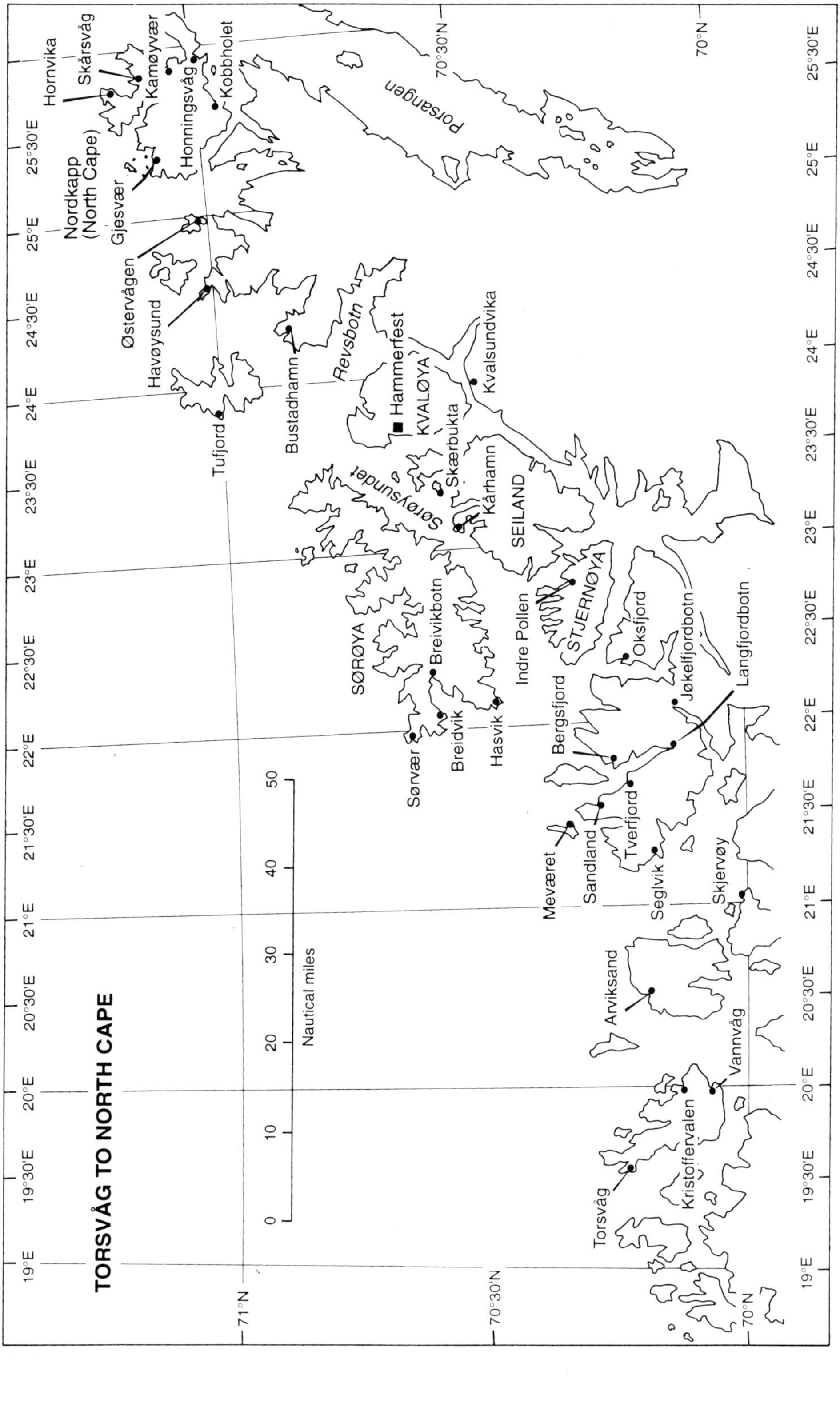
TORSVÅG TO NORTH CAPE
Nautical miles
0
10
20
30
40
50
Hornvika
Skårsvåg
Kamøyvær
Honningsvåg
Kobbholet
Nordkapp
(North Cape)
Gjesvær
Østervågen
Havøysund
Tufjord
Bustadhamn
Revsbotn
Hammerfest
KVALØYA
Kvalsundvika
Skærbukta
Kårhamn
SEILAND
Sørøysundet
SØRØYA
Breivikbotn
Breidvik
Sørvær
Hasvik
Indre Pollen
STJERNØYA
Oksfjord
Jøkelfjordbotn
Langfjordbotn
Bergsfjord
Meværet
Sandland
Tverfjord
Seglvik
Skjervøy
Arviksand
Vannvåg
Kristoffervalen
Torsvåg
Porsangen
71°N
70°30'N
70°N
19°E
19°30'E
20°E
20°30'E
21°E
21°30'E
22°E
22°30'E
23°E
23°30'E
24°E
24°30'E
25°E
25°30'E

Seglvik
Charts 93, 95   70° 12′ N, 21° 13′ E
Seglvik, at the W tip of a large mainland peninsula, is a pretty mole harbour with quays and good anchorage.

Jøkelfjordbotn
Chart 95   70° 07′ N, 22° 04′ E
From the small quay at the end of the fjord, there is a good view of the glacier, which comes down almost to sea level.

Meværet (E Loppa)
Chart 95   70° 20.7′ N, 21° 27.5′ E
Small moles make a good harbour, with a fine old grocery shop. There is also said to be good anchorage off the church. Most of the W and NW sides of Loppa is a Bird Reserve, out to 500 m offshore.

Sandland
Chart 95   70° 16′ N, 21° 36′ E
Just SW of the island of Silda, an attractive and scenic small mole harbour with quays and anchorage, but sometimes with little room for a yacht; one can also anchor outside the harbour, exposed to the NW and N. Shop and PO. Enter heading SE, passing SW of the varde in 5 m.

Bergsfjord
Chart 95   70° 15′ N, 21° 48′ E
Just SE of the island Silda, a sheltered harbour with anchoring room in 8 m off the fishing quay; PO and shop 3 km along road. The entry from the N is easy once the first varde is seen.

Tverfjord-S (S Tverfjorden)
Chart 95   70° 13′ N, 21° 44′ E
A sheltered quay, and a shop.

Langfjordbotn (Langfjorden)
Chart 95   70° 08′ N, 21° 52′ E
Berthing is available at quays at an attractive village, and there is an excellent hike to the glacier.

Hasvik (SW Sørøya)
Chart 97   70° 29′ N, 22° 10′ E
A nice mole harbour with fishing boats

Gullvika, Lofoten. (Photo: Hallgeir Pettersen)

berthed alongside quays, and a new pontoon. Water and fuel can be delivered, and it has been known for a good-sized *torsk* to be offered in welcome. The S coast of Sørøya also has several coves suitable for anchoring.

There follow three small mole harbours that might be particularly useful on a return passage from Svalbard:

Sørvær (W Sørøya)*
Chart 100   70° 38′ N, 21° 59′ E
Breidvik (W Sørøya)*
Chart 100   70° 36′ N, 22° 07′ E
Breivikbotn (W Sørøya)*
Chart 100   70° 35.5′ N, 22° 18′ E

Note that the following areas on Sørøya are Bird Reserves out to 200 m offshore: SW of the peak Andotten, which is SxE from Sørvær; Storgalten to Lyngøya, in E Galtefjorden, NW central Sørøya; around Lille Kamøya, N Sørøya.

Øksfjord
Charts 96, 97   70° 14.5′ N, 22° 21′ E
A pleasant substantial town at the NE of Øksfjorden cutting S into the mainland, with many large quays and a small-boat harbour. Extensive supplies, a boatyard with aluminium welding and even a doctor are available. Ytre Lokkarfjorden, 3 miles ExS, offers a good isolated anchorage with pleasing walks under dramatic overhanging mountains.

Alta / Bossekop (in Altafjorden)
Chart 96   69° 58′ N, 23° 15′ E
Bossekop, an old trading post at the foot of Altafjorden, is the harbour for Alta, Finnmark's largest town. There is a slate-quarrying museum that also has exhibits of Sami (Lapp) artefacts. A principal attraction is Hjemmeluft 3 km SW, the site of the most extensive prehistoric rock carvings in N Europe. It is an interesting walk up to the historic Northern Lights Observatory (907 m) at Halden. Bossekop is a mole harbour with several quays and extensive pontoons, where one is likely to find guest space (showers). Bukta, 1 mile NE, is not at all scenic and is the site of an airport and cargo terminal. Talvik, 7 miles NW, is an attractive village anchorage with bus connection to Alta, a PO and shop.

Indre Pollen (SW Rognsundet)
Chart 97   70° 19.5′ N, 22° 49′ E
A beautiful completely sheltered pool, with good anchorage in 4 m; mooring bolts on the island.

Kårhamn (N Seillandet)
Chart 98   70° 32.5′ N, 23° 10′ E
A small fishing village in a bay open to the NE, with PO and shop. Anchor off the fish factory in 12 m. Sandan, 2 miles SSE, is a pleasant anchorage in 6–8 m sand, with a few holiday cottages.

Skærbukta (Store Vinna)
Chart 98   70° 34′ N, 23° 21′ E
A small mole harbour that usually has a vacant mooring available. Factory and cottage ruins ashore, with good walking and fine views. Once a community of 400, destroyed in 1944. Note that Eidvågen, 3 miles SE, is a Bird Reserve out to 200 m offshore.

Kvalsundvika*
Chart 99   70° 30′ N, 23° 59′ E
A mole harbour in a small cove E and S of Kvalsundet, S of Kvaløya.

Hammerfest (NW Valøya)
Charts 98, 101, 489   70° 40′ N, 23° 41′ E
The world's N-most mainland city, with extensive facilities. Berth at a quay or at the city harbour pontoon inside the commercial pier, to starboard on entry; check to see if the yacht will need to be moved as others come and go. There are

boat-club pontoons to the N (size and depth unknown), and fuel and water. Showers are available at the Hammerfest Hotel. You can purchase membership of the Royal and Ancient Polar Bear Society, as long as you're not expecting to actually see a real *isbjørn* in Svalbard. There are notable views from the top of the zig-zag road to Salen.

Bustadhamn
Charts 99, 102   70° 51′ N, 24° 19′ E
On the mainland just S of the small island Reinøya, this deserted village has rather dilapidated quays but is a pleasant, interesting and secure harbour. One may find a few summer residents, and may see Samis with their reindeer. Government centralisation encouraged abandonment in about 1960, subsequently the fish plant was burnt down, and then another house was burnt by a fisherman whose boat had capsized, in order to attract attention to his plight. There is also anchorage in the N part of the harbour. There is a Bird Reserve in the area of Reinøykalven to the NW, up to 200 m offshore.

Tufjord (W Rolvsøya)*
Charts 101, 102   71° 00′ N, 23° 54′ E
A large sheltered harbour.

Havøysund (S Havøya)
Chart 102 inset   71° 00′ N, 24° 40′ E
This pleasant small community has numerous quays and fishing boats in a sheltered sound. Shops, bank, PO and a Second World War museum. The crew of the rescue boat can provide local information. Note that the N-most mile of Hjelmsøya, 9 miles NxE, is a Bird Reserve out to 500 m offshore.

Østervågen (SE Måsøya)
Charts 102, 103   71° 00′ N, 25° 02′ E
This pleasant harbour has several quays inside a mole, and a fine old church to visit. The school is also an interesting visit – with four teachers for 13 children. There are strong tidal streams. Shipyards, slips and a dry-dock.

Gjesvær (W Magerøya)*
Chart 103   71° 06′ N, 25° 23′ E
A good fishing harbour, approached from the NW or NE, then swinging SW. The three islands a couple of miles N of Gjesvær are a Bird Reserve, up to 500 m offshore.

Kobbholet (S Magerøya)
Chart 103   70° 57.5′ N, 25° 42′ E
An attractive natural anchorage, deep, with the holding perhaps not the best.

Honningsvåg (S Magerøya)
Chart 103 inset, 104   71° 00′ N, 26° 00′ E
A busy and sometimes noisy port with many quays, a guest harbour N of the commercial harbour, and a pontoon in the main harbour available for visitors' shopping. There is a bus service to the exhibits at Nordkapp, 34 km distant, said to be interesting but noisy and expensive. The helpful harbourmaster may be able to obtain ice/weatherfax charts from Tromsø, if one is bound for Svalbard. Showers in the SAS hotel. The museum is said to be interesting.

Kamøyvær (E Magerøya)*
Charts 103, 104   71° 03′ N, 25° 55′ E
A small fishing harbour, approached from the E.

Skarsvåg (NE Magerøya)
Charts 103, 104   71° 07′ N, 25° 50′ E
A picturesque fishing village, the most northerly in the world outside Siberia, only a few kilometres SE of Nordkapp. The small mole harbour is approached from the NE, with mooring alongside fishing boats to port after entry. Shopping by bus or a ride hitched from a tourist. This departure point for Svalbard is only 20 miles closer than Torsvåg, 155 miles WSW.

Hornvika (NE Magerøya)
Charts 103, 104   71° 09.5′ N, 25° 48′ E
Before there was a road to Nordkapp, this cove was used to land tourists. There is a dilapidated quay that may not extend down far enough at LW, and the bottom is large stones, thus mooring may be difficult. There is a steep 300 m climb up old wooden steps, with remnants of iron railings, to the plateau of Nordkapp.

7 Nordkapp to the Russian Border

County: Finnmark

Because the sailing lies offshore rather than in sounds, this coastline is less scenic than that farther W. Very few yachts venture so far E, unless bound for Murmansk.

CHARTS

Charts 324 and 325 at 1:200 000 provide the overview; the recommended detailed coverage is provided by charts 104, 108, 109, 114 and 116 at 1:50 000, and chart 294 at 1:100 000. Charts 105 to 107, 110 and 115 would also be needed for exploration far into some of the fjords.

TIDES AND CURRENTS

The greatest spring tides run slightly over 3 m at Nordkapp and Berlevåg, and 3.5 m at Vardø and Kirkenes. At Nordkapp, HW is 3 hours 20 minutes after Bergen; at Berlevåg, HW is 5½ hours after Bergen; at Vardø and Kirkenes, HW is 6½ hours after Bergen. The stream is reported to reach 3 knots close by the point at Slettnes Light.

HARBOURS AND ANCHORAGES

Descriptions follow of the harbours most used by yachts, and very brief mention is given of harbours less often used but potentially useful if needed for shelter. Note that Sværholtklubben halvøya, halfway between Nordkapp and Køllefjord, is a Bird Reserve, out to 500 m offshore.

Kjøllefjord*
Chart 108   70° 57′ N, 27° 21′ E
A large mole fishing harbour entered from the NW.

Skjøtningberg*
Chart 108   71° 01′ N, 27° 23′ E
A small harbour open to the NE.

Sandfjord*
Chart 108   71° 06′ N, 27° 38′ E
Good anchorage, open to the NW.

Mehamn*
Chart 109 inset   71° 02′ N, 27° 51′ E
A mole harbour entered from the NW.

Gamvik
Chart 109 inset   71° 03.5′ N, 28° 15′ E
A small fishing harbour with good shelter, fine for a passage stopover. Enter from the ESE, turn to the N, and berth at N quay near a fish plant. From here it is an interesting walk to visit the old lighthouse at Slettnes. Note that the area between Avløysingsbukta and Finnkongkeila, a couple of miles SE, is a Bird Reserve, out to 500 m offshore.

NORDKAPP (NORTH CAPE) TO THE RUSSIAN BORDER

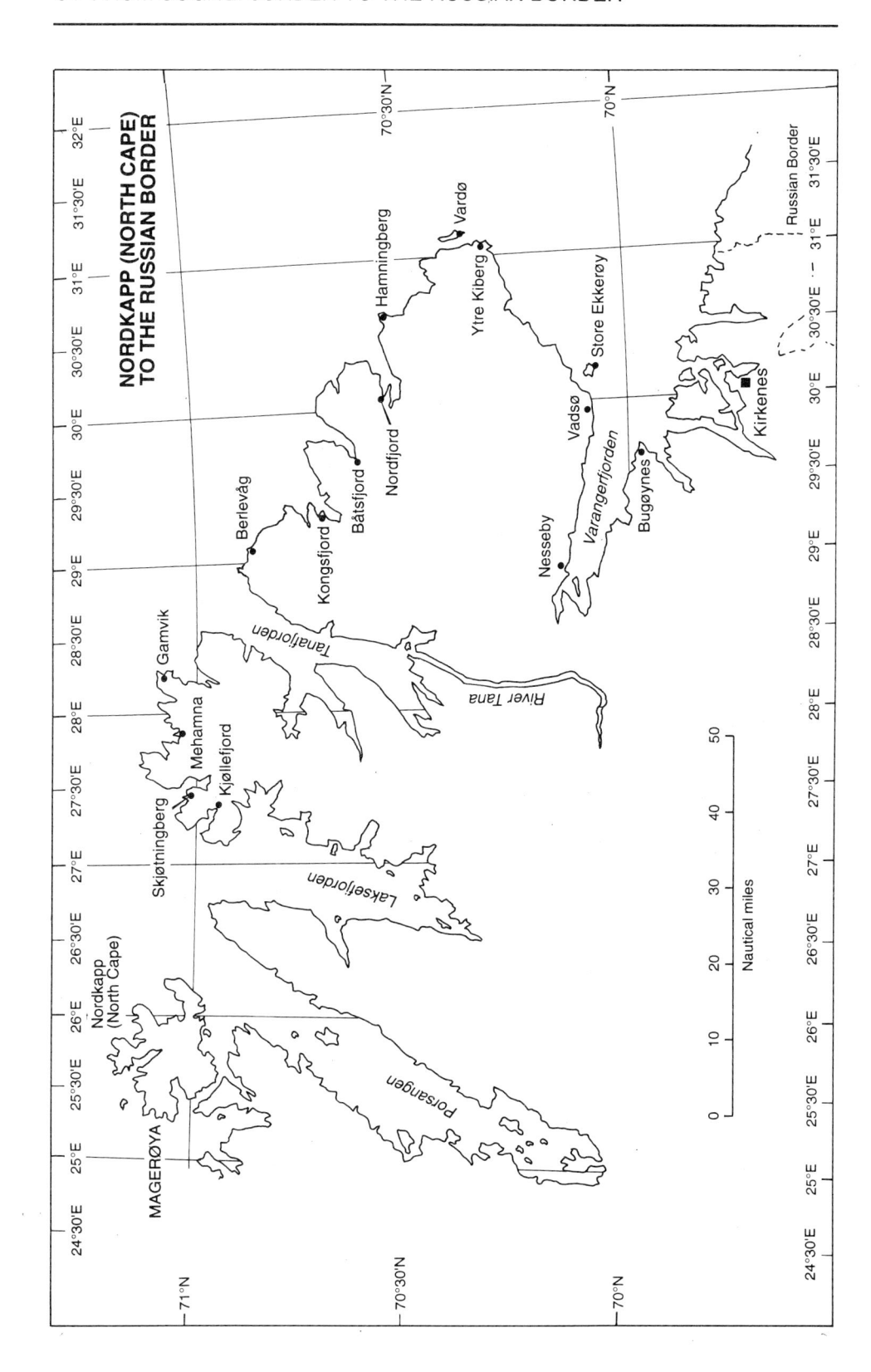

Berlevåg
Chart 294 inset   70° 51′ N, 29° 06′ E
A large fishing harbour with an elaborate French-designed mole replacing the previous one that was destroyed in storms. Good shelter and shopping. Often very busy day and night, making sleep difficult. Enter from the NE, and berth at the SW or alongside a fishing boat as the quays may be difficult for a yacht. There is a museum to the E.

Kongsfjord (in Kongsfjorden)*
Chart 294 inset   70° 43′ N, 29° 19′ E
A large mole harbour entered heading WSW, then N and NE. Note that the three islands lying 3–4 miles E are Bird Reserves, out to 200 m offshore.

Båtsfjord (in Båtsfjorden)
Chart 294 inset   70° 38′ N, 29° 44′ E
A large attractive harbour, with good shelter and supplies. Enter the outer harbour from the E, watching for fish farms, and berth at one of the many quays or the pontoon to the S. Note that the area 10 miles ENE, between Molvika (SE of Makkaur Light) and Sandfjorden, is a Bird Reserve, out to 500 m offshore.

Nordfjord (in Syltefjorden)*
Chart 294 inset   70° 33′ N, 30° 06′ E
A mole harbour with quays; enter from the SE.

Hamningberg
Chart 294 inset   70° 32′ N, 30° 37′ E
An interesting old Pomor trading centre; there are also Second World War fortifications on the top of the hill, built to attack the Murmansk convoys. The stone mole is not suitable for berthing, but there is good anchorage either side of the peninsula.

Vardø (SE Vardøya)
Charts 114, 294 insets
70° 22′ N, 31° 06′ E
A very old town and harbour with an ancient Danish fort, a nice stop with

When sailing in this sort of scenery (near Grøtøya) winds can be unpredictable! (Photo: Hugo Svendsen)

good supplies. Approach from the N or SE, enter from the N, and berth at the pontoon immediately to port. The island is connected by a tunnel to the mainland. It might be worthwhile to call Vardø Radio and ask about a visit to their facility. There is a very large bird colony at the N of Reinøya; this island and the three just SE are Bird Reserves. The most easterly harbour in Norway, Vardø is E of both Istanbul and Alexandria.

Ytre Kiberg*
Chart 114 inset   70° 17′ N, 31° 00′ E
A mole fishing harbour. Enter from the SSE or SxW, then head ENE.

Store Ekkerøya
Chart 114   70° 04′ N, 30° 06′ E
A very pleasant stop. Shelter is available to the NE of a small mole at the W of the peninsula, and berthing (with permission) at the high quay of the trading-post museum. There are large bird colonies on Store Ekkerøya, with the N and S coasts being a Bird Reserve out to 200 m offshore.

Vadsø*
Charts 114, 115 insets
70° 04′ N, 29° 45′ E
A large mole harbour W of the small isthmus to Vadsøya, entered from the SW. There is a small pontoon and easy waterfront shopping.

Nesseby*
Chart 115   70° 09′ N, 28° 53′ E
A small mole harbour; enter from the SW.

Bugøynes*
Chart 115   69° 58′ N, 29° 39′ E
A large mole harbour; enter from the N or SE.

Kirkenes
Chart 116   69° 44′ N, 30° 03′ E
The end of the line, unless one is headed for Murmansk. After the preceding outposts, this town of 6000–7000 may seem a real metropolis. The SW big-ship quay is a good central berth if there is space available; rather far to the E is a small-boat harbour. There is an interesting Second World War underground bunker museum.

PART 3

Svalbard

8 Cruising Spitsbergen Bjørnøya and Jan Mayen

A voyage to the Svalbard archipelago is a unique high-Arctic adventure. Nowhere else can such high latitude, only 600 miles from the Pole, and such spectacular glaciated mountain scenery be reached so easily by a yacht, in such generally moderate weather conditions, usually without serious danger or difficulty from ice, and in continual daylight. Having said this, however, it must be realised that a yachting voyage to within 600 miles of the Pole is a serious undertaking, requiring a yacht and crew capable of coping with the extreme conditions that the high-Arctic can present at any time. The 300 mile W coast of (Vest-)Spitsbergen island is generally free of extensive pack ice from June to November; however, the 'yachting season' tapers off during mid-August to avoid the rapidly increasing likelihood of severe weather. The coast is cut by deep fjords that offer many anchorages, often with beautiful blue glacier ice drifting about. The distant scene encompasses hundreds of square miles of huge glaciers separated by jagged mountain peaks, and the foreground often includes a glacier snout several miles wide with a beautiful ice-cliff several mast-heights high. One might see arctic fox, reindeer, walrus, whales, seals or polar bear. Svalbard abounds in seabirds and migratory birds, including the arctic tern, which enjoys both the Arctic and Antarctic summers.

Although there are approximately 3000 Norwegian, Russian and Polish residents on Spitsbergen, they are concentrated in four large settlements with summertime populations of 200–1200, three small settlements each with 4–15 people, and a half-dozen trappers' huts, leaving an overall impression of great isolation. The 22 000 tourists visiting annually by cruise ship and aeroplane are also concentrated, and although one might occasionally share a fjord with a cruise ship, most of the time solitude will prevail. From time to time one may see a yacht (a few dozen visit each year), or a kayaker, climber, trekker, rower, geologist, archaeologist or other visitor, but one is unlikely ever to feel crowded.

At the same time, fuel, water and supplies are available, as well as hospital and dental services should they be needed. VHF and MF Radio weather and communications services, and some degree of emergency assistance by ship or helicopter, are also available. But bear in mind that although the passage to Spitsbergen is less difficult than those to E Greenland or Antarctica, none the less when conditions in the high-Arctic environment turn harsh, or an accident occurs, the situation can quickly become far more serious than in lower latitudes. The cold and isolation places more stress, both physical and psychological, on crews, and tight schedules are likely to be disrupted if conditions deteriorate.

In some years it is possible to circumnavigate Spitsbergen island, venturing into more remote places and difficult conditions than those prevailing on the W and NW coasts. There are likely to be problems with drift ice, and more difficult navigation, perhaps in constricted straits with drift ice in 8–9 knot tidal streams. Much of the area is only now becoming thoroughly charted. Search and Rescue insurance, or the posting of a bank bond, may be required in order to enter these waters.

Bjørnøya (Bear Island) can be used as a way-stop between Norway and Spitsbergen, and although in some respects the island is bleak and desolate, it also has a unique beauty and exotic appeal and is well worth exploring. The coastline teems with seabirds, and the eroded stacks (and even a sea cave) add to the scene. The dozen men and women of the weather and radio station are always keen to have visitors to their extensive facility, and in suitable weather this is a most interesting stop.

The volcanic island Jan Mayen lies roughly 500 miles W of NW Norway and Svalbard, 250 miles E of Greenland and 300 miles NE of Iceland. This is just as isolated as it sounds, a destination for the serious seeker of out-of-the-way places. The ice-free season is similar to that in Vest-Spitsbergen. The island is 30 miles long and barren, with an impressive high glaciated volcanic cone (last eruption in 1970). The incidence of fog and rainy conditions is great in the summer months. The small staff of the Loran and Radio installation welcomes visitors. There are no all-weather anchorages on Jan Mayen. *Den Norske Los*, volume 7, describes the coastline in considerable detail; this is not included in this book.

Although the primary attraction of Svalbard lies in its remote spectacular scenery, some knowledge of its history and cultural infrastructure may add greatly to one's voyage. The two English language guidebooks to Svalbard, listed in the Bibliography, are highly recommended. Although not absolutely necessary, the very fine Arctic Pilot and Visitors' Guide *Den Norske Los*, volume 7, written in both Norwegian and English, is highly recommended for both its detailed pilotage and its extensive general coverage of history, climate, ice, flora and fauna, geology and weather; it would be a shame to sail to Svalbard without this volume.

ICE CONDITIONS

The ice conditions in Svalbard are a balance between the warming influence of the Gulf Stream and the pressure of the pack ice drifting down in the prevailing SW current. In most years the passage from Torsvåg to Bjørnøya to Sørkapp is likely to be free of ice in early June, but in the infrequent bad years it may be well into August before ice is no longer

JA aboard Kyrah *close in to the glacier snout in Ftitjovhamna, Bellsund, Spitsbergen. Not a place to hang about! (Photo: Ben Armitage)*

a problem. A June passage can be planned, but the schedule must be adjustable according to the ice reports in late May and early June. And although the passage to Sørkapp may be ice-free early in June, the SW coast of Spitsbergen, and the inner fjords, may still be obstructed by ice, making late June or early July the most usual passage time. In some years, a few weeks after the W coast of Spitsbergen is clear of ice, the winds may bring new pack ice around Sørkapp, temporarily blocking Hornsund and possibly even Bellsund and Isfjord. In most years there is little difficulty with pack ice W and N of Spitsbergen below $80°$ N except early in the season, but during a bad year the fjords on the W and NW coasts of Spitsbergen may be clogged with glacier drift ice until later in the season.

In some years, the NW and N coasts can be temporarily beset with pack ice in strong N winds, opening back up again with the easing of the wind. There is usually some drift glacier ice in most of the fjords and anchorages of Spitsbergen throughout the summer, with a few larger bits drifting out along the coast. This ice is often very beautiful, but it does require a sharp lookout when under way (especially in foggy conditions) and it can sometimes force a shift in anchorage; however, with continual daylight, this is less of a problem than it would be in darkness.

The impressive and beautiful glacier snouts are often closely approached by yachts and dinghies, but bear in mind that this is not without risk. In addition to the immediate ice-fall and wave produced, there is a possibility of a huge chunk of ice resurfacing some distance out from the snout.

PROTOCOL

Norway has absolute sovereignty over Svalbard and Jan Mayen under a treaty originating in 1920, and the Sysselmann in Longyearbyen governs the territory. Under the treaty, Svalbard may not be wholly integrated as a part of Norway, and is a non-military zone. The signatories, especially the Russians who had mining interests in Svalbard at the time of the signing, have specified rights under the treaty.

Tourism, including yachts, is rapidly increasing in Svalbard, and the government is very concerned. Svalbard's arctic landscape and ecology is extremely fragile, primarily because it takes many years before disturbance to the soil is obscured by weathering, there is little vegetation to hide scars, and reproductive rates of the flora are low. Although there are areas where severe damage has already been done, in some cases even in recent years and by sanctioned activities, most areas away from the few inhabited centres are relatively pristine, and a rapidly rising level of attention is now being given to avoiding further damage and repairing existing damage when possible. Official policy is to discourage the development of mass tourism, and firmly to control even limited tourist activity in order to avoid damage to the environment. Regulation is stricter than in Norway, and is becoming more so each year. The regulations are designed to ensure that one's visit leaves no traces. It is important for yachts to be seen to be aware of and to be adhering to the regulations; every instance of protocol violation or poor seamanship requiring official intervention increases the likelihood of restrictions that could reduce future yachting access to Svalbard.

The document *Environmental Regulations for Svalbard and Jan Mayen* should be requested by writing to: Sysselmannen på Svalbard, 9170 Longyearbyen, Svalbard, Norway (Tel: (47) 79 02 31 00); also, request any other information relevant to a visit by a yacht. It is important to be up to date on the latest changes in the regulations. Briefly, animals and nests should not be disturbed. (To moderate fierce diving attacks by arctic terns, hold up a stick overhead to give them a diversionary target; it is, however, prohibited to strike at them.) Any artefacts or evidence of man's earlier activity, including old whale bones and walrus bones, should be left as found. It is permitted to collect fossils outside the National Parks (in Bellsund, Isfjorden and Kongsfjorden). A primary concern is the exclusion of human activity between 15 May and 15 August within 300 m of all the Bird Sanctuaries, within 300 m of Moffen between 15 May and 15 September, and within 500 m of Kong Karls Land all year round.

Each visitor is required by the regulations to notify the Sysselmann of plans involving travel within National Parks and Nature Reserves; these include SW and NW Spitsbergen, areas likely to be visited by yachts (also included are all areas E of Spitsbergen). Arrival in Svalbard waters should be announced to Bjørnøya Radio and Svalbard Radio on VHF. If visiting Longyearbyen, one must register at the Sysselmann's office in person or, if not by VHF-telephone ((47) 79 02 31 00) during business hours via Svalbard Radio. Be sure to notify the authorities upon leaving Svalbard to avoid receiving an embarrassing enquiry back home to confirm your safe departure.

It is recommended that you carry a hand-held VHF radio and small EPIRB on shore expeditions. Remember that dense fog can develop quickly, and a hand compass could be useful. Walking on areas of glaciers with snow cover or steep ice is likely to be extremely dangerous unless one's crew is properly experienced and equipped with crampons, ice axe and rope.

Passport requirements for Svalbard are as for the rest of Scandinavia, and no special permit is required. There is no customs clearance, but yachts are officially required to clear Customs (usually in Tromsø or Honningsvåg) upon return from Svalbard. Svalbard is a rabies area.

POLAR BEARS (ISBJØRNER)

There are approximately 3500 polar bears in Svalbard, and if one goes on shore outside the few populated areas, they pose a danger. This danger is taken very seriously by the authorities. Although polar bears are not aggressive unless hungry, they may well be hungry, particularly in the summer on the W coast or in the interior away from their usual prey of seals on the pack ice. Without natural enemies, they are fearless, and their great curiosity may change to aggression unexpectedly. They can move unbelievably quickly, up to 60 km/hr for short distances, and may swim faster than one can row a dinghy. During the summer, polar bears are regularly seen along the W coast, and frequently along the N coast, and although one may not be fortunate enough to see one during a visit, the possibility of an encounter is very real. In 1994, we saw one in Hornbæckpollen (in Liefdefjorden), and the same day five more were seen in Krokvika 12 miles NE, including a mother with two cubs, and the day after that a bear was seen swimming across Liefdefjorden.

In the heavy-ice summer of 1993, 20 bears were seen at the Polish Station, during a season usually entirely without bear visits.

Polar bears are protected from hunting, and harassment of one is a serious offence. All visitors are required by the authorities to be adequately armed to protect against an attack, but to take every reasonable measure to avoid an attack, and to shoot a bear in self-defence only when there is no alternative in protecting human life. Protection of property is not usually considered justification for shooting. Any shooting of a bear must be reported immediately; all parts of the carcass belong to the state. Large fines have been imposed in cases of shootings that were deemed avoidable; an experienced local guide suggests that shooting at a range longer than 30 m is likely to be considered unjustified.

Adequate weapons are magazine rifles of at least calibre .308/7.62/30-06, or magazine shotguns using 12 gauge single-slug ammunition (unobtainable in Norway). Semi-automatic assault rifles, and automatic shotguns, illegal for hunting in Norway, are ideal for defence, but are usually expensive. Although a powerful pistol in the hands of an expert may be considered adequate defence against a polar bear attack, pistols of any size are illegal for this purpose. Obviously, each armed person must also be able to use the weapon effectively. Warning shots will sometimes frighten away a polar bear, as may flare guns and/or thunder-flash grenades. If one must shoot to kill, it is suggested to shoot at the chest or shoulder, and follow up immediately with a second shot. A curious bear will often shuffle about sniffing from side to side, but a lowered head and stalking advance usually indicates a charge is imminent.

Each weapon is expected to have documentation that authorises use of the weapon and showing ownership. Although foreigners are not permitted to purchase weapons in Norway, it is permitted for a licensed Norwegian to loan a weapon to a foreigner (as of 1994, the law limits the period of the loan to 30 days, but local exception may be made by the Police Chief, and the law will probably be amended to permit longer loans for the purpose of self-defence in Svalbard). Mauser .308 rifles may be rented for Nkr 300 per week (1994 rate) from YAMAHA/Ing G Paulsen, Postboks 490, 9170 Longyearbyen, Svalbard, Norway, Tel: (47) 79 02 13 22, Fax: (47) 79 02 18 10; a reservation is highly recommended. Rifles may also be rented in Tromsø from Andresens Vaabenforretning, attn: Randi Andresen, Storgt 53, 9000 Tromsø, Tel: 47 776 82 403, for Nkr 35 per day and Nkr 1500 damage deposit (1994 rate). Thunder-flash grenades are available in two sizes at moderate cost from Engelsrud Fyrverkeri Fabrikk, Postboks 387, N-1701 Sarpsborg, Norway, Tel: (47) 69 14 11 00, Fax: (47) 69 14 17 34; shipping charges may exceed the cost of the grenades.

CHARTS

The only single Norwegian chart that covers the waters between the mainland and Sørkapp on Spitsbergen is chart 515; at 1:2 000 000. British Admiralty chart 2228 at 1:1 000 000 is also available as a passage chart.

The entire archipelago of Svalbard, including Bjørnøya, is covered by Norwegian charts 505 and 507 at 1:750 000 and 1:600 000. British Admiralty chart 2751 at 1:823 000 covers the same area as far E as 28° in one chart. Coverage at these scales is not especially useful unless a circumnavigation of Spitsbergen is envisaged, or exploration well E of the more usual areas, in which case charts 533, 535 and 537 at 1:100 000 should also be considered as well.

The W and N coasts of Spitsbergen are covered at 1:350 000 by charts 509 and 510. These charts are recommended as useful for overview and planning, for Wijdefjorden on the N coast, and for several detailed insets of anchorages.

SW Spitsbergen is covered by chart 504 at 1:200 000, which is recommended.

Central Spitsbergen is covered by chart 503 at 1:200 000 and, along with NW Spitsbergen, is covered by charts 521 to 524 at 1:100 000; all are recommended. With 504, 522, 523 and 524, chart 503 is redundant, but may be found convenient none the less.

Chart 513 at 1:15 000–1:60 000 is recommended as useful for its detailed coverage of Ny Ålesund, Longyearbyen, and especially Forlandsrevet, and for the intricate navigation into Sveagruva.

Bjørnøya is covered by chart 501 at 1:40 000, which is recommended because of Bjørnøya's role as a mid-passage haven.

Passage from NW Norway to Jan Mayen is covered by chart 303 at 1:3 500 000, and Jan Mayen is covered by chart 512 at 1:100 000.

Svalbard has been extensively mapped topographically at 1:100 000, and at 1:10 000 in a few areas. These maps may be useful for venturing ashore, and for sailing in the relatively uncharted waters E of Spitsbergen. There are also special maps describing geology, flora and fauna. All maps, as well as aerial photographs, are available at the Norsk Polarinstitutt, Rolfstangveien 12, 1330 Oslo Lufthavn, Norway, or in Longyearbyen.

As from 1994, Svalbard is being resurveyed, and charts are being revised and newly published; many of the present (1995) charts are often based on old surveys, and off the main leads cannot be trusted to show every hazard. Before sailing to Svalbard, it is worth checking with Statens Kartverk to see if there are any new charts or revisions since the last update of the catalogue.

TIDES AND STREAMS

The table below gives the range of the greatest spring tides and the times of HW. Mean Spring range is around 80 per cent of this greatest range, and Mean Neap range around 50 per cent, but note that in some parts of Svalbard the tidal range at neaps is reported to be less than usual compared to the range at springs. Spring tides occur one to two days after the new/full moon.

RANGE OF GREATEST SPRINGS AND TIMES OF HW

Bjørnøya 1.2 m 3:00 after Bergen
(SE) Kvalvågen 1.2 m 1:10 after Bergen
(SW) Hornsund 1.5 m 2:00 after Bergen
(W) Longyearbyen 1.8 m 2:20 after Bergen
(NW) Magdelenefjorden 1.2 m 3:20 after Bergen
(NE) Hinlopen Strait 1.0 m 4:30 after Bergen
Jan Mayen 1.4 m 2:00 after Bergen

Tidal streams are generally moderate except to the E of Spitsbergen, but when added to currents the net speed can sometimes reach 2 knots, even in open water.

Near Bjørnøya, the stream is stronger, especially around the S of the island, around Framneset at the E, and around Kapp Duner at the W where it may reach 3 knots. During the flood tide, the stream runs N along the E and W coasts, and W along the N coast, reversing on the ebb. The waters surrounding Bjørnøya may be disturbed by tidal eddies for some distance off, are often rough, and dangerous in severe weather. Indeed, all of the waters between Norway and Sørkapp are generally rougher than would be expected from the wind strength alone, and a somewhat lumpy passage is usual.

The ocean currents in this area seldom exceed 1 knot, and are quite complex. N of Troms, the current sets mostly NE, with eddies. S of Bjørnøya, the current sets NE in general. W and NW of Bjørnøya, the current sets N, up the W coast of Spitsbergen. The current that sets S along the SE coast of Spitsbergen sweeps W around Sørkapp to join the N setting current, and is the major cause of the pack ice (often with polar bears riding along) on the SW and W coasts of Spitsbergen for eight months of the year.

The stream may reach 6 knots in the sounds N and S of Axeløya in Bellsund, and 4 knots in Forlandsrevet.

The combined stream and current around Jan Mayen sets SW at 0.5–1.5 knots, but may reverse on the spring flood tide.

PASSAGE

The most common route to Svalbard is via the coast of Norway through the Lofoten area, stopping at Tromsø for final provisioning, fuelling and weather information (see the section on Tromsø), then departing via Torsvåg. With a moderate increase in the offshore distance, departure can be made directly from Lofoten or Vesterålen. Although sailing farther ENE towards Nordkapp before departing offshore may be worthwhile *per se*, no significant offshore mileage will be saved.

Bjørnøya lies slightly N of halfway between Torsvåg and Hornsund, and offers the possibility of temporary refuge if the weather becomes unpleasant, as well as a very interesting stop. Although Bjørnøya has no all-weather harbours, there are anchorages on all sides of the island and suitable shelter can be found. Bjørnøya breaks the voyage into roughly two legs of two days each.

It is often foggy near Bjørnøya and Sørkapp, and indeed to some extent in all of Svalbard. Decca and Loran are of marginal value, if any, in Svalbard; new Loran stations, though, may change this in the future. As one progresses N along the W coast of Spitsbergen, the magnetic compass will probably become more and more sluggish, perhaps even useless at around 78° N. Fluxgate and small hand compasses may be affected less. This presents no problem in fair weather, but in poor visibility, radar and GPS are very welcome. Autopilot compasses may be affected, producing sluggish or erratic performance.

During much of the passage, Vardø Radio or Bjørnøya Radio will be within VHF range or, failing that, within MF range (along with Svalbard Radio) if one has that capability. As Hornsund is approached, the Polish Polar Station can be called on VHF. There is a gap in VHF coverage between the Polish Station and Svalbard Radio's aerial at Bellsund, and once out of range of their aerial at Ny Ålesund, only MF will be useful (or HF to Rogaland or some more distant station).

There are a significant number of logs, sometimes as large as 1 m in diameter and 10 m long, floating in the Barents Sea and in the coastal waters of Svalbard. These logs are very difficult to see unless it is quite calm, even if a closer lookout than usual is being kept. Except possibly for a yacht with a metal hull, these logs constitute a hazard that must be recognised when sailing these waters.

In clear weather, Sørkapp is often seen more than 75 miles off. In poor visibility, bear in mind that the low-lying land and shoals at Sørkapp reach nearly 10 miles S of the high ground. There is a racon beacon (Morse K) on Sørkappøya at 76° 28.7' N, 16° 32.3' E. Sørkapp is known as an area of significantly augmented E and W winds and waves. Should immediate shelter be wanted in E winds, anchoring at Stormbukta, 14 miles NNW of Sørkappøya, is straightforward and will give calm waters – although strong winds will blow down from the glacier. Otherwise, intricate navigation is needed for the anchorages indicated on the chart.

Hornsund offers the first sheltered easily accessible anchorages, in addition to scenery among the best in Svalbard, and an outstandingly warm welcome to be expected from the Polish Polar Station, making it an excellent passage destination. However, keep in mind that Hornsund is particularly susceptible to being blocked by pack ice early in the season, and by glacier ice when there are strong E winds. Beware the 2 m shoal Hovdenakkgrunnen, 2.5–3 miles off the coast at the entrance to Hornsund.

WEATHER AND CLIMATE

The winds in the Svalbard area during June, July and early August are usually moderate, but there may be exceptions. Local topography has a great effect, with an extreme variation in wind strength and direction found over a short distance. Heavy rain is unusual, but drizzle, low overcast and fog are common; fortunately, these weather patterns are interspersed with crystal-clear periods. The yearly variation is great, and the fortunate may have a relatively warm, clear and mildly windy summer with few problems caused by ice, while the less fortunate may have a great deal of cold fog, very strong winds, and unpleasant, perhaps dangerous, problems caused by ice. In this respect, the summer of 1992 was fairly typical, with little ice, winds sometimes touching Force 7 for short periods, mixed overcast, fog and clear spells. The summer of 1993 had exceptionally heavy pack and glacier ice throughout most of the summer, which caused great difficulty for visiting yachts, but idyllic clear sunny weather. The summer of 1994 was 'the worst in 32 years', according to expert local opinion, with an intrusion of heavy pack ice off the SW coast in mid-July, day after day of thick fog, substantial blizzard snowstorms, and more than a few days of sustained winds to Force 8–9 with topographically caused sustained gusting to Force 12. Boat and crew must be prepared for whatever conditions are encountered. The temperature along the coast ranges usually between 0 and +10°C, although 20° may be reached in sheltered inland areas. During the latter half of August the weather usually becomes less settled and substantially more severe, and by waiting for conditions to improve one risks being forced eventually into a memorably unpleasant passage S.

Although not bitter cold as the latitude might suggest, the wind-chill while sailing requires excellent windproof and waterproof gear – including ear and head protection, thick warm waterproof gloves, and boots large enough to enable several pairs of thick socks to be worn. Snow-mobile boots, moon-boots or the like can be a blessing, but the liners should be removable for drying. A cabin heater is necessary for comfort for all but the very hardy. For going ashore, the best gear seems to be knee-high sturdy fitted rubber boots with a heel and lug tread, used with a removable insole pad and several pairs of heavy socks; a surprising amount of hiking can be done in these, and often the terrain is wet, to say nothing of getting in and out of the dinghy. Such boots are widely sold in Norway, and probably elsewhere, under the 'Viking Off-Road' label. Deck boots are much less suitable. Waterproof insulated flotation deck suits, although fairly expensive, would be useful in stormy conditions or a sinking, and are probably a better choice than a full immersion suit not useful for deck wear. The standard local gear for Zodiac use is an insulated flotation drysuit with integral boots, but this is so bulky to store and expensive, and so hot to hike in, that it is less appropriate for use by a yacht.

ANCHORING TECHNIQUE

The wind and drifting glacier ice conditions in Svalbard are often extremely local, and a shift of anchorage of only a few miles will often bring dramatically different conditions. With no darkness to complicate shifting anchorage should conditions change, one can often use an anchorage that would not feel comfortable on a dark night. However, wind and drifting ice conditions can change rapidly, something to keep in mind when leaving one's boat unattended while on a shore expedition. Anchoring in the least depth available will help to limit the size of pieces of ice that drift into the boat.

Several of the anchorages on Spitsbergen are foul with thickly growing kelp, and it may often require several attempts to get the anchor well set. A fisherman (stock) or CQR-type anchor may bite through the kelp into the bottom better than a Bruce- or Danforth-type anchor, and a heavier anchor than standard may help. It is sometimes recommended to pay out the rode to a long scope before putting any strain on it. It is essential to be certain that the anchor is into the bottom and not just caught in a thick mass of kelp. A very effective technique, and one that I use and recommend for all conditions (not just in kelp), is to set the anchor normally using reverse engine, then let the boat come ahead one or two boat-lengths, and then smartly back down straight aft so that the momentum of the boat hitting the rode at several knots puts a strong surge strain on the anchor. The bow will dip sharply if the anchor is setting, and if it is not setting this will be evident earlier rather than later when the wind comes up. Unless the yacht's engine and propeller are unusually large, simply backing against the anchor in reverse does not put sufficient strain on the anchor to tell if it might be hooked into kelp or poorly hooked into the bottom, and it is surprising how often the surge will pull out an anchor that the static pull in reverse would have indicated as holding strongly. If the anchor cannot be set to hold against the surge, then one must decide whether to try further, or to use the poorly set anchor knowing that it may not hold if conditions deteriorate. A long, sharp serrated bread knife can be useful for clearing kelp from the anchor prior to having another try. Several anchorages have very soft mud, which will probably require a Danforth-type anchor to develop sufficient holding power for severe conditions.

The best shelter is found behind low moraine spits, which break the waves without causing gusting of the wind. Anchoring in the lee of high, steep mountains often leads to severe gusting, so instead of a steady Force 7 the wind will alternate between lulls of Force 3 and sustained williwaws of Force 9 to 12 or even greater.

HARBOURS AND ANCHORAGES ON BJØRNØYA

All of the anchorages on Bjørnøya are in sand, usually in 4–6 m. Many offer access for very interesting walks. Much of the rock is extremely crumbly, presenting risk in approaching cliffs closely by yacht or dinghy, and in climbing. Listed anticlockwise from the S:

Sørhamna (SE Bjørnøya)
Chart 501   74° 22′ N, 19° 10′ E
This is the best anchorage on Bjørnøya and quite dramatically scenic; it is 2 miles NE of the S tip of the island. It is dangerous in S winds, but well sheltered from winds with a N component, and is one of the richest seabird habitats in the world. There is a small sandy beach, with a short climb up the crumbly cliffs; this requires care. Perleporten, the tunnel under Kapp Kolthoff 1.5 miles SW, is featured in Maclean's thriller *Bear Island*. The sea cliffs SW of Sørhamn are spectacular, and in suitable sea conditions are worth seeing close up.

Kvalrossbukta (SE Bjørnøya)
Chart 501   74° 23′ N, 19° 10.5′ E
Just NE of Sørhamna, open to the NE. There are ruins scattered about from the 1908 whaling station. It is easy to walk up on to the island from the sandy beach by the stream. Less rolly than Sørhamna in W winds.

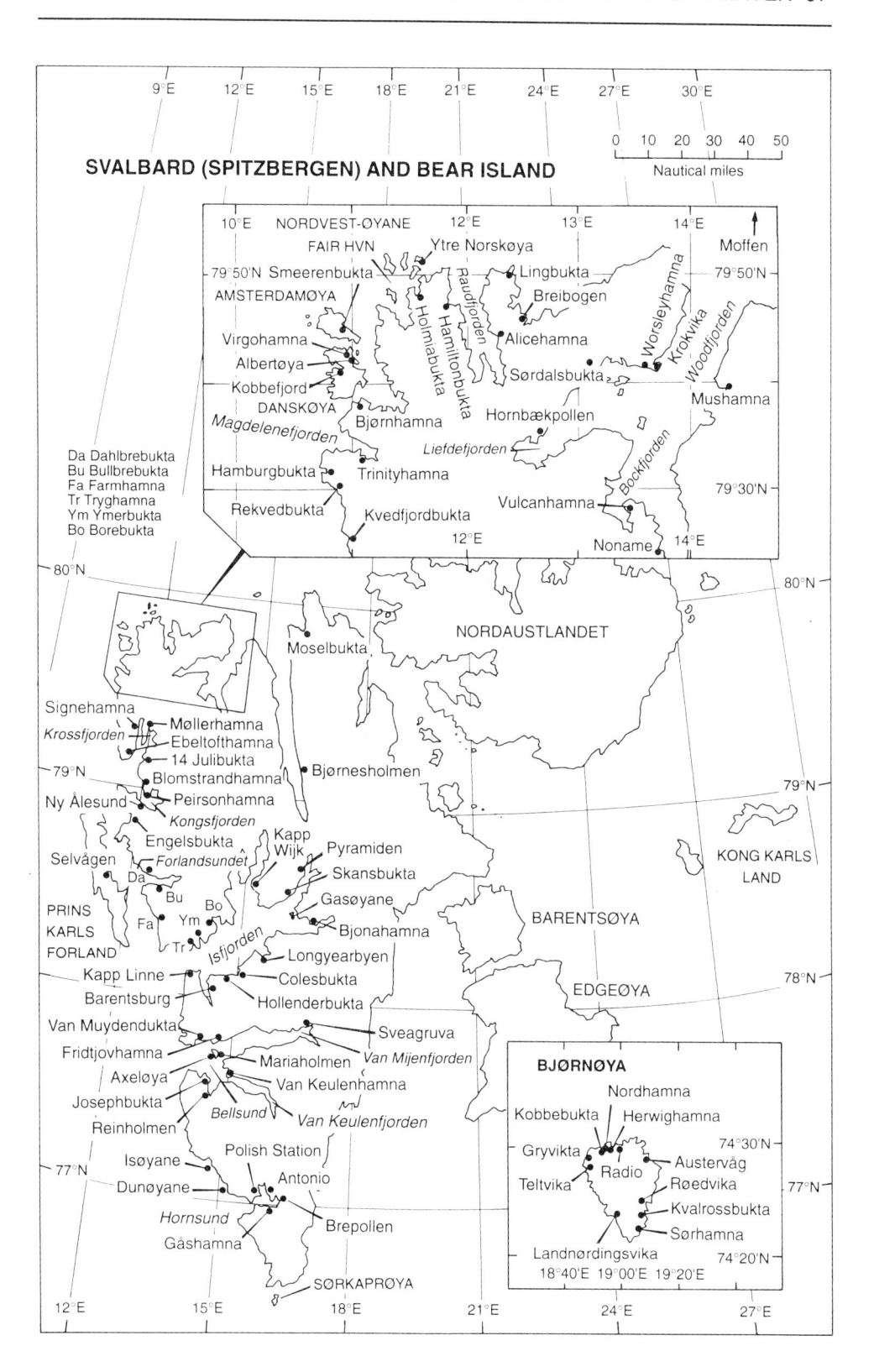

CRUISING SPITSBERGEN BJØRNØYA AND JAN MAYEN 97

Lognvika (SE Bjørnøya)
Chart 501   74° 23.1' N, 19° 10.8' E
A scenic tiny anchorage, ⅓–½ cable wide, not 1 cable as stated in *Den Norske Los*, volume 7; several anchors or shore lines may be required, but the shelter is excellent. Has a sandy beach, a stream and access to the shore.

Røedvika (SE Bjørnøya)
Chart 501   74° 24' N, 19° 10.5' E
This is a bay open to the E, just N of Kvalrossbukta, providing the safest shelter in strong westerly conditions, according to *Den Norske Los* (which states that the winds will then be even; however, strong gusting has been reported by yachts). Beware Miserygrunnen 3 m, 5 cables NE.

Austervåg (NE Bjørnøya)
Chart 501   74° 29' N, 19° 11.5' E
A bay open to the NE. Access up on to the island is next to the small stream. Just S lie the extensive ruins of the Tunheim coal mining operation, which had a population of 250 in the early 1900s. It is an extremely interesting walk of a couple of miles over unusual rocky terrain to the Radio Station; the walk along the cliff-top (beware crumbling edges) is smoother and offers dramatic views of the coastline. **Kolbukta**, just N, may be less rolly than Austervåg, but without immediate access to the island.

Herwighamna (N Bjørnøya)
Chart 501   74° 30.3' N, 18° 59.7' E
At the centre of the N coast, this anchorage is the landing place for Bjørnøya Radio Station. Inside the small point at the W of the bay there is a small quay with 2 m depth. In most sea conditions, this is not a secure yacht anchorage, and adjacent Nordhamna or an anchorage on the W or E coasts, with a walk of a few miles, may be safer. The facilities are extensive and interesting, and the welcome warm. The oldest building in Svalbard, Hammerfesthuset, dating from 1823, is nearby, and there is a small museum created by the station personnel. There are souvenirs for sale.

Nordhamna (N Bjørnøya)
Chart 501   74° 30.3' N, 18° 58' E
Kobbebukta (N Bjørnøya)
Chart 501   74° 30.0' N, 18° 53' E
W of Herwighamna on the N coast, these two bays open to the N offer large anchoring areas, with some protection from E and W swell.

Gryvikta (NW Bjørnøya)
Chart 501   74° 28.5' N, 18° 46' E
Just N of Kapp Duner at the NW of the island, this small cove offers shelter from easterly and southerly weather, without access to the island.

Teltvika / Lunkevika (NW Bjørnøya)
Chart 501   74° 28' N, 18° 47' E
Just S of Kapp Duner at the NW of the island, these coves offer shelter in weather from the E and N. Both have sandy beaches and access to the island.

Landnøringsvika (SW Bjørnøya)*
Chart 501   74° 22.8' N, 18° 57' E
This open bay on the SW coast, between Kapp Kåre and Kapp Harry, offers shelter from easterly weather, but it may be rolly. Anchorage is in the middle of the bay in 12–15 m, with the outermost large stone at Skrednesset (6 cables SE) in line with Kapp Harry; *Den Norske Los* states that it is foul inside this line.

9 SW Spitsbergen

Polish Polar Station / Isbjørnhamna (NW Hornsund)
Chart 504   77° 00′ N, 15° 33.5′ E
The position of this anchorage is not very evident from the chart; but as one approaches, the buildings will be seen to port. Circle round with the cross on Wilczeodden to port, watching the depth off the rocks S of the point, and anchor in front of the buildings in 8–10 m; one can anchor in 5 m, but then it may be difficult to avoid several isolated rocks that cover and uncover with the tide. Beware a dangerous isolated rock that just uncovers, in the centre of the approach, an unexpectedly far 2 cables from shore, bearing 090° from the blue building. This anchorage is somewhat better sheltered than might be expected from its open character, but conversely it can often be surprisingly rolly. As with many anchorages in Svalbard, in some wind conditions there may be too much glacier ice for this one to be usable. When within VHF range, the Polish Station can advise on ice and swell conditions, but bear in mind that conditions change rapidly and the station personnel may not fully appreciate a yacht's requirements. The time I spent at the Polish Station was the highlight of my 1992 voyage to Norway and Svalbard, and many other voyagers have had a similar experience.

There may be a policeman from the Sysselmann's office stationed in a hut near the Polish Station, in order to check visiting yachts into the tourist registration system.

Antonio Pigafettahamna (NW Hornsund)
Chart 504   77° 00′ N, 15° 40′ E
The retreat of Hansbreen over the past few decades has created a new lagoon harbour, with all-round shelter, a sizeable anchoring area in 2–6 m (stony with thin mud overlay – be sure the anchors are well set), and fine views of the mountains and very nearby glacier snout. The entry, at the E edge of Hansbreen, and the centre and SE part of the lagoon, seem to have no unexpected rocks, but extra care should be exercised; some rocks do uncover in the SW part of the lagoon. In some winds, the harbour might become filled with drift glacier ice, in which case Gåshamna might be an alternative. In August 1994 there was an interesting flume cut by the stream in the ice at the edge of the glacier, easy to explore on the grit-covered solid ice and safe to walk up for a bit without any special glacier gear. The name *Antonio Pigafettahamna* has been requested for this harbour, honouring Magellan's supercargo who reported on the first global circumnavigation, and the catamaran *Antonio Pigafetta*, which explored the harbour in 1994.

Gåshamna (S Hornsund)
Charts 504, 509 inset
76° 56.4' N, 15° 52.5' E

A fine and scenic anchorage across the fjord from the Polish Station, with an extensive area for anchoring in 4–5 m. There are several streams, brick ruins of the 1899–1901 Russian degree measurement expedition, a more recent and still serviceable wooden hut, and archaeological ruins and burial sites from the extensive Greenland Right-Whale tryworks from around 1620. There are several huge whale bones near the hut, and a most impressively large number near the small ruin about a mile distant at the W end of the bay.

Brepollen (E Hornsund)
Chart 504   77° 00' N, 16° 18' E

This area, and indeed the entire length of Hornsund, is especially scenic, and is often said to offer some of the finest scenery in Svalbard. At times it can be difficult because of strong winds coming down from the glacier and from drifting ice. Beware of a 2.3 m shoal 1.2 miles SE of Treskelodden (this will be shown on the new chart issued in 1995). One can anchor on either side of Treskelodden. *Den Norske Los* states that in strong E winds the large amount of calf ice from Brepollen can force vessels to leave Hornsund, and that even with storm force winds in Hornsund it may be nearly calm outside just to the N and S.

Dunøyane
Charts 504, 509 inset
77° 04' N, 14° 56' E
Isøyane
Chart 504   77° 08.4' N, 14° 45.5' E

Dunøyane are low islands rather far offshore, and Isøyane lies just off the large Torrellbreen. Both are good anchorages. Isøyane, as the name suggests, may be subject to a lot of drifting glacier ice. One can also anchor off Torrellbreen N of the charted streams to the E. Dunøyane and Isøyane, and Olsholmen a few miles NW, are Bird Sanctuaries that must not be approached closer than 300 m between 15 May and 15 August.

Josephbukta (Renardbreen–W Recherchefjorden)
Charts 504, 503   77° 31.5' N, 14° 33' E

Very fine scenic and sheltered anchorage in the moraine bay formed by the retreating glacier. Anchor in the centre, or behind the spit to the N.

Reinholmen / Vestervågen (SW Recherchefjorden)
Charts 504, 503   77° 30' N, 14° 33' E

The charted anchorages are very secure, but they may be rolly with a NW swell, and are subject to violent gusting. One can also anchor temporarily off Calypsobyen (3 miles N) to see the ruined buildings dating from around 1920. Anchorage on the shelf NW of Calypsobyen provides shelter from S and SE winds. Beluga are sometimes seen in this area. There is a harbour chart 1:20 000 for Vestervågen in the 1990 *Den Norske Los*, volume 7.

Van Keulenhamna (NW Van Keulenfjorden)
Charts 504, 503   77° 37' N, 14° 55' E

This is a secure anchorage with good holding, but in bleak surroundings. The sound N of Eholmen is clear with 14 m depth. There are numerous anchorages in Van Keulenfjorden charted and described by *Den Norske Los*, including Fleur de Lyshamna and Burbonhamna just SSE.

Axeløya (S)
Charts 504 inset, 503 inset
77° 41.5' N, 14° 44' E

At the S tip of Axeløya is the hut of the

Færoese trapper Louis (Hiawatha) Nielson. Just WxN of the hut there is a charted anchorage between Axeløya and a ragged skerry that offers fair shelter, rather distant from the hut. For the venturesome, there is a sheltered but kelpy anchorage in the lagoon N of the hut, gained with local knowledge. The 1:70 000 inset on charts 504 or 503 will be helpful.

Mariaholmen (entering Van Mijenfjorden)
Charts 504 inset, 503 inset
77° 40.7′ N, 14° 49′ E
This anchorage at the SE side of the smaller island S of Axeløya offers good shelter except in E winds, in 4–5 m. The stream runs up to 6 knots through the sound. The high steep Midterhuken teems with birds and is remarkably green; in calm conditions the small anchorage Gåsbergkilen charted 1:20 000 in the 1990 *Den Norske Los*, volume 7, would be a fine stop, as might the anchorage shown on charts 503/504 just S of Midterhuken.

Fridtjovhamna (entering Van Mijenfjorden)
Charts 504 inset, 503 inset
77° 46′ N, 14° 37′ E
There is secure anchorage in very sticky mud inside the thin peninsula Hamnodden. Enter heading NW, to the NE along Kapp Schollin, as shown on the 1:70 000 inset on chart 504 or 503, or the 1:20 000 chart in the 1990 *Den Norske Los*, volume 7. There are extensive trappers' huts and equipment on the peninsula. Egil Lindberg, on the yacht *Framanjo,* spent the winter of 1993–4 in this harbour, frozen in the ice for eight months. In northerly winds there is good anchorage in the small cove halfway along the NE coast of the fjord. The tidal stream in the sound N of Axeløya reaches 6 knots.

Sveagruva (NE Van Mijenfjorden)
Charts 504, 503, 513
77° 53.5′ N, 16° 43′ E
This sizeable coal mining village is presently inactive, but is being kept in good condition by a small maintenance crew. There are laundry facilities, and a quay for berthing, and anchoring ground. The entrance is quite foul for a large ship, but less so for a yacht; entrance using chart 513 is straightforward, but not very easy without it. A large cave has recently been discovered nearby, which may be explored with a local resident as guide (crampons may be required).

Van Muydenbukta (N Bellsund)
Charts 504, 503   77° 45′ N, 14° 05′ E
Whale bones have been found on the shore of this anchorage open to the S, just E of Kapp Martin Light. The bottom may be stony, with not the most reliable holding. Beware the many dangerous uncharted rocks NW of Reiniusøyane.

10 W Spitsbergen

The large and rather open **Isfjorden** contains Svalbard's three large settlements, and several branching fjords. The geology is somewhat different from that on the SW and NW coasts, here tending towards colourful massive stratified mountain masses rather than sharp spiry ridges and peaks.

Kapp Linne / Randvika (entering Isfjorden)
Charts 524, 509 insets, 503
78° 04′ N, 13° 38′ E
This anchorage for Isfjord Radio and weather station is not well sheltered from the strong winds that often blow out of the fjord. Approach on the two-cairn transit 149.5°, and anchor in 4 m depth; farther in, the transit leads over a rock awash half a cable off the shore. The surrounding area is a Bird Sanctuary that must not be approached closer than 300 m between 15 May and 15 August; enquire locally for the boundaries. Svalbard's second largest and very scenic lake, Linnevannnet, is situated between the mountains SE (chart 503).

Barentsburg (E Grønfjorden)
Charts 523, 503   78° 04′ N, 14° 14′ E
This is the one of the two Russian settlements in Svalbard, with a population of around 1200. The Russians are eager for foreign contact and currency. There is a large quay and small pontoon, at which berthing might be arranged, possibly for a fee. Laundry facilities may be available. There have been reports of yachts having engine troubles as a result of using the very cheap diesel that may be available. Barentsburg boasts a 30 000 volume library, a 450-seat theatre hall, a substantial museum, and an extensive sports facility. A modern building houses a large 27°C salt-water swimming pool open (except Monday) from 1100 to 2300; the pool is surrounded by many indoor plants that provide a startling contrast to the view outside. There is also an agricultural complex that includes a herd of 35 cows. Many yachtsmen have found this a very interesting stop from a cultural point of view.

There is reasonable anchorage available on either side of Finneset, 2 miles S; *Den Norske Los* suggests it is better to the S of the point, but the anchoring shelf seems to be larger to the N. See the inset on chart 509. If there is a lot of ice drifting about, the tidal streams by the point may cause difficulties.

Colesbukta (S Isfjorden)
Charts 523, 503   78° 07′ N, 14° 56′ E
Den Norske Los recommends the centre of this bay as excellent anchorage, but the depths of 30–40 m are more suitable for ships than for yachts. There is a derelict quay with 6 m depth, not con-

nected to the shore, on the E side of the bay, which can be used in mooring. Until 1967, this was a busy Soviet coal port. Hollenderbukta, which is 5 miles W, offers good anchorage in some wind directions.

Longyearbyen (Adventfjorden)
Charts 523, 503, 513
78° 14′ N, 15° 38′ E

In addition to being a mining town, Longyearbyen is the Norwegian administrative centre for Svalbard, with a population of around 1200. Although some visitors describe the town as unattractive, others are quite enthusiastic (the scene from the anchorage is rather industrial, but once ashore it is much nicer). The town is expanding substantially, and is even about to displace Tromsø as the world's most northerly university site. Water is available at the quay, and diesel is obtainable at about two-thirds the Norwegian price. The quay is usually busy, not available for berthing; quay improvements are needed and were in progress in 1994. The anchorage shelf is not large, and in heavy weather is not secure; better depths may be found NW towards the Coal Quay. There is a church, a bakery, a substantial grocery and souvenir shop at tax-free prices, handicrafts, fur and leathergoods shops, a restaurant, a bank, a PO, a telecommunications centre, a library, accommodation, a campsite, an excellent museum, a Sunday evening cinema, a swimming pool at the school, car rental, taxi and airport bus service, hire facilities for bicycles and windsurfing boards, a tour of a mine, and a hospital. The world's N-most diamond polisher lives in Longyearbyen. Ing G Paulsen at Yamaha provides trekking tours, a remarkably extensive supply of camping gear and clothing as well as rifle hire, assistance with boat equipment procurement and repair, and a large crane for emergency haulout and repairs at reasonable prices. 'Info-Svalbard' is the tourist information office, and the Norsk Polarinstitut sells a variety of maps and aerial photographs. Relatively inexpensive meals may be had at the mine cafeteria. A full-service hotel was under construction in 1994. Hardware is available at the shop near the quay. If not already checked into the tourist registration system, the master of a visiting yacht must check in at the office of the Sysselmann (Governor). Even if already registered, a visit to the Sysselmann's office is likely to prove interesting and productive.

Bjonhamna (entering Tempelfjorden)
Charts 523, 503 78° 24′ N, 16° 53′ E

This frequently used yacht anchorage offers good shelter and holding, next to impressive cliffs with huge scree slopes. Enter heading NW, then swinging to the NE not too close around the point. There is said to be good hiking here, and fossils especially to the NE. Cruise ships often anchor to the E off the mine ruins at Kapp Schoultz. SSE lies Fredheim (Home of Peace), built by trapper Hilmar Nois who spent 50 summers and 39 winters on Spitsbergen, often accompanied by his wife; his home is now maintained by the Sysselmann.

Gasøyane (entering Billefjorden)*
Charts 523, 503 78° 27′ N, 16° 17′ E

There is a clear passage with 5 m depth midway between the point and the E-most small islet. If rounding to the W, note the rock awash 3 cables W of the largest island. One can anchor NE in Anservika. Gasøyane itself is a Bird Sanctuary that must not be approached closer than 300 m between 15 May and 15 August.

Skansbukta (entering Billefjorden)*
Charts 523, 503   78° 32′ N, 16° 02′ E
This small cove offers good anchoring, open to the S. At the E are ruins of a gypsum quarry.

Pyramiden (NW Billefjorden)
Charts 523, 503   78° 39′ N, 16° 24′ E
This Russian mining centre is only slightly smaller than Barentsburg, with the world's most northerly swimming pool, a hospital, a greenhouse and sports facilities. Many find it more attractive than Barentsburg, and the surrounding scenery is more dramatic. There is a large quay, with berthing by arrangement and possibly a fee. Anchoring is sometimes possible in Petuniabukta to the NE. The Nordenskiøld glacier to the E has an especially impressive snout.

Kapp Wijk (NE Nordfjorden)*
Charts 523, 503   78° 35′ N, 15° 13′ E
A mile SSW of the cape is the hut of trapper Harald Soleim. Anchoring is possible ENE of the cape, but beware of the strait becoming blocked if there is a lot of drifting ice.

Borebukta (NW Isfjorden)
Charts 523, 524, 503
78° 21′ N, 14° 16′ E
The sills at Borebukta and off Sveabreen (8 miles NxE) are both good for anchoring, but open to the SE. The tiny spit charted W of the sill has become submerged, and several yachts have grounded on it. Note that Boheman to the NE, including the islets S of Bohemanflya, is a Bird Sanctuary that must not be approached closer than 300 m between 15 May and 15 August.

Ymerbukta (NW Isfjorden)
Charts 523, 524, 503
78° 16′ N, 14° 00′ E
There is fair anchoring on a narrow shelf in the NW part of this bay, but the kelp grows thickly. It is open to the S. Borebukta is probably preferable.

Tryghamna (NW Isfjorden)
Charts 523, 524, 503
78° 16′ N, 13° 47′ E
Who can resist 'Safe Harbour'? Much used in the seventeenth century as a refuge by whaling boats, and so named because the pack ice seldom entered from Isfjorden. The best anchorage seems to be at the NE, near the stream.

Prins Karls Forland provides 40 miles of sheltered water between Isfjorden and N and NW Spitsbergen. With high mountains and glaciers on both shores, the views are especially beautiful. Navigating through the Forlandsrevet shoal area is straightforward with GPS or in good visibility. At the SW of Forlandet are the Planke-Holm and Orlandsøy Bird Sanctuaries which must not be approached closer than 300 m between 15 May and 15 August.

Farmhamna / Eidembukta (SE Forlandsundet)
Charts 524 and 509 insets, 503
78° 19.68′ N, 12° 51.13′ E
This fine well sheltered anchorage in 2–8 m lies off the cabin of the Danish trapper Hanks Lund. Enter heading SSE, sounding carefully, and anchor NE or, with great care, SE of the hut. In N winds, anchorage a couple of miles N offers better shelter. There are harbour charts 1:20 000 in the 1990 *Den Norske Los*, volume 7.

Bullbrebukta (SE Forlandsundet)
Charts 524, 522, 503
78° 30′ N, 12° 37′ E
The small unsurveyed bay N of Bullbreen can be entered E of the island blocking the mouth of the bay, with around 2 m depth at mid-tide; there is a large rock awash at mid-tide in the E

side of the passage, so favour the W side. The channel W of the island dries at low tide. In the bay, there is anchorage in sand 1.5–15 m.

Dahlbrebukta (SE Forlandsundet)
Charts 524, 522, 503
78° 34′ N, 12° 23′ E
A quite well sheltered anchorage behind the little spit just N of Ankerneset, with beautiful mountains rising close behind and fine views of the glacier.

Selvågen (SW Forlandsundet)
Charts 524, 503   78° 33′ N, 11° 17′ E
This anchorage at the W of the sound is open to the E, but has good holding. The deep innermost part of the bay is closed off by a sill with 1.5 m depth. Hermansøya across the sound to the E is a Bird Sanctuary that must not be approached closer than 300 m between 15 May and 15 August.

Forlandsrevet (in Forlandsundet)
Charts 513, 522, 503
78° 43′ N, 11° 18′ E
There is a channel 5 cables wide with 4 m least depth through this shoal that otherwise blocks Forlandsundet, and 15 cables wide for a least depth of 2 m. Although not difficult in good conditions, care is needed. There is a visual transit 021.5°/201.5° along the centre of this channel, with a notch in the mountains and rock buttress downslope 'Jessiefoten' over the point 'Aurtangen', shown in a sketch on the charts. Even in good visibility, the exact location of Jessiefoten is not entirely clear till one is nearly on the transit, whereupon it becomes evident. There are beacons usually present at each side of the sound, and sometimes small buoys are set. These coordinates are recommended for those with GPS, with the usual caveat regarding reliance on any single navigational datum: (EUROPE ED-50 datum; insignificant offset from WGS-72 or WGS-84) 78° 41.50′ N, 11° 15.20′ E and 78° 44.75′ N, 11° 21.50′ E. The longitude scales on charts 524 (1991), 513 (1970), 503 (1975) and 522 (1974) disagree; unless a note on the chart instructs otherwise, to get longitudes that agree with chart 524 and with my (JA) GPS observations while on the visual transit, subtract 0.9′ from longitudes charted on chart 513, subtract 1.0′ from longitudes charted on 503, and subtract 2.0′ from longitudes charted on 522. The tidal stream reaches 4 knots, and care must be taken not to be set too far off the line. The timing of the stream has not been measured, but it is probably not too different from that offshore, which turns N around 3 hours before HW. The bottom to the W is rocky, but to the E is sandy, so if in doubt favour the E. There is good anchoring on the sandy bank E, perhaps useful in poor conditions to await better ones. Once N of the shoal, there is also good anchoring along both shores for some distance, with Engelsbukta, 78° 50′ N, 11° 55′ E, offering shelter from drifting ice (and a small cave at the S). There may be walrus in the NE of this area. There is a huge guillemot colony just SW of Fuglehuken, the N tip of Prins Karls Forland.

11 NW Spitsbergen

Kongsfjorden offers fine views of the huge Kongs glacier and Tre Kroner mountains, as well as the settlement of Ny Ålesund.

Ny Ålesund (S Kongsfjorden)
Charts 513, 522   78° 56′ N, 11° 56′ E
The population of the Norwegian research station at Ny Ålesund varies from 50 in the winter to 200 in the summer, with scientists visiting from many countries. There is a small museum, always open and charging a modest fee, and the site of Amundsen's *Norge* polar Zepplin launch. The ruins of the huge mine explosion are interesting to examine. Through the Kongs Bay Coal Company, services are available: diesel at even lower cost than in Longyearbyen, water, washing machines and dryers, and showers. Enquire at the office, hours 0800–1200 and 1300–1630 (Tel: 79 02 71 11). Rather high berthing and watering fees are posted, often waived (enquire) for a yacht taking on diesel and berthing for only a short time or anchoring off. There are telephones on both quays and in several buildings. One can post cards here from the world's N-most PO (1230–1330). Most staple food supplies can be purchased from the chef on the second floor of the canteen (marked 'Private Mess – No Admittance'); prepare a clear list of what is wanted beforehand, as visitors are not allowed into the stores. There is a souvenir boutique. Ny Ålesund is best avoided when a large cruise ship is disembarking upwards of 800 passengers, unless one especially enjoys people-watching. There is good anchorage both NW and SE of the quays or between them, open between NW and SE; chart 513 will be found helpful here. It is possible to berth inside the New Quay, but the quay is too high for a yacht, and the basin may prove an uncomfortable refuge in heavy weather. Mietheholmen and Prins Heinrichøya, and Lovenøya and Eskjert a few miles E, are Bird Sanctuaries, not to be approached closer than 300 m between 15 May and 15 August.

Blomstrandhamna (NE Kongsfjorden)
Chart 522   79° 00′ N, 12° 05′ E
This anchorage may offer shelter in conditions unsuitable for Ny Ålesund or Peirsonhamna, but it often suffers from poor protection from calving ice. Beware the 1 m shoal Austnesbåen, 2 cables SE of Austneset. It is possible to anchor in the entrance, particularly at the N with shelter from calf ice, as well as in Nordvågen and Sørvågen, and also along Kongsfjordletta NW towards Kapp Guissez. There is often a trekking tent camp in the area. Breøyane and Guissezholmen are both Bird Sanctuaries that must not be approached

closer than 300 m between 15 May and 15 August.

Peirsonhamna / London
(NE Kongsfjorden)
Charts 513, 522   78° 57.8′ N, 12° 03′ E
This is a pleasant small cove a couple of miles NE of Ny Ålesund, with good anchoring in sand mixed with stony areas, open to the SSW. There are interesting ruins of the marble quarry that operated in the 1920s by an Englishman until it was found that the marble splintered after being installed for a time; in addition to machinery, a couple of the cabins are preserved as historic monuments. Ragnar Thorseth and his family overwintered a couple of miles ENE, just S of Gerdøya. It may now be possible to circumnavigate Blomstrandhalvøya.

The splendidly scenic **Krossfjorden** divides into several subsidiary fjords, with many impressive views, and several anchorages.

Ebeltofthamna (SW Krossfjorden)
Chart 522   79° 09′ N, 11° 37′ E
One can anchor in 7 m, N of the rock awash in the middle of the entrance, as suggested in the Pilot, or alternatively one can enter part way into the bay to the S where there is 3–4 m. Open to the E and SE.

Fjortende Julibukta (SE Krossfjorden)
Chart 522   79° 07′ N, 11° 50′ E
This is a very scenic anchorage, very close to the 14th of July Glacier. One can anchor in 2–3 m inside the point, taking care of the depth during entry. There are remains of a hut, and often many seals.

Møllerhamna (NW Møllerfjorden)
Chart 522   79° 17′ N, 11° 51′ E
This anchorage in the NW arm of the fjord shelves very steeply, so one may need to anchor as deeply as 15 m. However, one can anchor in less depth nearby, with less shelter, to either side of **Regnardneset*** immediately E, or to the E across the mouth of Kollerfjorden, S of **Speidarneset***. There is also good anchorage along the S shore of Tinayrebukta. In 1973 H W Tillman painted the name of his Bristol pilot cutter *Baroque* on a conspicuous 20 m high boulder at the E side of the NW arm, which might make an interesting pilgrimage: there is anchorage off the boulder.

Signehamna (W Lillehøøkfjorden)
Chart 522   79° 16.5′ N, 11° 32′ E
This well sheltered beautiful anchorage at the W side of the fjord is considered an excellent place for hiking, especially in the lake valley SSW. There are said to be arctic char in both the harbour and in the lakes, and there are large colonies of guillemots and kittiwakes S of Nilspynten. One can anchor quite far into the cove, probably in 4 m. There is also excellent anchorage in the tiny cove immediately S, in more than the charted 2 m (watch for rocks), but with the possibility of ice closing off the entrance. There is also anchorage off Øyenrabben 3 miles N, but this might be too close to the Lillehøøk glacier, which calves large bergs – especially in August. The Lillehøøk snout and floating ice are especially scenic.

Kvedfjordbukta
Chart 522   79° 25′ N, 10° 53′ E
Rekvedbukta
Chart 521   79° 30′ N, 10° 46′ E
These bays are open to the NW and SW respectively, but under appropriate conditions they offer good anchorage.

Hamburgbukta
Chart 521   79° 32′ N, 10° 42′ E
This curious cove, only 4 cables in diameter, has a very narrow entrance

over a 2 m sill, and once inside there is poor anchoring in 8–16 m with squally winds likely. The sill breaks in all but very calm seas, so one could be trapped inside. There are several interesting burial sites nearby.

The really fine scenery in famous **Magdalenefjorden** makes it a prime target for cruise ships. The Waggonway glacier produces a lot of ice, which in E winds can cause problems. The tidal stream runs strongly off Magdelenehuken, N on the flood.

Trinityhamna (S Magdelenefjorden)
Charts 521, 510 inset
79° 33.5′ N, 11° 02′ E
This delightful yacht anchorage has a substantial area of sand 4–5 m behind an enclosing sheltering spit; however, E winds may fill the anchorage with drift ice. The holding on the W side of the spit is steep and stony and not good. Passage is safe S of Donkerholmane, and landing ashore is easy. The Sysselmann often has a patrol stationed in the nearby hut. On some days there may be several cruise ships in the fjord, some disembarking hundreds of passengers. There is a monument and also burial sites nearby. At the NE corner of the fjord, there is a colony of little auks believed to number 200 000–250 000 (photo p. 13).

Several large, high islands create a NW corner of Spitsbergen that is quite different in character from the W and N coasts. Although the islands are not extensively glaciated, the scenery is very fine, and sailing in the sounds sheltered from the sea is welcome. The distances are on a shorter scale, with much variety. The high steep islands may create extremely strong local winds.

Bjørnhamna (W Reuschhalvøya)
Charts 521, 510 inset
79° 38.5′ N, 11° 00′ E
This anchorage S of Danskøya, inside a little spit, has an abandoned hut and relics, and is open to the NW, N and NE. It is foul except for a channel 1 cable wide and 5 m deep along the W side. The Sysselmann often has a patrol stationed in the nearby hut. Moseøya to the W, and the small islands Skorpa off Harpunodden to the NW, are Bird Sanctuaries that must not be approached closer than 300 m between 15 May and 15 August. *Den Norske Los* recommends anchoring as charted off the SW coast of Danskøya, but yachts have reported difficulties with very heavy kelp. There is also anchorage to the E in 12 m in **Scheibukta*** , and in 6 m in **St Laurentiusbukta*** , both open to the N.

Albertøya (NE Danskøya)
Charts 521, 510 inset
79° 43′ N, 10° 59′ E
It is possible to anchor in 2–3 m SW or W of Albertøya, an area known as **Krunglebukta*** , and to navigate the narrow channel W and NW of the island, half a cable E of Danskøya, and thence into Danskegattet; however, yachts have reported less depth than indicated on the chart in this area. The plan on chart 510 is useful for navigation of the E end of Danskegattet. The recommended transit 265° is Oddskjeret (the islet off the point at the N centre of Danskøya) in line with Fugelsteinen (the small islet three-quarters of a cable S of the larger Likholmen).

Virgohamna (N Danskøya)
Charts 521, 510 inset
79° 43.3′ N, 10° 56′ E
This anchorage, at the S of Danskegattet, was the launching site for the Andrée

balloon and Wellman zeppelin, and there are interesting extensive ruins from this activity. There are also remains from whaling. There is anchorage in 4 m E and W of the small island. The withdrawn British Admiralty chart 3203 (1897) shows 1 fathom carrying into the innermost little cove, passing SW of the island, whereas *Den Norske Los* states that 'only small boats can go right into the inner part of the harbour, E and S of the low islet'. On the shore of Amsterdamøya to the NE are the ruins of Smeerenburg (Blubber Town), which had a population of 1200 in the 1630s; there is good anchorage off Smeerenburg in N winds.

Smeerenbukta (NE Amsterdamøya)
Chart 521   79° 45.5' N, 10° 55' E
Anchorage in 5–10 m is available in this bay open to the NE; in strong S winds there will be ferocious gusting.

Kobbefjorden (W Danskøya)
Chart 521   79° 41.8' N, 10° 51' E
This large cove, open to the W, has several good anchoring locations: just SW of the island, in 3–4 m; in 4–6 m on the extensive shoal between the island and the spit to the N; in 2–4 m E of the spit; in 6 m off the shore SE from the spit. The small island Postholmen was formerly used as a post-drop by whalers. There may be shoals a bit farther from Kapp Guenert than is indicated on the chart.

Two sounds provide passage to the E: **Norskøysundet** with a rock of depth 1.7 m to the N (the location may be discernible); and **Svenskegattet**, with a narrow channel close to the S of Sabineodden to avoid the foul ground NxE of Steggholmen (the sounding 3 m, 3 cables E x S of Cummingøya, has a depth 1.2 m). This foul area contains the

Weathered turrets of ice in Magdalenefjorden, Spitsbergen.

only hidden dangers in the approaches to Holmiabukt. Svenskegattet may also be entered via the channel well S of Steggholmen and then NNE; beware the rock awash 8 cables SW of Steggholmen. There is a large area NE of Steggholmen for anchoring in 4–5 m, rather far from shore. There are very many birds in this area.

Holmiabukt (N Vasahalvøya)*
Charts 521, 510 inset
79° 48′ N, 11° 34′ E
The sheltered inner reaches of Holmiabukt range between 10 and 30 m depth except for 7–5 m N and S of the point on the W shore.

Ytre Norskøya (Nordvestøyane)
Charts 521, 510 inset
79° 51.3′ N, 11° 37.5′ E
This pleasant cove, open to the E, offers good shelter in SW winds. This island is especially fine for hiking, with reindeer and fox, many burial sites at the SW, and a large bird colony to the N. There are many similar anchorage possibilities throughout the Nordvestøyane, depending on the wind direction, but in some cases the steepness of the ground may lead to severe gusting.

Raudfjorden, along with Liefdefjorden to the E, is one of the most beautiful fjords in Svalbard. Beware the shoals to the N of both sides of Raudfjorden, as they may extend a bit farther than charted.

Hamiltonbukta (W Raudfjorden)
Chart 521   79° 48′ N, 11° 50′ E
A particularly spectacular anchorage, with good anchorage off the NW shore if not too clogged with drift glacier ice. The Hamilton glacier calves especially actively. There are numerous anchoring possibilities, but the area is not well charted and some inventive care must be exercised.

Alicehamna (SE Raudfjorden)
Chart 521   79° 44′ N, 12° 14′ E
A fine anchorage, except that in S winds when there is calving from the Raudfjord glacier, lying NE of Bruceneset is preferable. There is especially fine hiking along the lakes to the NNE. Beware Svalisbåen, depth 1 m, to the W of Alicehamna.

Lingbukta*
Chart 521   79° 50′ N, 12° 24′ E
The charted hut is gone, but one can anchor either side of the point.

Breibogen / Vesle Raudfjorden
Chart 521   79° 46′ N, 12° 32′ E
There is often a trekking tent camp in this area. It is possible to take a dinghy into Morenelaguna to the W, and possibly through the stream into Richardvatnet; an adventuresome shoal-draft yacht entered Morenelaguna in 1994 at HW and found good anchorage in 3 m inside. The large low peninsula to the E, Reinsdyrflya, is populated with 1000 reindeer, and also offers an anchoring shelf around its perimeter.

Moffen
Charts 521, 510   80° 01′ N, 14° 30′ E
This small island is a Walrus Reşerve, and approach closer than 300 m is prohibited between 15 May and 15 September. It is possible to anchor on the extensive sand banks surrounding the island.

Liefdefjorden is one of the most beautiful fjords in Svalbard, with several excellent anchorages, and often a good deal of drifting glacier ice. This fjord is also frequently visited by cruise ships. **Bockfjorden**, a volcanic area, has the attraction of hot springs.

Krokvika (N Liefdefjorden)
Chart 521   79° 41.8′ N, 13° 42′ E
There is more depth than charted in this

A yacht at anchor is dwarfed by its surroundings in Hornbækpollen, Liefdefjorden, Spitsbergen.

excellent anchorage, 4 m sand into the cove inside the crook of the spit. Very sheltered, with good hiking to see reindeer, fox and perhaps polar bear.

Worsleyhamna (NE Liefdefjorden)
Chart 521   79° 41.5′ N, 13° 37′ E
Sørdalsbukta (N Liefdefjorden)
Chart 521   79° 41.3′ N, 13° 02′ E
These are open anchorages along the N shore of Liefdefjorden. There is also a superb anchorage for shallow-draft yachts, or bold deep-draft yachts with the tide, in the W lagoon of Andøyane (1.2 m sill, 3.5 m anchorage).

Hornbækpollen (W Liefdefjorden)
Chart 521   79° 36.2′ N, 12° 39.2′ E
An especially fine, well sheltered and beautiful anchorage. The anchoring shelves are not very wide, it is 20 m in the centre, and some of the bottom is very soft mud, so some care is required to get secure holding. There is good hiking, and a glacier close by. A streamlet may provide fresh water with a bit of hydraulic engineering. A short easy scramble up to the top of the moraine shelf at the N side of the anchorage, below the large kittiwake colony, puts one in the midst of extensive fox territory.

Mushamna (E Woodfjorden)
Chart 521   79° 39.6′ N, 14° 15.6′ E
A fine all-wind anchorage in a lagoon. Enter heading SE, then NE with the coast close to starboard, then N and NW to anchor. There is an uncharted submerged rock near the centre of the NE coast. Nearby is the handsome log home of trapper Reidar Hovelsrud. There is also a trapper's hut 8 miles NNE at Gråhuken, where six Norwegian hunting vessels were trapped by ice in 1872, with 19 people perishing from scurvy before the remaining 38 were rescued.

Vulkanhamna (E Brockfjorden)
Chart 521   79° 28′ N, 13° 25′ E
This anchorage is across Brockfjorden from Jotunkjeldane, an area of hot spring activity, and off which it may be possible to anchor temporarily in fine weather. There are two cool hot springs at Jotunkjeldane, not far from an extinct volcano cone, with warmer springs a very meandering 7 km SSE, with several streams to be waded (high boots needed), shown on *Blad* B5 of the 1:100 000 topographic maps at Trolkjeldene, 79° 23.3′ N, 13° 28.5′ E.

Unnamed anchorage (S Woodfjorden)
Chart 521   79° 26.0′ N, 13° 43.2′ E
A scenic anchorage, especially useful in S winds, just N of a small sand spit. There is a large kittiwake colony high above.

Wijdefjorden, long and sheer, penetrates 60 miles S, to within 15 miles of Pyramiden in Isfjorden. To the E lie the highest mountains in Svalbard, Perriertoppen and Newtontoppen, both 1717 m.

Mosselbukta / Mossellaguna
(NE Wijdefjorden)
Chart 510   79° 52.8′ N, 16° 03′ E
At this anchorage often used in whaling days, there are ruins on the small island Polhemodden, from the 1872 overwintering expedition of 67 men led by Nordenskiøld. There is a trapper's hut in the area. The anchorage is outside the unnavigable lagoon shown in the photograph in *Den Norske Los*, and offers better protection in W winds than might be supposed. As described by *Den Norske Los*: 'Enter at a suitable distance from the N-ern shore. One will then catch sight of an islet which is now connected to land about 5 cables from the head of the bay. On the top there are the remains of Nordenskiøld's over-wintering house 'Polhem'. Due S of Polhemodden, and separated from it by an unnavigable sound, are two small islets, and a little SE of them, a steep islet with a heavy iron bolt on the top (note: the bolt is now bent over). Smaller vessels can go S of the two islets – which are really two almost connected skerries – and anchor between them and the steep 'Boltholmen' in 4–6 m water. Vessels have also anchored in 13 m, 5 cables off.'

Bjørnnesholmen (E Austfjorden)*
Chart 510   79° 07.5′ N, 16° 09′ E
The sound E of the islet is navigable, with anchorage off the trapper's hut.

PART 4

Sognefjorden and south to the Swedish Border

12 Sognefjorden

County: Sogn og Fjordane

The Sognefjord is entered through the Sognesjøen, either through the inner leads from N or S, or direct from the sea. With a relatively shallow and uneven bottom, seas here can be extremely unpleasant in rough weather, until the relative protection of the fjord proper is reached. This is the longest fjord in Norway, extending 80 miles inland from Rutletangen Light, where the fjord proper begins, to the end of the main fjord, and a great deal farther up some of the long side branches, notably the Lustrafjord. As the Sognesjøen extends for 15 miles from the sea to the mouth of the fjord, the main inlet is thus some 95 miles long, and the heads of some of the branches are well over 100 miles' steaming from the sea. This is a wild, grand and harsh part of the world, with depths of up to 1300 m many miles inland, and with snow-capped mountains over 1400 m high standing close to the water's edge on both hands. Squalls are frequent and can be very violent, even in fine weather, and Norwegian yachtsmen tell frightening tales of the *fallende wind* – a sudden blast of cold air that can roll down a mountainside, felling trees before it, and strike down almost vertically on to the water, forcing a yacht over until it is horizontal.

The more usual difficulty, however, is areas of total calm, and it would be most unwise to visit this or any other fjord without reliable power, particularly as good havens and anchorages are few and far between.

CHARTS

Charts 24, 251 and 252, and also chart 124 if exploring the Nærøyfjord or inner Aurlandsfjord. Note that charts 251 and 252 are on a scale of 1:75 000 as opposed to the standard Norwegian scale of 1:50 000, so distances are greater than they may appear at first glance.

PASSAGE

With the above general notes on the Sognefjord in mind, the passage up the

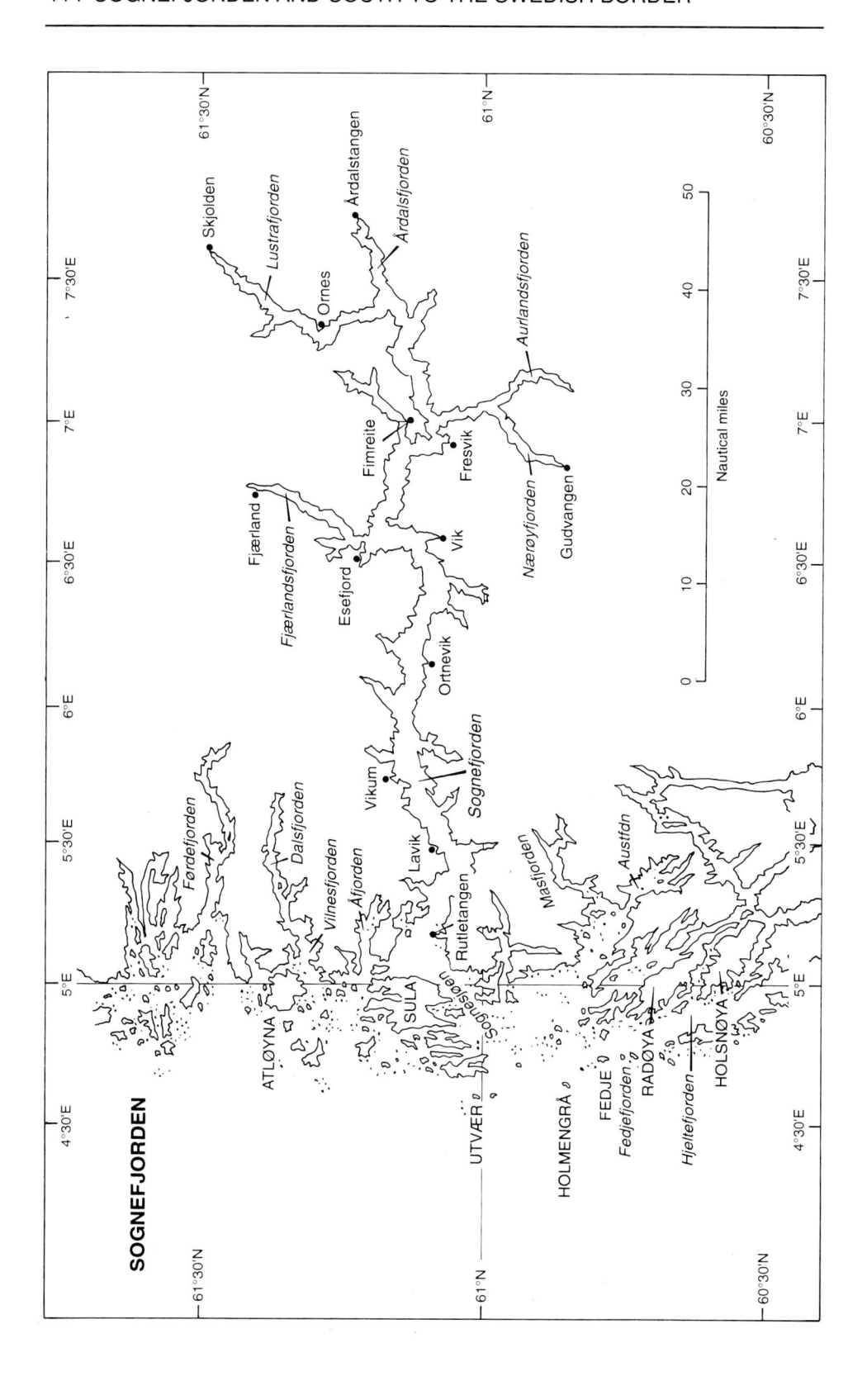

114 SOGNEFJORDEN AND SOUTH TO THE SWEDISH BORDER

fjord is straightforward, with no offshore hazards whatever once the skerries and rocks either side of Rutletangen (inset on chart 251) have been negotiated. Of the side fjords, there are three of major importance. Fjærlandsfjord branches off to the N in 6° 35′ E, and there are good views of glaciers from its head. The mouth of the fjord is 46 miles from Rutletangen Light, and the fjord is 14 miles long. The next branch, the Aurlandsfjord, is to the S in 7° 01′ E, 57 miles from Rutletangen, and it has its own branch, the Nærøyfjord, some 6 miles inland on the W side, which extends about 9 miles to the SW.

This is one of the most spectacular fjords in Norway, narrowing to under 400 m in places and towered over by almost vertical cliffs over 1000 m high. It should clearly be avoided in bad weather, and as the entrance of the Aurlandsfjord is 58 miles from Rutletangen and the head of the Nærøyfjord 73 miles, this is therefore a major expedition in an area of highly uncertain weather, and the reader should consider carefully whether he or she should not enjoy the similar but less remote scenery of the Lysefjord (p.134) unless virtually unlimited time is available.

The final important branch of the Sognefjord is the Lustrafjord, running off to the N in 7° 24′ E, about 69 miles from Rutletangen. Its main point of interest is that as it is 22 miles long, its head is 91 miles from Rutletangen, and 106 miles from the sea.

HARBOURS AND ANCHORAGES

These are listed clockwise round the coast, from the N side of the entrance, up the fjord including the N branches, and back along the S side in the same way.

Lavik
Chart 251 61° 06′ N, 5° 30′ E
Although once a useful harbour, two new ferry quays have restricted anchorage space so severely that it is now best regarded as for emergency use only. This is a pity, as the village has a telephone kiosk, shop, bank and PO.

Vikum
Chart 251 61° 09.5′ N, 5° 40′ E
One of the best harbours in the outer Sognefjord, providing sheltered anchorage in all but SE winds. The best anchorage is between the island of Hamnaholm and the mainland. Beware a dangerous wreck that lies alongside the N-most 25 m of the island and extends out for about 10 m: this covers at HW, but is otherwise plainly visible. There are several mooring posts on both the island and the mainland only 30–40 m away, so take a bow line ashore in the direction of the expected wind and drop a stern anchor towards the opposite side. Good holding in sand and clay. There is also a mooring buoy, in the pool, which may be available for use in conjunction with shore lines. There is a shop in the village, but the walk from this berth is rough. Better to motor round into the main bay and put a shopper ashore on the rough stone quay below the village (photo p. 115).

Esefjord
Chart 252 61° 13′ N, 6° 32′ E
A small fjord at the mouth of Fjærlandsfjord. Anchor some 100 m SE of the large red mooring buoy on the N side of the fjord about ¼ mile in from the entrance (see inset on chart 252). Clay bottom, depth about 6 m. Make sure you are well W of the W-most shore marker indicating a submarine cable. Exposed in winds between ESE and SSE. Supplies at Balestrand on S side, and also a bank and hotel. A tourist resort.

Vikum, Sognefjorden. A typical varde may be seen top left.

Fjærland
Chart 252   61° 24′ N, 6° 59′ E

Moor at a quay as space allows: least depth 2 m alongside the shorter (shop) quay, 3.2 m on the longer. This harbour gives access to the magnificent Jostedal glacier. A guide may be available through the hotel, or Anders Øygard (Tel: 57 69 31 18) speaks English and guides. JA went up unguided in 1992 and says, 'Visit the glacier museum – not cheap, but worth it for the dizzying films shot by helicopters flying down into crevasses, then walk a few km to around 200 m past Anders' farm (61° 27′ N, 6° 48′ E) and turn left on to a wide and obvious trail. Within half an hour you will see a signpost above to your right, from which follow the steep but well trodden and safe path up the rocky ridge (not the wide trail up off to the left, not the gully straight up, and not the trail off to the right). Eventually you may come to snow, depending on snowpack and time of year, where hiking boots will be needed, and you will see the peak of a hut roof above. This was built by Anders. It would be unwise to proceed farther on to the glacier itself without a guide, but the views all the way up are fantastic. From fjord to hut is a 900 m climb, making a strenuous and worthwhile day, but remember that a sudden change in the weather or a sprained ankle could be potentially disastrous, so a compass and sensible boots are vital, and someone in the village should know your plans.' Note that this is a serious expedition, involving a 914 m climb, which even the fit find taxing (MB). *Den Norske Los* warns that severe squalls may be experienced when it is blowing hard from the NW (photo p. 3).

Fimreite
Chart 252   61° 09′ N, 6° 59′ E

A good sheltered anchorage at the

bottom of Sogndalsfjord. Anchor NE of the village: good holding, clay and sand, depth 10–15 m.

Skjolden
Chart 252 61° 29′ N, 7° 36′ E
Lying at the head of the Lustrafjord, Skjolden's principal claim to fame is that it is the farthest from the open sea that you are ever likely to get and yet find yourself still in a tidal salt-water port. Moor to one of the quays (see large scale inset on chart 252 for the approach and entrance), or anchor 600 m S of the town in 20 m, mud and rock. Shop, hotel and PO.

Ornes
Chart 252 61° 18′ N, 7° 19′ E
In fair weather one may berth at the (partly ruined) wooden quay or anchor as charted 1 cable SSW of the point. Note the rock awash close SW from the point. Ashore is the oldest wooden church in Norway, built in the twelfth century.

Årdalstangen
Chart 252 61° 14′ N, 7° 42′ E
A mainly industrial harbour at the end of the Årdalsfjord, which is the name given to the last stretch of the main Sognefjord. Numerous quays, but considerable commercial traffic. It may be possible to find a berth in the small boat harbour where there is a least depth of 2.2 m. The harbour is well protected. Shops, hotel, bank, etc.

Gudvangen
Chart 124 60° 53′ N, 6° 51.5′ E
A village at the head of the Nærøyfjord, with very heavy tourist traffic. Berth alongside as space allows, or anchor off in about 20 m, but the bottom shelves very steeply. A place for a daytime visit rather than an overnight stay. Shop, PO and hotel. *Note*: if exploring the Nærøyfjord, an additional chart, chart 124, will be needed.

Fresvik
Chart 252 61° 04.5′ N, 6° 56′ E
This harbour should be avoided in NW winds, when an unpleasant sea builds up in the bay. Anchor close in to the E shore of the bay about 1½ cables N of the village and take a line ashore to one of the two mooring bolts, or berth alongside the quay if room. Good shop.

Vik
Chart 252 61° 05′ N, 6° 35′ E
A town with a population of 3600, several shops, bank, etc. Exposed in northerly winds. Anchor on the E side of the bay NW of the cannery (see large scale inset on chart 252) or berth alongside one of the six quays, least depth at any 2.1 m. The wooden Hopperstad stave church dates from around 1200, and is well worth a visit.

Ortnevik
Chart 251 61° 06.5′ N, 6° 08′ E
A shoal extends from the E side of the bay, marked by a varde and two iron posts. Keep well over to the W shore until past the more southerly post, and anchor in 15 m. Good holding, sand and clay. This is a particularly attractive anchorage. There is a shop by the quay on the W side of the bay. *Den Norske Los* says that strong E or NW winds create a sea in the bay: the former may also produce heavy squalls.

13 Sognefjorden to Bergen

Counties: Sogn og Fjordane and Hordaland

PASSAGE

Charts 24, 23

There are two main alternatives available, each having a number of variants. The simplest route from Rutletangen Light is to proceed down Sognesjøen and make for the conspicuous lighthouse on Holmengrå. Leaving this ½ mile to starboard, a SE course leads into Fedjefjord, and thence into the Hjeltefjord which connects at its southern end with the W branch of the Byfjord, leading to Bergen. Alternatively, one can pass under the Knarrevik bridge (49 m) and proceed to Kviturspollen (the best harbour from which to visit Bergen).

The second route is farther inland, and in far more sheltered waters. Turn S out of Sognesjøen either side of the island of Hisarøya. If on the more westerly route, continue S to the W of Store Vassøya and Sandøya, while if on the E of Hisarøya turn W, pass through the narrow channel between Grimstadholm and Storholm, and then proceed S along the narrow channel to the E of Sandøya. From the W channel steer S or, from the E one, WSW, until the varde on Hageskjær is identified, then steer to leave this close to port. One can then proceed between Bakkøya and Keiløya (bridge clearance 25 m) or through the still narrower passage between Bakkøya and Ulvøya. This has a very narrow bridge with only 15 m clearance, and strong tide eddies are experienced in the channel, so it should only be attempted under power and with sail lowered. Continuing SE, Kalvshovudet is left close to port, and then after 3 miles the S-going channel is taken, which leads into the Radsund. From its narrow S entrance, the way to Bergen by way of Kvernafjord, Salhus Fjord and Byfjord is straightforward. (Byfjord, by the way, means City Fjord, which is why there are so many of them – but then Norway is full of identically named islands and fjords, often spelled somewhat erratically, which can cause confusion.)

The main variant on the Hjeltefjord route avoids the necessity of crossing about 7 miles of unprotected water, while preserving the advantage of the long run down Hjeltefjord, which is wide enough to provide good sailing. Take the W alternative of the inner passage until clear of Vikingneset, on the SE tip of Byrknesøy. Thence steer WSW until the varde on the N end of Harsøy is identified, whereafter leave Harsøy, Rotøy, Langøy, Lauvøy and Ulvøy close to starboard. Emerge between Geitarøy and the mainland, steer S between Kluftholm, and Dyrnes varde, continue S and pass through the well buoyed channel between Knopesteinen and Vardeholm (conspicuous lighthouse) and then turn W until Hjeltefjord opens up. In a brisk W or NW wind, this route provides good sailing almost all the way, while avoiding the heavy seas that may be found in the outer reaches of Sognesjøen. Distances to Bergen from Rutletangen Light: 50 miles by the E (inshore) route, 59 miles by the Hjeltefjord. To Kviturspollen: 62 miles by the inshore route, 63 miles by Hjeltefjord. The inshore route is thus much shorter if a visit is to be made to Bergen itself, but the two are much the same if (as I would recommend) Kviturspollen is used as the base from which Bergen is visited.

With reasonable wind the outside passage can be sailed from end to end, while the inshore one is subject to blanketing from the surrounding mountains. In 1976 MB sailed the whole of what I have described as the 'main variant' of the outer passage under jib alone with a Force 7 N wind, and had a most enjoyable sail without undue sea.

TIDES AND CURRENTS

Den Norske Los tends to make little or no distinction between tidal stream and current, and this is scarcely surprising as the currents created by wind and meteorological factors tend to be strong enough to hold up or even reverse the tidal stream. HW Bergen is about 1 hour before Dover, and the flood runs S in the waters N of Bergen, and N from Kviturspollen and E along the Byfjord. One should therefore allow for up to 2 knots of tidal stream in these directions, added to a steady current of at least as much if there have been strong winds from the same quarter for a few days. Thus in a period of stiff northerlies, for example, the current might vary

Unusually gentle scenery for W Norway: fields and islands near Kviturspollen, HQ of the Bergen Sailing Club.

between nothing on the ebb to 4 knots southerly on the Radsund, with both tidal streams and currents being weaker in wider waters such as the Hjeltefjord. The reader will readily see that accurate prediction, if possible at all, can only be carried out with detailed local knowledge. My experience is that even the locals often turn out to be wrong when trying to predict exact currents.

HARBOURS AND ANCHORAGES

Inshore route

Eivindvik
Chart 24   60° 59′ N, 5° 05′ E
The main quays lie at the W end of the village, N of Fonnevik on the island of Fonna. Moor alongside one of the small quays W of the large steamer quay, and then seek local advice on obtaining permission to stay. The harbour is sheltered in all but strong westerlies, when the wind funnels along the sound and kicks up a heavy sea. In these conditions anchor in the bay opposite the E end of the village, on the W side 1 cable S of the bridge in about 20 m. Clay bottom, good holding once the anchor has dug in. Fuel and water from hose at E end of steamer quay, excellent shop by quay with PO next door. There is a bank about 250 m up the hill: keep right at fork in road. A pleasant and pretty little village.

Ramsvik
Chart 24   60° 58′ N, 04° 58.5′ E
A useful and pretty small anchorage in 5–8 m, mud bottom. Fully sheltered. No facilities.

Vikingevågen
Chart 24   60° 52′ N, 04° 55′ E
A charming landlocked anchorage offering perfect shelter in all weathers. Keep to N in entrance to avoid rock (1 m) in S of channel. Once in, keep to the S side and anchor before the bluff on the N shore. Good holding on mud bottom, numerous mooring bolts. Complete seclusion. No facilities.

Mastrevik
Chart 23   60° 47.5′ N, 04° 56.5′ E
See also Passage notes regarding tide eddies in the narrows to the N. The harbour is in the bay to the W of Viksholm. The main pier has fenders that are set too high for the average yacht, which may drift under at LW, so it is safer to berth alongside the factory quay 200 m to the S, if permission can be obtained; 4.5 m alongside, complete shelter. Fuel near the steamer quay. Excellent shop in the village, up the hill and second on the right from the recommended mooring.

Grunnesundet
Chart 23   60° 40.5′ N, 5° 06′ E
This delightful anchorage must be approached from the N end of Radsundet, as there is only about ½ m at LW in the narrows ½ mile SE of Askelandstangen. Keep slightly to the starboard side of the channel as far as the first bay on the N side, where one can anchor in 10 m, taking a line ashore. Better, however, is to proceed a further ½ mile, keeping to mid-channel, where a larger bay will be found where one can lie in absolute protection and seclusion with a line to a rock on the islet and another to one on the mainland, and no need for an anchor. There is a minimum of 3 m in the channel to the first anchorage; 2.5 m to the second, where the depth is 3.5 m. Very beautiful and lonely, no facilities.

Alverstraumen
Chart 23   60° 35′ N, 5° 13′ E
Lie alongside one of the three quays, minimum depth 2.7 m. The stream here

SOGNEFJORDEN TO BERGEN

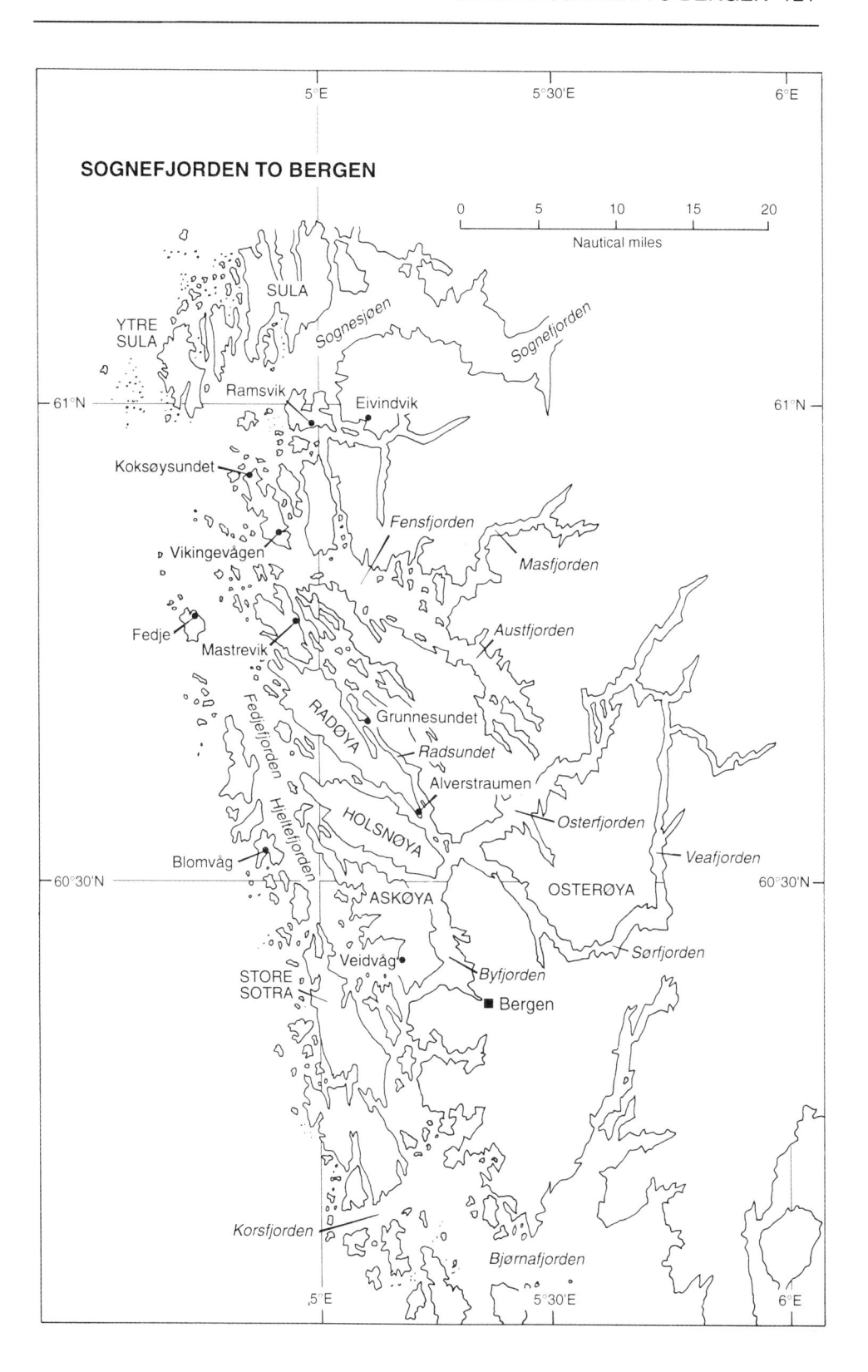

can reach 6 knots, according to *Den Norske Los*, and although the rate is much affected by wind (see above) it is one place where it is well worth arranging to pass through with a fair tide, particularly near springs. It runs N on the flood and S on the ebb. A charming little town with PO, shops and café.

Outer route

Koksøysundet
Chart 24   60° 56' N, 4° 48.5' E
A narrow but well marked sound with several good anchorages towards its W end. Good holding in sand and clay, with numerous mooring bolts. The anchorages are completely sheltered, but the entrance is rough in strong winds from W to NW, when it is safer to proceed through Bårøyosen and approach from the E (three overhead cables, min clearance 20 m). A pretty anchorage with no facilities.

Fedje
Chart 23   60° 46.5' N, 4° 44' E
This island is invaluable in bad weather on this rather exposed route, as it has two excellent harbours close together, one exposed only to the N and the other to the SE. Fedje harbour itself is very busy and crowded, but there is excellent anchorage in Rognsvåg in 4 m well up the inlet halfway down the W shore of the bay. Good holding in sand with several mooring bolts (see large scale inset on chart 24). It may also be possible to berth on the concrete public quay, least depth 2.2 m. In strong N winds this anchorage is to be avoided, but then Sildevåg, whose entrance lies about a mile to the SE, becomes ideal. Keep along the SW shore of the inlet once past the varde as the hazards are on the NE side, and anchor when the depth is suitable. Several mooring bolts on both shores. Both anchorages are within walking distance of Fedje; Rognsvåg is no more than 200 m from the centre, and Sildevåg about ¾ mile. Bank, PO, shops and restaurant.

Blomvåg
Chart 23   60° 31.5' N, 4° 53' E
Reached by way of the Ulvsund (bridge, 20 m clearance) and the Rorsund. On no account attempt to use the Straumesund, which has only 1 m. The anchorage offers complete shelter in all weathers. Anchor in Dalsvåg, the extreme N arm of the harbour. Good holding in sand and mud, several mooring bolts. PO, shop and hotel in Blomvåg village, about ½ mile SW of the anchorage.

Veidvåg
Chart 23   60° 25.5' N, 5° 09' E
A landlocked anchorage in a small bay near the S of Askøya. Approach to the N of the islet in the middle of the entrance, and anchor in the W of the bay (12 m) or go alongside quay if room. Shop in Hetlevik (½ mile).

Bergen
Charts 23, 21   60° N, 5° 19' E
Like most major commercial ports in large cities, this is an uncomfortable and noisy place, and Kviturspollen, the HQ of the Bergen Sailing Club, is far more to be recommended for a long stay (see next section). A reasonable berth can often be found at the extreme SE end of Vågen, the more northerly of the two harbours, but there can be considerable movement from the wash of ships manoeuvring, and from swell if the wind is NW or N. All possible shops, etc, with beer freely available though expensive.

The aquarium (on the point of Nordnes, the headland dividing the two harbours) is famous and well worth a visit, as is the Hanseatic Museum on

Grunnesundet. The narrows mentioned in the text live up to their description!

Bryggen, the road running along the NE side of Vågen. Also, do not miss a trip up the funicular, which runs up from near the SE corner of Vågen, with incredible views from the top on a clear day.

There is a service centre with toilets, showers, washing machines and dryers in the new building on quay 70 – Zachariasbryggen – entered from Torget, the square at the end of the Vågen part of the harbour. It is kept locked: keys available from 'Bon Appetit', which occupies part of the same building. There are good open air fish and vegetable stalls on Torget. All repairs and services are available: Båt & Motorservice (Tel: 05 31 16 68), Dolviken Båtservice (Tel: 05 12 30 50) or Bjordal & Madsen (Tel: 05 12 17 00) will help or advise. Fuel from Blaauw Marine, quay 66 in Vågen.

14 Bergen to Haugesund with the Hardangerfjord

Counties: Hordaland and Rogaland

PASSAGE

Charts 21, 19, 17 (main route)   22, 117, 118 (Hardangerfjord)

There are only minor variations on the passage S until one reaches the latitude of 60° 10′ N, where three main choices offer themselves. One can continue SSE down the rather dull wide sound called Langenuen, coming out at the NE end of the Bømlafjord, just where it joins the group of fjords known as the Hardangerfjord. (It is worth noting that, unlike Sognefjord, all the waters in Hardangerfjord have their own individual names, so although charts 117 and 118 are named Outer and Inner Hardangerfjord, the name appears nowhere else on the charts.) The second choice is to continue S, passing W of Huftarøya, either side of Selbjørn, and proceed across Selbjørnsfjord and down the Nyleid, emerging into the middle of the Bømlafjord, while finally one can turn W through Korsfjord into the open sea, and so S.

Another possibility for those intending to explore the Hardangerfjord is to bear round to the E at the top of Langenuen, proceed up the short but wide Bjørnafjord, and then turn sharply S through the narrow and spectacular Lokksund that leads out into the Hardangerfjord itself.

The passage up the Hardangerfjord with its various arms is quite straightforward, but the trouble is that one has to go many miles inland before the scenery becomes anything out of the ordinary. Flat calms and violent squalls are commonplace, and unless time is virtually unlimited I feel that the outer skjærgård, with a trip up the short but spectacular Lysefjord, is likely to prove better value.

Continuing S, one proceeds SW down Bømlafjord, emerging into open sea protected only by a group of relatively small islands. Even these give out after a couple of miles, and there is a gap of totally unprotected sea some 2 miles long, which can be most unpleasant to cross in heavy weather from the W. After that, however, the protection builds up again until one slips behind the islands just N of Haugesund. In the approach, one should start from a position about 1 to 2 cables off Kvalen Light, having kept well inshore all the way S, as the dangers are all farther off. A SSE course will then lead into the eastern entry channel, narrow but well marked. Alternatively, WSW clears the rocks to the NW of Sørhaugøya and leads to a red buoy marking the W side of the main channel. This entry should be used at night, as it is well marked by the white sectors of two successive lights.

Storsundet in Hardangerfjorden.

TIDES AND CURRENTS

The strongest streams are likely to be found in the N of this area, particularly in the Vatlestraumen, the narrows between the N of Bjørøya and the mainland. The flood runs N and the ebb S, but as always the rates can be much affected or even reversed by wind. Farther S the streams are more and more wind-based, with a tendency to a southerly set, at least in summer.

HARBOURS AND ANCHORAGES

N of Hardangerfjord

Grimstad
Chart 21   60° 19′ N, 5° 14½′ E
There is an anchorage in the small bight just to the E of Grimstad village. Good holding in about 5 m, shell and sand. This is just W of a large tanker berth, so there is a rather commercial atmosphere, but it is a useful place to wait for a fair tide through the Vatlestraumen. There is also a new marina. The village is notable for its numerous bakeries.

Hjellestad
Chart 21   60° 15′ N, 5° 14′ E
The marina here has visitors' berths and all facilities including fuel. Dues are charged. Shop and PO. Beautiful walks in the vicinity.

Kviturspollen
Chart 21   60° 16′ N, 5° 15′ E
Both *Den Norske Los* and the chart use the spelling Kviturdpollen, but the inhabitants use the above, although sometimes with two Ts, so I have preferred it. This shows the problems of trying to establish spelling in Norway, although considerable progress has been made on standardisation since the first edition of this book was published.

This charming lagoon is the HQ of the Bergen Sailing Club, and the approach is well marked. On arrival, pick up a vacant mooring and then check at the clubhouse, which has showers. Moderate charges. The lagoon is perfectly sheltered, often from wind as well as sea, which can encourage the unwary to set out in conditions that prove to be wild outside. Bus service to Bergen. Fuel and supplies at Hjellestad (see above). (Photo p. 119.)

Kvalvåg
Chart 21   60° 00¾′ N, 5° 05′ E
This small harbour on the N of Stolmen Is provides complete shelter in all winds, although an uncomfortable swell sets into the harbour in strong winds from the NW to N. The church on the W side of the harbour is conspicuous. Steer to leave it well to starboard, and proceed down the starboard side of the harbour. There is 3.5 m in the outer part, and 2.5 m in the inner. The harbour is shoal on the E side and the available width is therefore very restricted, so care must be taken with a following wind as it can prove difficult to bring up. Berth along the quays along the W wall of the harbour, 1.9 m or more alongside. Shop and PO. A charming place, and has a salmon fishery, so salmon (*laks* in Norwegian) can be bought cheaply. Enquire at the shop.

Landrøyvåg
Chart 21   59° 59′ N, 5° 24′ E
A landlocked anchorage on the E side of Langenuen. Keep well to the starboard side of the narrows in the entrance, to avoid the shoal with two ½ m rocks projecting S from the islet, and anchor on the E side of the S branch of the lagoon in 11 m, sand. No facilities.

Godøysund
Chart 22   60° 04′ N, 5° 35′ E
A useful stopping place for those using the Lokksund route to Hardangerfjord. The approach from the W is strewn wit hazards, but well marked. Most of the dangers are on the N side of the approach, so keep at least ½ mile S of Vesøyane until the marker S of Rundeskjær is identified, whence a course of 105° T leads into the well marked channel, which *Den Norske Los* states is suitable for vessels of up to 3.5 m draft. There are pontoons off the Godøysund Fjordhotel, on the S side just past the first narrows in the sound. These were reported as being expensive in 1994. There are also many good anchorages in bays and creeks in the area, notably Hamnavika, some 2 cables NE of the hotel on the N shore, entered close E of the islet that lies in the jaws of the bay.

Koløystø
Chart 19   59° 51.5′ N, 5° 18′ E
This harbour lies at the N end of Koløyosen and has three quays, least depth 2 m. The town has a PO, bank and shop. It is not usually possible to

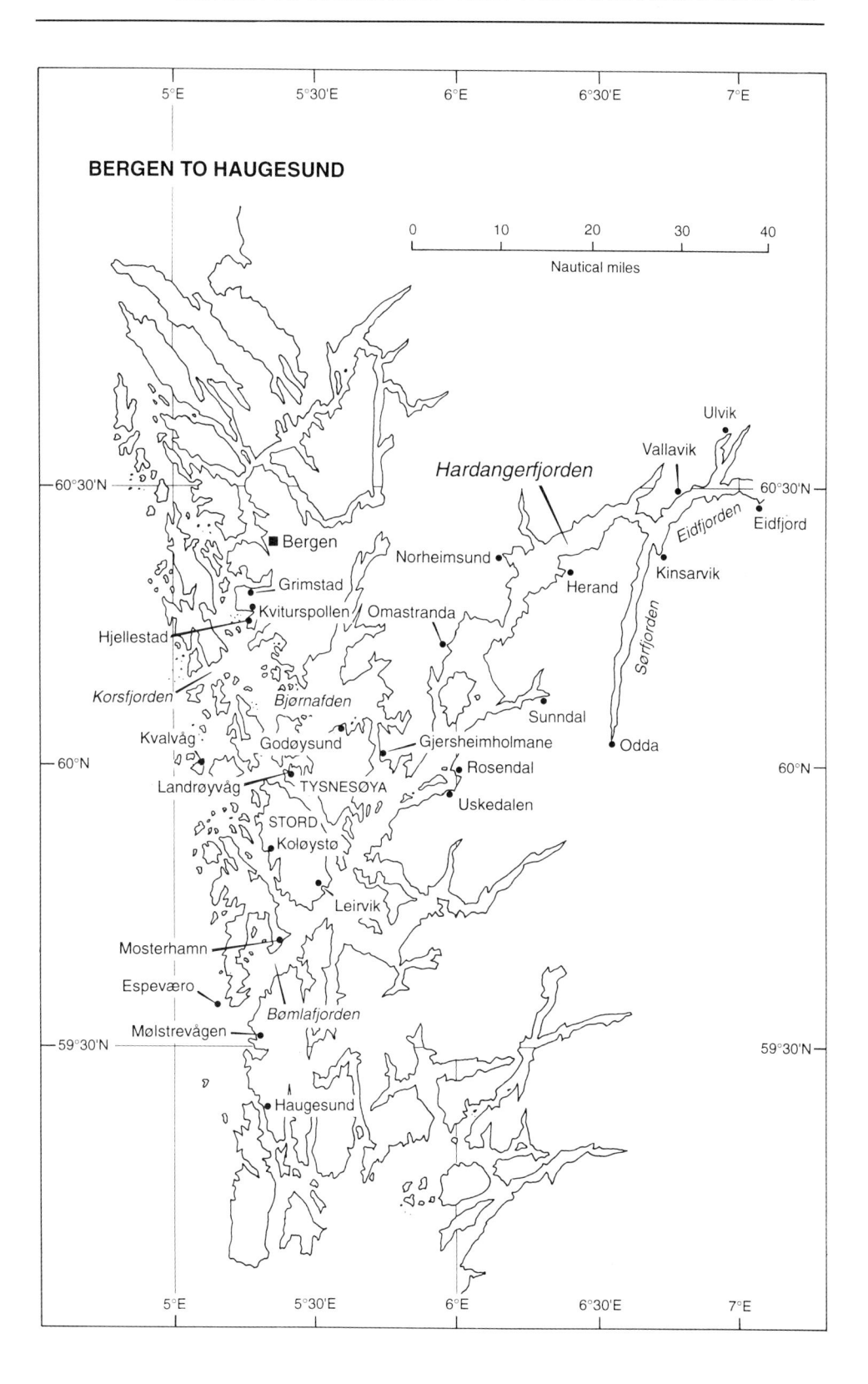

BERGEN TO HAUGESUND WITH THE HARDANGERFJORD 127

berth for the night at a quay, but there is good and sheltered anchorage in Koløyosen in attractive surroundings. Mooring bolts are provided both on Koløyna and the Stord mainland: sand and clay, 10–15 m. Approach either side of Dåseholm, as shown by the leading line on the chart. Yachts drawing less than 2 m can also pass N of Koløyna.

In Hardangerfjord

As with Sognefjord, the harbours covered below are arranged clockwise around the shore of the fjord and its branches.

Gjersheimholmane
Chart 20   60° 00.5′ N, 5° 43.5′ E
A good anchorage at the S end of the Lokksund, on the E side. Anchor between the islet and the mainland in 8 m, sand and mud, with mooring rings. A most beautiful berth, but no facilities.

Omastranda
Chart 117   60° 13′ N, 5° 59′ E
A pleasant anchorage inside the islet of Omaholm. Anchor in 6 m, mooring bolts, sand and mud bottom. Shop, bank and PO.

Norheimsund
Chart 117   60° 22′ N, 6° 09′ E
A considerable small town with all kinds of shops (including chandlery), hotels and restaurants. There are several quays and pontoons, or one may anchor in the bay N of the islet, 8 m, sand and clay. Beautiful scenery, good connections to Bergen. There is an impressive waterfall, Steindalsfossen, 2 km out of the town.

Vallavik
Chart 118   60° 29′ N, 6° 50′ E
An apparently exposed anchorage, but protected by the surrounding mountains. There is a rough quay with 4.6 m, but better to anchor 2 cables to the NE near the Måsestein. There are mooring bolts both on it and the mainland; 10 m, sand and clay bottom.

Ulvik
Chart 118   60° 34′ N, 6° 55′ E
A large village set in beautiful scenery at the head of the Ulvikfjord. There may be room to berth at the quay in front of the Brakanes Hotel, from whom permission to stay should be asked, or one may anchor in the bay SW of the church. Exposed in SE winds. There are numerous shops, bank, PO and hotels.

Eidfjord
Chart 118   60° 28′ N, 7° 04′ E
The most easterly anchorage in Hardangerfjord, well protected and offering impressive scenery. Anchor in the bay W of the town, where about 20 m can be found, clay bottom, or try for a berth alongside. Hotel, bank and shops, and a church dating from 1309. With snow-capped peaks running up to 1600 m in close view, this is a beautiful but often stormy place.

Kinsarvik
Chart 118   60° 22.5′ N, 6° 43′ E
A somewhat exposed but safe anchorage near the entrance to the Sørfjord, perhaps the most remarkable branch of the Hardangerfjord as it runs in an almost exactly straight line for nearly 20 miles. Anchor in the SW of the bay, 15–20 m, sand and clay. Bank, shops and PO in the town, interesting twelfth-century church near the quay.

Odda
Chart 118   60° 04′ N, 6° 33′ E
A large town at the extreme end of the Sørfjord (see above). There is a pontoon with room for eight to ten yachts in the bay W of the river, with water and electricity. Washing machine available; enquire at the Tourist Information office: they will also advise the energetic

Herand
Chart 117   60° 20.5′ N, 6° 22′ E
Anchor NW of the quay in 10 m, good holding in sand. S of this line the holding becomes bad (smooth rock) until near the quay, where fine sand occurs again and there are eight mooring bolts. So make sure the anchor is well dug in. Bank, shop and PO in the village. If stores are not required, the anchorage inside Herandsholm a mile to the W may be preferred. Good holding in sand and clay, with mooring bolts on Herandsholm and the skerry to the E. Fully protected, but no facilities. Keep an eye out for fish cages when entering the anchorage.

Sunndal
Chart 117   60° 07′ N, 6° 16′ E
A beautiful village lying on the S shore of the Maurangerfjord, a short branch off the SE side of the main Hardangerfjord. Berth at the quay if no ferry expected, otherwise anchor in the bay W of the quay or E of the river mouth. The water is deep and the holding (soft sand and clay) is poor, so this is a place to visit in good weather only. There is a shop and PO in the village.

Rosendal
Chart 20   59° 59′ N, 6° 01′ E
I mention this harbour mainly to warn against it. It is a famous tourist centre, and locals tend to recommend a visit. *Den Norske Los*, however, says quite flatly that this is a poor harbour, with doubtful holding in deep water. Those who do decide on a visit in settled weather should anchor no further N than the transit of Kalvtangen with the S-most point of the Nes, as the holding beyond is dangerous: within this limit, as far N as possible. For a short time a berth may be possible at the quay. There are also two small pontoons off the Fjordhotel at Stølen, ½ mile to the S, where it may be possible to berth. Bank, hotel, shops.

Uskedal
Chart 20   59° 56′ N, 5° 52′ E
A charming village on the S side of the Storsund. The whole area is subject to severe mountain squalls, especially with strong SE winds, but it is beautiful in settled weather, and a good place to visit to get the flavour of the Hardangerfjord without going up too far.

There are two small marinas, W and NW of the church, where it may be possible to berth, or it is possible to anchor close in to the SE point of Flatholm, 15 m, fine sand. Shops, PO and bank in the village. If there are any problems finding a berth, excellent anchorage will be found 1 mile to the N on the other side of the sound in Skorpevågen, 10–15 m, sand and mud. This anchorage is sheltered in almost all conditions.

W and S of Hardangerfjord

Leirvik
Charts 19, 20   59° 47′ N, 5° 31′ E
A large and fully sheltered natural harbour on the SE end of the large island of Stord. There are several entrances, all well marked. Once in the bay, steer for the end of the breakwater that projects N from the S shore. Round this, but not too close as there are numerous mooring buoys for small boats just past the end, and the yacht harbour will be seen beyond. The berths are convenient for the numerous shops, restaurants, etc. Fuel and water in the yacht harbour. Leirvik is a large and rather dull town, but excellent for stocking up.

The Lokksund, one of the entrances of Hardangerfjorden.

Mosterhamn
Chart 19   59° 41.5′ N, 5° 22′ E

A charming and useful harbour on the island of Mosterøy, on the N side of the Bømlafjord. A slight swell occurs in strong SE winds, otherwise perfectly protected. Enter close to the S of Kaninholm Light, and leave two perches close to port. A low rock shelf projects from the N side of the inlet. Moor at the wooden quay of Moster Marina (depths from 2.9 m to 0.5 m at the N end) where all facilities are on offer, or elsewhere as opportunity allows. A charming little village with shops and bank, and the oldest stone-built church in Norway.

Espevær
Chart 19   59° 35.5′ N, 5° 09.5′ E

This perfectly sheltered and charming little fishing village is now more inhabited by pensioners than active fishermen, which adds to its charms for yachtsmen. The main approach from the S presents no problems. It is also possible to enter from the E between Ådnesøyna and Skardholmen or from the N via Kjeholmsundet (see inset on chart 19). The latter route breaks in northerly gales, but is useful in strong southerlies. There are normally plenty of berths alongside, but it is also possible to anchor in a bay at the SW end of the harbour, or a larger one on the other side of the narrow sound that runs on S and W. The village has shops, bank and PO. A museum in Baadehuset can be reached by means of a tiny cable ferry, and there are pleasant inland walks.

Mølstrevågen
Chart 17   59° 31.5′ N, 5° 15.5′ E

A useful stopping place between the Bømlafjord and Haugesund, although the entrance is dangerous in strong winds between SW and NW, and should not be attempted in those conditions.

The entrance is well marked, and lit by night, and shelter can be found in any conditions once in. Anchor 1½ cables SE of the lighthouse in 18 m, sand; or go farther in down the S-most branch of the inlet where there is 9 m, with mooring bolts and good holding.

Haugesund
Chart 17 59° 25′ N, 5° 17′ E
One of the largest towns after Bergen and Stavanger on the part of the W coast of Norway covered in Part 4, Haugesund had 27 000 inhabitants in 1988. The rather tricky approach from the N was covered in the introduction to this section: once inside, the entrance itself is straightforward, between Hasseløy and Risøy, leaving one buoy to starboard. Berth alongside any quay on the mainland (E) side as space allows: those farther S are usually the best bet. However, bear in mind that this is a busy commercial harbour, and all berths are subject to wash. There is also a yacht harbour just N of the N bridge, which has a clearance of 13.5 m. If this is too low, it can be reached by turning N between Hasseløy and the islands to its W, then E before the main N breakwater to close the mainland shore, and then S towards the bridge, when the yacht harbour will be seen. All facilities, and good shops nearby. The southern bridge has clearance of 22.5 m, and this channel provides a short cut to the Karmsund. The town is old and beautiful, with all possible chandlery and repair facilities as well as excellent shopping.

15 Haugesund to Stavanger with the Lysefjord

County: Rogaland

CHARTS

Charts 17, 16 and 205
Chart 205 is 1:100 000, but quite adequate for exploring the Lysefjord and the area round Stavanger.

PASSAGE

Apart from the few who may wish to visit the offshore islands, of which Utsira is the largest and probably the most interesting, yachtsmen are unlikely to use the open sea passages over this section, as besides being exposed it is also considerably longer than the inshore route. The normal route to Stavanger takes one out of the southern entrance of Haugesund (see above), down the Karmsund, and then southeasterly to Kvitsøy Fjord, the Byfjord and Stavanger itself. Continuing to the Lysefjord takes one E, leaving the Marøystein with its conspicuous beacon close to port, and on between Uskje and Kalvøy. From here one passes S of Lille Teistholm, and N of Brattholm and Tingholm (conspicuous lighthouse), and so into the Høgsfjord. The entrance of the Lysefjord lies about 7 miles up the Høgsfjord on the NE side, and care should be taken to identify the buoy that lies about 2 cables SE of the point that lies on the NW side of the entrance, and leave it to port when entering. Once past the comparatively shallow entrance there are no hazards apart from a shoal, resulting from an old landslide, off Geitanes, about 2 miles before the end of the fjord.

Though there is not space to deal with the area in this book, it is also worth mentioning that N and E of Stavanger lies a whole maze of fjords known collectively as Ryfylkefjordene. From N to S they extend almost 50 miles, and about half that from E to W, and the system is so complex that a whole season would be needed even to begin to acquire a detailed knowledge of it. All the waters are sheltered from the sea, so it is an excellent place to spend some time exploring, particularly while waiting for an improvement in the weather before making the exposed passage S to Lindesnes.

TIDES AND CURRENTS

The strongest tides are met with in the northern part of the Karmsund, and in the narrows by Sallhusstraumen bridge the average spring rate is $2^1/_2$ knots, but as always the rates are much affected by wind, and in a strong and established blow the lee-going tide can reach up to 4 knots. The N-going stream begins about $3^3/_4$ hours after HW Bergen, and the S-going about $2^1/_2$ hours before. Farther S, wind-driven currents tend to

HAUGESUND TO STAVANGER WITH THE LYSEFJORD 133

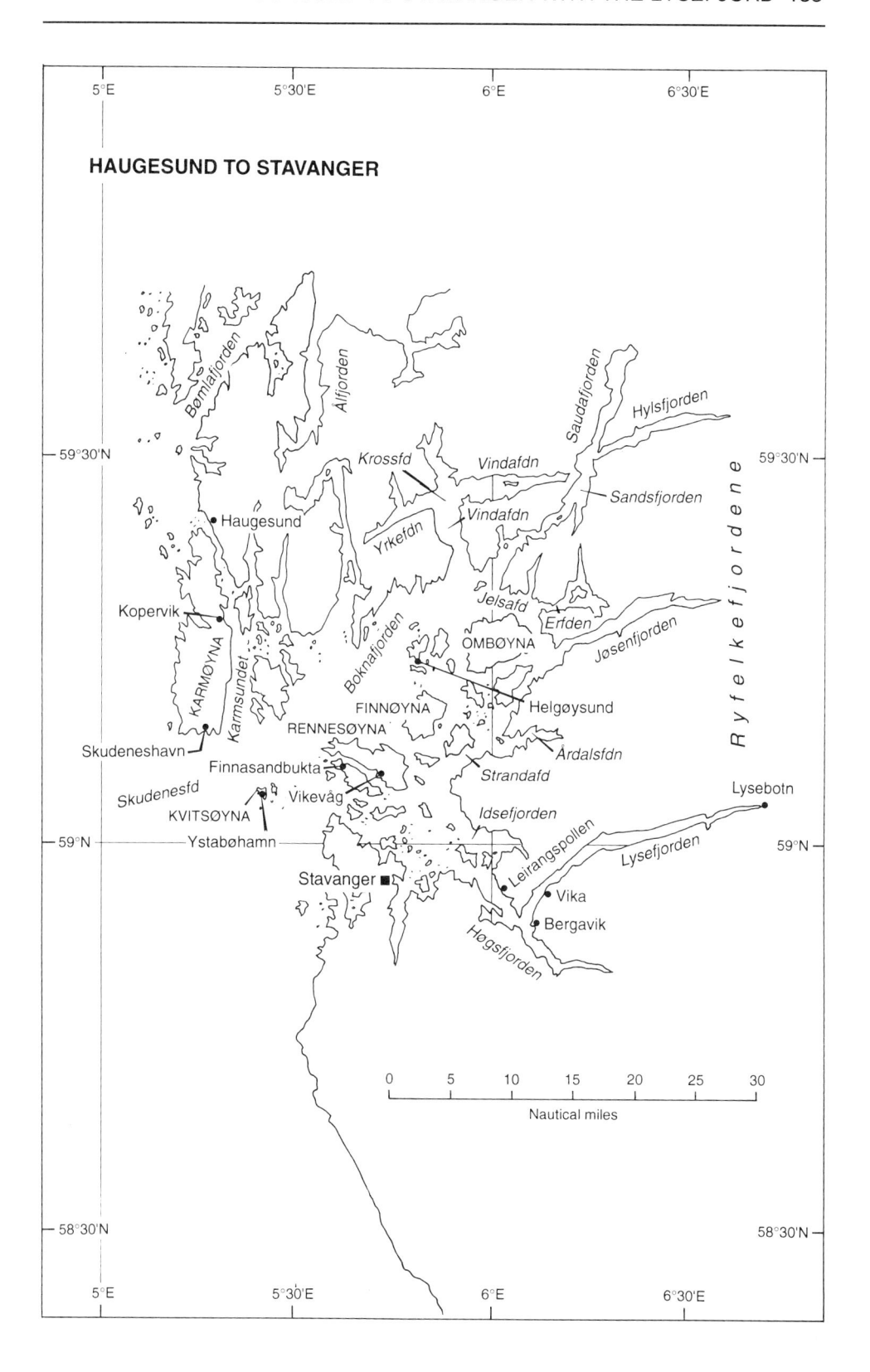

take on more importance than tidal streams.

HARBOURS AND ANCHORAGES

Kopervik
Chart 17   59° 17′ N, 5° 19′ E
A pleasant town of some 7000 inhabitants (1989) with a good harbour offering complete shelter in all weathers. Approach from the Koparnaglen Light if coming from the N, or from the off-lying buoy from the S. There are two main harbours, the northern one of which should be used (there is also a shallow bay farther N, which should be avoided). Proceed well up to the W end of the harbour, where a 32 m length of wooden quay is reserved for visiting yachts 15 July–15 August: otherwise, berth where possible. Fuel, water and good shopping. A rather dull town, but more comfortable than Haugesund.

Skudeneshavn
Chart 16   59° 09′ N, 5° 15.5′ E
This is an attractive and interesting town, with a beautifully sheltered harbour. The entrance appears rather alarming from a first glance at the chart, but the main approach from the SE is perfectly simple in practice. Coming from the N, round the islets off Beiningholm about 2 cables off; from the S, steer on the conspicuous tall white tower E of the town and close it until the islands of Vikaholm and Søreholm appear separate. Steer to leave Vikaholm, the more northerly of these, about 100 m to port, and enter, using the large-scale inset on chart 16. Moor at the extreme end of the harbour. Good shops, restaurant, bank, etc.

Helgøysund
Chart 16   59° 13.5′ N, 5° 50.5′ E
A little off the beaten track, some 20 miles ENE from Skudeneshavn, this harbour none the less makes a charming detour. A bridge (14 m) joins the islands of Talgje and Helgøyna, and the marina lies on the W (Talgje) side N of the bridge. Fuel and water, and shop. Beautiful walks on both islands. Note that the island is technically Nord-Talgje, and must not be confused with the larger Talgje 7 miles to the S off Rennesøy.

Ystabøhamn, Kvitsøyna
Chart 16   59° 03.5′ N, 5° 24′ E
Kvitsøyna is the main island in a group lying some 6 miles SE of Skudeneshavn. The group is easily identified by the conspicuous lighthouse 45.2 m high standing almost in the middle of the low islands. Visitors may find the large scale chart 471 useful, particularly if they have no magnifier. Enter from the W via Revingsund (two fixed red leading lights) or Sagaskjersund (W sector of Ystabø Light), or from the SE passing close SW of Sandholm, and then W of Pikskjer Light ½ mile to the NW. The latter entrance is sheltered in W winds. All the channels are well marked, and easier to follow than would appear from the chart. The final approach to the harbour itself, Ystbøhamn, is through the sound immediately to the W of Rossøyna. Berth alongside the NW arm of the pier (3 m), or at one of the quays as space permits and where permission can be obtained. Least depth at any quay 1.9 m. This is an attractive and unusual place, specialising in lobster fishery. Stores, fuel and water available. The westerly entrances, particularly the Revingsund, are dangerous in a sea, and if the sea is breaking over the rock (1.5 m) NNE of Revingen varde, the channel is impassable and the SE entrance should be used.

Note: About 6 NM ENE from

Kvitsøyna is Klosterøyna and the entrance to the Mastrafjord. Anchorage can be found in Finnasandbukta, just N of the narrow deck in the island a mile E of its W-most point that divides it from the larger Mosterøyna. From here it is a mile walk westwards to Utstein Kloster, an interesting restored medieval monastery, mentioned in the sagas, from where English monks once tried to convert the Vikings. Some 3 miles E of this anchorage on Rennesøyna, **Vikevåg*** has a yacht harbour with visitors' berths offering good shopping and facilities. Although unvisited by either MB or JA, it appears completely sheltered except perhaps in heavy weather from the S.

Stavanger
Chart 16   58° 58′ N, 5° 44′ E
This is one of the main cities and ports in Norway, with a population of 97 400 in 1989, and estimates of up to 120 000 by 1995. The approach down the Byfjord is straightforward, but it is as well to keep well over to the SW side to avoid the traffic, which is sometimes heavy. The main visitors' berth is at the S extremity of Vågen, the narrow bay on the W side of the harbour, inside the floating wharves. A white van, open (in season) 1600–2000 Mon–Fri and 0900–2000 Sat and Sun, acts as a tourist centre, sells charts, etc, and can provide fuel. Water is also available. These berths are noisy (numerous discos), disturbed by wash and rough in N winds. It may also be possible to find a berth in the Stavanger Sailing Club marina on the S side of Sølyst, the island just N of the town E of Vågen, now connected to the mainland by a bridge. The marina, which has a good slip, is about 20 minutes' walk from town, or there are buses from the bridge. YC Tel: 51 86 33 36. All possible facilities in town, and tourist boat trips up the Lysefjord. Do not miss the beautiful thirteenth-century Gothic cathedral, and the museum and (separate) maritime museum are both worth a visit. In spite of its size, Stavanger has considerable charm with many old buildings.

Leirangspollen
Chart 16   58° 56′ N, 6° 02′ E
This sheltered lagoon just N of the peninsula of Leirangshamaren was once an excellent yacht anchorage and a good base from which to make a day trip into the Lysefjord. However, there has sadly been considerable development by an experimental station, and with a fish farm and a submarine cable in the cove it is now probably only usable if permission can be obtained to use one of the station's numerous quays and jetties. An alternative, though less well sheltered from the W, is **Indra Skeidvika**, 5 cables to the SE. Bottom shell and sand. Fish farm.

Bergavik
Chart 205   58° 54′ N, 6° 05′ E
A possible alternative to Leirangspollen/Skeidvik as a base from which to explore the Lysefjord is the Lysefjord Marina at Bergavik. The pier has 2.3–3.3 m along its N side and 2.8–2.0 on the S side for lengths of 17 m and 13 m respectively. However, the other wooden jetties have depths varying between 1.5–0.5 m, so for yachts of seagoing size there are only two berths or three at the most; if full, though, one can always continue to Vika (below). The marina has diesel, water and a shop.

The Lysefjord
Chart 205
58° 54′ to 59° 03′ N; 6° 05′ to 6° 40′ E
Which? magazine would undoubtedly make this its 'best buy' among the fjords of S Norway, on a basis of value for

distance run. All the most spectacular features of the inner waters of the great fjords can be enjoyed in its length of only just over 20 miles, and in particular the numerous waterfalls are exceptionally beautiful and grand, while the extraordinary Prekestolen (Pulpit Rock) about 6 miles into the fjord on the N shore is a nationally famous beauty spot. There is no anchorage, but in good weather it is possible to put some of the crew ashore to make the steep but fairly easy climb to the summit, from which remarkable views can be enjoyed. The only safe anchorage in the fjord is at Vika, 3 miles in from the entrance, but in reasonable weather it is also possible to come alongside the quay at Lysebotn, at the head of the fjord (see below). As with all the fjords, it is a wild place in rough weather: areas of flat calm give way to violent blasts from unpredictable directions as the wind funnels down from the mountains, so really reliable power is essential, and boomed sails should be used with caution.

After entering, the islands of Store and Lille Bergholm are best left to star-

Waterfalls cascade down the steep sides of Lysefjorden.

board, after which Vika will soon be identified as the first deep bay on the starboard hand. The anchorage is sheltered by the surrounding land, but can be gusty in some conditions. The next 5 miles or so as far as Mulen offer much of the best scenery in the fjord, and once the point is rounded there is a grand view right down the remaining 11 miles of its length. If time is short, it is well worth going this far and then turning back, but the final 3 or 4 miles will repay making the extra effort. The cliff walls rise to almost 914 m, while the fjord itself narrows to little more than half of that. Thin cataracts pour down on both sides of the gorge, often in deep gullies so that they can be seen for only a few seconds. And then without warning the walls open out, and the fjord ends in a straight shingle beach with the village beyond. It is a sail that my family and I (MB) will certainly never forget.

Vika
Chart 205   58° 57′ N, 6° 08′ E

This deep bay on the S shore of the Lysefjord, some 3 miles from the entrance, provides the only safe berth in the whole length of the fjord. The anchorage is deep, about 13 m, and the holding in fine sand and mud with some weed can prove difficult to get a grip on, but is reasonably good once the anchor is well dug in. This is one of the places where a CQR holds better than a fisherman. There is a wooden quay, but the depth alongside shallows to 0.9 m, and the deep part is used by a small steamer, so it is best avoided. No supplies.

Lysebotn
Chart 205   59° 03′ N, 6° 39′ E

Lying at the head of the Lysefjord, this berth is exposed to an uncomfortable amount of swell in strong winds from a westerly quarter. There are two quays. The N one is used by a steamer, but the S one, which is wooden and rather rough, is available for visiting yachts. There is a good shop behind the house facing the N quay, and also a PO. In calm weather it is possible to berth overnight and walk up to the snow line in some seasons. Take local advice before leaving the boat unmanned: the last ferry is about 1800 hours.

16 Stavanger to the Naze (Lindesnes)

Counties: Rogaland and Vest-Agder

PASSAGE

Charts 16, 14, 13, 12, 11

The skjærgård disappears a few miles S of Tananger, which lies W of Stavanger on the outer coast, after which there are no alternative routes, and many fewer harbours. In heavy weather from the W the coast is completely exposed, and the passage should only be attempted under such conditions in a well-found vessel with a strong crew.

From Stavanger, proceed NW up the Byfjord, keeping about ½ mile off the SW shore and leaving two red buoys to port. With Tungenes (which has a conspicuous lighthouse) abeam, continue so as to leave Bragen Light, which lies about ½ mile offshore to the NW, close to port, and then steer for the N of Alstein until the black buoy marking the W end of the Tungeflu shoal has been passed. From this position a course just E of S will lead past the red Bjørnaflu and Dalshaugflu buoys, both of which should be left to starboard, and Lysbøye Light, which should be left close to port. From here, the entrance to Tananger is open.

Continuing S, Laksholm with its offlying light and Flatholm are left to the S, after which course is altered to pass about ½ mile W of Ausa Light. This course should be held until Sørskot is on the starboard beam, after which course should be set for the Jærens Rev light buoy. Once the shoals off Jærens Rev have been rounded, the passage of the coast becomes relatively straightforward. Raunastein, about 1½ miles beyond Kvassheim Light, should be given a berth of a mile to avoid the offlying shoals, and in heavy weather from between S and W the Siren Grund shoal should be avoided. This shoal, lying in about 58° 15′ N, 6° 20′ E, has rocks carrying as little as 10 m up to 2 miles offshore, and while these are too deep to be a direct danger to yachts, the sudden shoaling can produce dangerous seas in these conditions.

After this point, the coast can be followed reasonably closely to Lista Light. The tall lighthouse standing on low ground is very conspicuous (see drawing on the chart) and can be picked out from many miles away in good visibility. About 3 miles beyond Lista, at Døsen, the land falls away into rocks and islands until the great headland of Lindesnes is reached. Pilotage on this leg can be tricky, and a good offing should be maintained if the visibility is suspect.

Norwegian yachtsmen tend to speak of the Naze, as the English called Lindesnes for hundreds of years, with a good deal of awe, and indeed the seas there can be impressive in strong westerly weather, when it is worth passing the point at least 2 miles off, to avoid

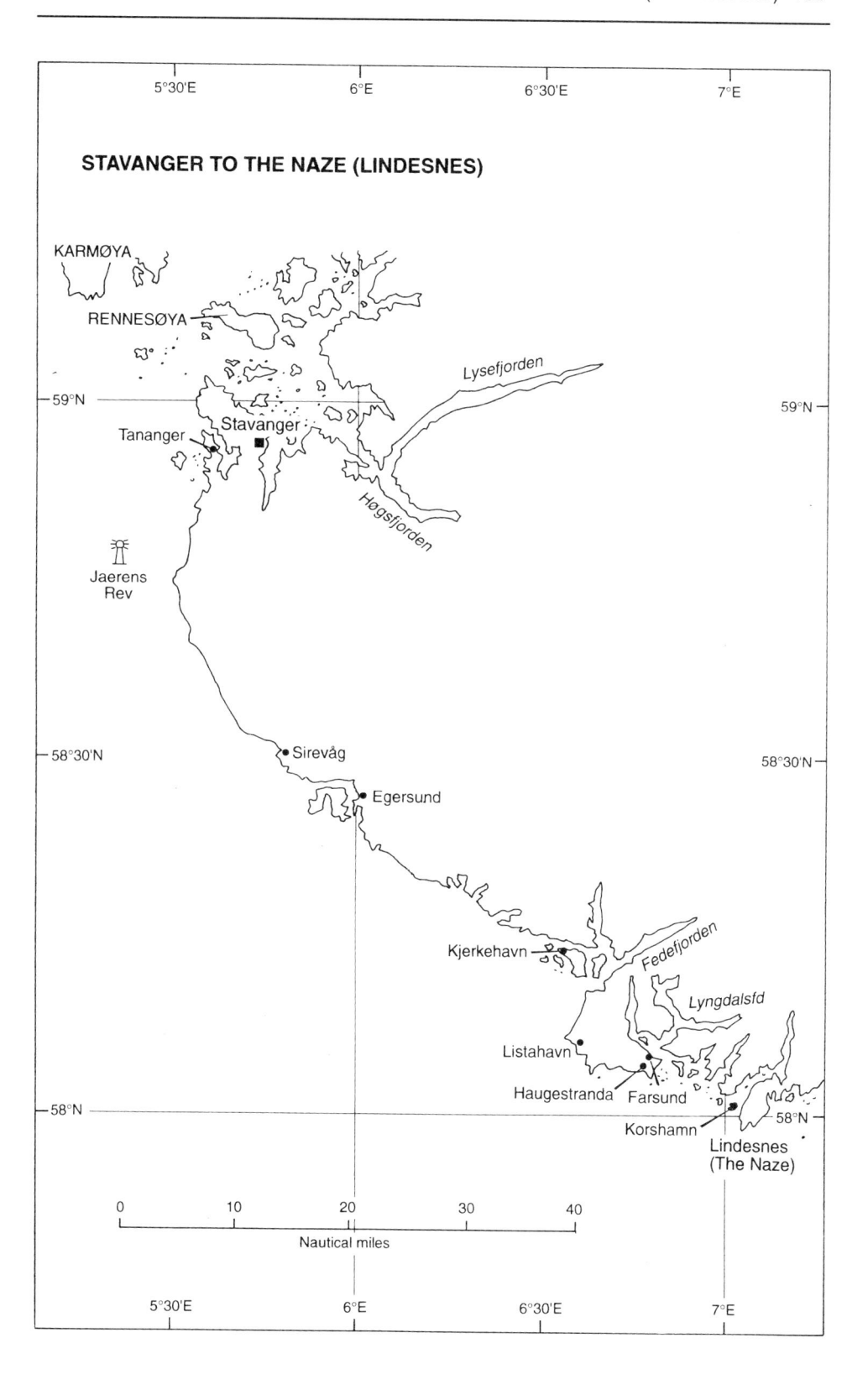

STAVANGER TO THE NAZE (LINDESNES)

passing over the Neskletten, a shelf with about 25–30 m over it where the sudden shoaling can produce particularly high seas. However, the seas are honest compared with those off many of the headlands on the S coast of England, and while they may be high, the sailing conditions are usually quite manageable in normal summer conditions. In strong NW winds, the worst seas are encountered off Lista rather than Lindesnes.

TIDES AND CURRENTS

There is a slight but appreciable tidal stream in the Byfjord between Tungenes and Stavanger, flowing inland on a rising tide (which begins about 5 hours after HW Bergen), and out on the ebb (Bergen – 1 hour). For the rest of the region, the general flow is W and N along the coast, at rates that can reach as much as 2 knots. Rates and directions are much affected by wind, and strong currents running in towards the shore have been experienced with onshore winds. There is no significant tidal stream S of Jærens Rev.

HARBOURS AND ANCHORAGES

Tananger
Charts 16, 14   58° 56′ N, 5° 35′ E
This excellent and attractive little harbour lies at the extreme S end of the skjærgård, and it is therefore a useful place to wait for suitable conditions for a passage round the Naze to the quieter waters of the SE coast. The entrance is straightforward: leave Melingsholm, which is connected to the mainland by a breakwater, close to port, and then round up sharply into the well marked entrance channel. There are twenty or more guest berths in the yacht harbour in the NE part of the harbour; it is also possible to berth bows on to the mole connecting Melingsholmen to the mainland, stern to buoy, W of the pilot boat berth, and it may be possible to find a pontoon berth on the long jetty in the NW bay. The harbour is perfectly sheltered and has excellent shops, services and communications, including buses direct to Stavanger Airport. Seven ton slip. Showers and toilets at Hummeren Hotel at W end of the N shore. First three days free. Interesting small fishing museum; universally preferred to Stavanger.

Note: Between Tananger and Sirevåg there are now several mole harbours along the coast. These could be of use in an emergency, but this type of harbour can be difficult to enter in heavy weather.

Sirevåg
Chart 14   58° 30′ N, 5° 48′ E
About 30 miles from Tananger, this is the first practicable stopping place on the way S. White leading marks, lit at night, lead into the narrow entrance. Anchor as far in as depth allows, or go alongside and enquire whether there is a vacant fisherman's mooring buoy. Shops, PO and railway station. Some swell in bad weather.

Egersund
Chart 13   58° 27′ N, 6° 00′ E
One of the best harbours on the open part of the SW coast, and an excellent choice for a first landfall. There are two entrances, one facing W and the other S, so one of them is sheltered in any weather. Approaching from seaward, the radio beacon on Skarvøy is an added convenience; although the nominal range is only 10 miles, I understand it has been picked up from as far away as 50 miles. It transmits on 301.1 kHz at 0, 6, etc with a call sign of GE (— — · ·).
Entering from the W, identify Eigerøy

Entering Egersund by the S entrance.

lighthouse (a conspicuous red and white tower) and make for a position about 2 cables from the NW point of the island of Midbrødø, on which the light stands. From here make for the varde on Gulholm to the NE and leave it close to port, after which the channel is well marked. An alternative approach to the N of Lureholm and Sundsgabholm can be made in good visibility, but the post on the Dyrøflu rock (0.7 m) is not easy to pick up, being rather thin and low. At night, the green sector of Grundsundsholm Light leads straight in along the main channel.

From the S keep well in towards the shore, even passing inside Svaaholm if convenient. The only hazard on this side is the Isakboen, least depth 3.5 m, but clearly marked by a black buoy. At night the white sectors of Skarvø Light provide safe approaches. There is a conspicuous fish factory on the E side of this channel about a mile S of the town: it can be smelly at times.

The current usually runs E and S in the sound, sometimes attaining as much as 2 knots.

Whichever entrance has been used (coming from the W there is a 23.75 m bridge to pass under), the harbour lies in a branch running E from the main sound, 2 miles N of the S entrance. Moor on the starboard side at the NE end of the harbour, on the pontoons of the Gjestehaven, or elsewhere as space permits. Fuel available on the opposite bank. A considerable town (9000 inhabitants in 1992) with all shops and facilities. Customs at the harbour office on the S bank near the entrance (Strandgaten quay 24). Note that there is no tidal range, but considerable changes in water level occur as a result of meteorological changes. Harbour dues somewhat above average.

Kjerkehavn
Chart 12   58° 14′ N, 6° 32′ E
On the W side of the island of Hidra, this harbour has several entrances, one of which is always sheltered. Note that I have used the spelling in *Den Norske Los*: most authorities spell it Kirkehamn. There is swell in strong westerlies. One can berth alongside a quay on the S side of the eastern inlet, or anchor in Kongshavn, the bay to the N just before the main harbour, 20–25 m, mud. Shop and fuel. Charming walks ashore. The harbour is a centre for mackerel fishing in summer, and is often busy.

Listahavn
Charts 11, 12   58° 05.5′ N, 6° 36′ E
This is an artificial harbour about 1 mile SE of Lista Light, formed by connecting the island of Brekneholm to the mainland by breakwaters, with an entrance left in the S one. The entrance is straightforward, and there are leading lights. A buoyed channel leads to the inner harbour, after leaving the E side of Brekneholm close to port, and one can lie alongside a suitable vessel if space permits. Alternatively, one may anchor in the outer harbour in 4–6 m; mooring rings are available. All facilities, including a boatyard capable of repairing wooden hulls. Depths alongside the quay in the inner harbour range from 3 m at the W end to only 1.5 m at the E end. A useful but not very attractive stopping place: in heavy weather from the SW, the outer harbour can become untenable for yachts owing to severe swell. Flights to Oslo and Stavanger from the nearby airfield.

Haugestranda
Chart 11   58° 04′ N, 6° 46′ E
A small artificial harbour, halfway between Lista Light and the Naze, and useful as it requires less of a detour than Farsund. Approach by identifying the peak of Skibhaugen, and steering on it when it bears NE if coming from the W, or nothing W of N if from the E. On closing with the land, the islet of Svartskjær will be identified, when course is altered to pass close to the S of it, after which steer NE leaving Lille Svartskjær close to port and continue to the harbour entrance. Coming from the W the Skaagskjærflu (2 m) must be avoided by holding course on Skibhaugen until the bearing on Svartskjær has increased to at least 045° Mag. It is possible to lie alongside the S mole, minimum depth 2 m. Or lie to anchor and a mooring ring, of which there are three on the S mole and one on the N shore. No facilities.

Farsund
Chart 11   58° 006′ N, 6° 48′ E
This is a sheltered and attractive harbour, well worth a visit if time can be found for the modest detour involved. The approach is simple, making close up to the now disused Søndre Kattland Light (conspic white stone building at 58° 03.5′ N, 6° 50.5′ E), then proceeding

NE to leave the buoy marking the E end of the Bukkene shoal to port. From here steer on the light on Langøy until a cable or so offshore, and then NW to pass between Store Håøy and Lille Håøy and so into the harbour. All hazards are well marked. Berth at the marina in the bay to the SW off the main harbour (Lundevågen); fuel, water and shop. Bus to Lista airfield for flights to Oslo and Stavanger. A considerable town: pop 9300 in 1992.

Korshamn
Chart 11   58° 01′ N, 7° 00′ E
A pleasant, totally sheltered harbour, and a useful place in bad weather to wait for a lull to round the Naze, which lies only 3 miles to the SE. From the W, approach along the N shore of Kjøpsøy, keeping Revøysund open ahead. This leads N of Sagebomflua (perch): once past this danger, curve SSE to pass E of Kreklingholm and so into the harbour. From the E, keep no more than 2 cables off the land N of Lindesnes until it turns E of N after 1 mile. From here steer between the lights on Lypskjær and Kleveholm, N between the red and green buoys at Musa, then close under Ulvasodden (the SW point of Revøy) and into the harbour. Berth alongside as space permits, and ask permission to remain. Fuel, water and stores. There are also several attractive anchorages within a few hundred yards of the main harbour.

17 The Naze (Lindesnes) to Larvik

Counties: Vest-Agder, Aust-Agder, Telemark

PASSAGE

Charts 10, 9, 8, 7, 6, 5

Once past the Naze there is a completely different feel to the geography, and usually to the weather as well. The skjærgård still exists, but the islands tend to be smaller and more scattered, and one tends to be cruising along the mainland coast inside a fringe of offshore islands, rather than having the choice of inshore sounds between large islands typical of the W coast. The land itself is rounder and gentler, and the weather is usually much better. Strong winds are most likely to blow from the shore and there is far less swell at sea, so the gaps in the island chain take on less importance.

These factors also make the passage more straightforward, as there are relatively few alternatives of any importance. From the Naze one can pass S of Udvaare, or else inside the Vaare group, passing N of Langeboerne and then leaving the Kvideflu buoy to port. Entering the skjærgård N of the island of Hille, one passes Mandal, and continues N of Skjernøya (bridge 19 m), but S of Skogsøya, which has low HT cables on its N side, and returns to relatively open water at Tånes. A course N of the vardes on Eids-Stangholm and Bøddelen leads into the Songvaarfjord. From here, leave Maageskjaer varde to port and proceed up the well marked Vestregabet between Ytre Flekkerøya on one side and the mainland on the other into Kristiansandsfjord.

Continuing E from Kristiansand, the shortest and most interesting passage leads close S of the island of Herøya, and then N of Stokken through the Randesund. This is narrow but well marked, and there is an inset on chart 9 giving an invaluable enlargement of the complex narrows N of Stokken. Passing close S of Stangodden (varde), cross the mouth of the Kvåsefjord to the Kårehausene buoy (light and whistle), and turn NE up the well marked channel that leads inside Nipe and Ramsøya to Natvigtangen.

From here the big-ship route lies in the open sea outside Tronderøya and the offshore skerries, close SE of Nødingen (varde), and so to Reierskjær Light, left close to starboard, and on NNE outside Justøya to Saltholm Light, just E of Skogerøya. However, to use this route would be to miss what local yachtsmen rightly regard as one of the most beautiful and interesting channels in all Norway – the Blindleia. This looks tricky on the chart, but is so well marked with vardes that in practice one is never in any doubt about the route, and indeed once (MB and family) succeeded in traversing the whole length of it under spinnaker, although this is only to be recommended in light airs from about SSW.

The Blindleia begins at Natvigtangen, and has a least depth of just over 3 m and a least height of 20 m, the clearance of the bridge at the N end between the mainland and Justøya. Steer N by W from Natvigtangen, and pass between Helleøya and Grimsøya (the latter is unnamed on the chart, but is the island with the varde immediately to the W of Helleøya). Pass S and W of Steinsøya, through the narrows between Indre Tronderøya and the mainland, whence a line of vardes leads to the channel W of Furøya. From here the channel is quite easy, running W of Ågerøya, Hellersøya and Justøya and emerging under the bridge into the Skallefjord. All vardes and perches have direction pointers and the whole passage is much easier than it looks, and is totally sheltered except perhaps in strong SE winds when a little swell can penetrate between Tronderøya and Kalvøya.

The Skallefjord leads to Lillesand, from where a simple passage leads via the Humlesund, and Havsteinen and Bergkirken vardes, to the channel inshore of Homborøya and so out past Indre Mågholm (varde) to the open sea. From here, unless visiting Grimstad pass well S of Håboskjær varde, and then about 3 cables W of Hesnesbregen Light. Pass close E of Hesnesøya leaving Tøndeholm varde to starboard, and so along the coast past Fevig, inshore of Torsken, Spaer and Ytre Torungen, with its conspicuous lighthouse and N into the Galtesund to Arendal. From here the Tromøsund leads out past Skinfeldtangen to another length of open sea. Keep close in past Mågeholm and Rendeskjær Light (both left to port), after which steer for the light on Tverdalsøen. From here a pleasant diversion may be made to Tvedestrand and back. Then proceed up the Havefjord between Borøen and Sandøen, pass close W and N of the varde on Store Bastholm, and so through the Lyngørfjord keeping inshore of the islets, and out between Sildeodden on the mainland and Store Sildeskjær varde.

The next leg of the course lies in the open sea, past Risør and a long stretch of open coast to the rather tricky entrance to Kragerø. It is not really as bad as it looks, however, as there are numerous buoys and perches, and once the Stangskjær and Fjordboen vardes have been identified it is simple, as one steers between them from just E of S, taking care to leave the Storbrottet beacon ($^{1}/_{2}$ mile to the S) to port. Once past these marks the channel to Kragerø is clear, after which proceed N of Berøya and Gumøya via the Langårsund (beware strong W current), and so between Store and Lille Fluer into the Eksefjord. Continue close S of Vittenskjul Light and Rødskjær (varde), and then strike across E for Tvistein Light. From here steer nothing N of E until the light and whistle buoy that marks the SE end of the Rakkeboene has been identified, when course may be altered to N to leave it to port, and proceed up Larviksfjord. The Rakkeboene is a dangerous shoal, as the current usually sets W on to it, so always guard against being carried W of the buoy until into the entrance of the fjord. This is a dangerous place, especially in poor visibility, and should be treated with respect. In places the current can reach 2 knots.

TIDES AND CURRENTS

The tide has no significant effect on the currents in this section, or indeed anywhere farther into the Baltic. The main current along the coast runs SW and W at between 1 and 2 knots, reaching this rate 2 or 3 miles offshore, and being somewhat less inshore. It is of course subject to wind effects, which can reduce or even reverse the flow temporarily. The inshore passages have unpredictable directions of current, that in the Blindleia being generally NE, in the opposite direction to the general flow. These currents are part of a circulation system that includes NE currents along the NW Jutland coast, and offshore navigators should study the pilot books carefully on this point.

HARBOURS AND ANCHORAGES

Åvik
Chart 10 58° 02′ N, 7° 13′ E
A landlocked harbour sheltered in all conditions, convenient for waiting to round the Naze to the W or for recovering from a tough run in the opposite direction. The entrance is clear and well lit, and the harbour lies just to the E of the mole connecting the most westerly islet N of the town on Svinør with the mainland to the N. Moor alongside the wharf, which has mooring rings, least depth 4 m. Fuel, small shop and PO.

Mandal
Chart 10 58° 01.5′ N, 7° 27′ E
A landlocked river harbour, protected and available in all conditions. An ideal choice as a first landfall from the S or W. There is a bar with about 3 m in the entrance, but this presents no problem as the water is sheltered from any direction. Keep to starboard until the channel turns NW, then get as far W as the outgoing traffic will permit, as the E side is shoal. Once in, the pontoons of the Sjøsanden Marina will be seen ahead and to port, on the W side of the river. Moor here on the first pontoon, bows to and stern to anchor, or elsewhere as space allows. Customs (in Store Elvegaten), showers at the marina, good shops, fuel, etc. Mandal is Norway's most southerly town, lying only 30 miles N of Inverness, and in 1992 it had a population of 12 400. The white sandy beach stretching for ½ mile W of the entrance is both conspicuous and famous: the town itself has many old wooden houses and a good museum.

Orpholmsund
Chart 10 58° 00.5′ N, 7° 35′ E
A sheltered anchorage between Skogsøy and Orpholm to the E. The approach from the S is easy; that from the NE requires a little more care. Anchor 100 m S of the skerry in the channel in 8–10 m. The holding is a little soft, mud and weed, and a fisherman holds best. A line can always be taken ashore to windward, which is a worthwhile precaution in heavy weather. The anchorage is protected by high ground on all sides, and is exceptionally quiet and beautiful. No facilities.

Ny Hellesund
Charts 9, 10 58° 03′ N, 7° 51′ E
A sheltered sound between Monsøya to the N, and Kappeløya and Helløya to the S. Anchor in about 18 m, sandy bottom, with a line to the land, as otherwise one is in the way of traffic through the sound; or go alongside a quay on the S side with permission, minimum depth 2 m alongside. No supplies.

Kristiansand
Chart 9 58° 08.5′ N, 8° 00′ E
This rather strange city, laid out geometrically on a reclaimed marsh, is one of Norway's principal ports. There are two harbours, one reached by passing W of the island of Odderøya, and the other to the E. Although it is not immediately

THE NAZE (LINDESNES) TO LARVIK 147

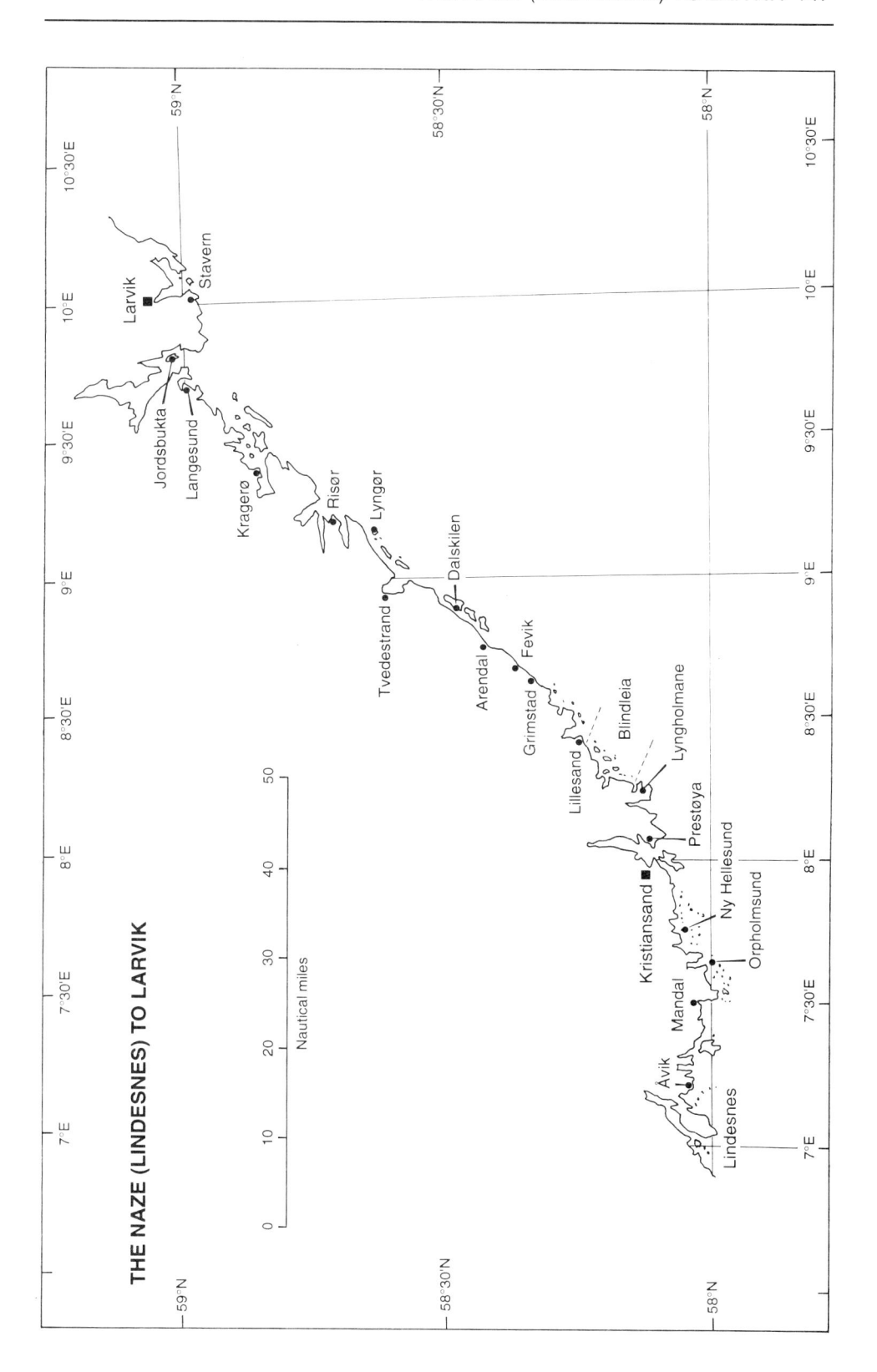

obvious from the chart, the two harbours are cut off from each other by a low bridge connecting Odderøya with the city, and so it is a journey of almost 2 miles by water from one to the other.

The best visitors' berths are in the E harbour roughly in the middle of the marina area, which takes up virtually the whole of the SE edge of the main city, just to the left (SW) of a flattish tower with a red conical roof. Depths are 1.8–2.4 m on the outside of the mole, but less inside. If full, try Nodeviga Marina: it lies at the SW end of the SE shore, and has four guest berths with 2.5 m. It also has diesel: the main marina (Kristiansholm Båthavn) has electricity, showers, toilets and water. Chandlery and repairs from J Lochner, 16 Vestre Strandgåt: a useful street that also contains the Customs at no. 23, bus station at no. 33 and railway station at no. 49. Founded in 1641 by Kristian IV of Denmark, the town had 66 000 inhabitants in 1992. The strict grid pattern of its design is unusual in Europe, and makes it imposing rather than friendly in feel, but excellent shops, hotels and restaurants, good communications and several parks and zoos give the visitor plenty to do and see.

Prestøya
Chart 9   58° 08′ N, 8° 03′ E

This sheltered anchorage is safe in all conditions, although the entrance may be slightly exposed in southerly gales. The anchorage lies between Prestøya and Sjursøya to the W. The two islands almost touch to the N of the anchorage, and the only entrance is to the S. Keep to starboard of the centre of the channel going in, to avoid an uncharted rock just below the surface on the W side of the entrance. Anchor in the middle: moderate holding in thick weed with soft mud underneath. A fisherman is almost essential as there is hardly room to dig in a CQR, but in strong winds a line to a rock or tree on the weather shore and a stern anchor will ensure security. No facilities, but the anchorage is only a couple of miles from Kristiansand and is a most convenient place from which to make daylight visits to the city. A most attractive and idyllic anchorage. There is also good anchorage to the E of the peninsula of Stokken, 2 miles to the SE, inside the islets that lie off its E side. This is an excellent jumping-off point from which to begin a passage NE up the Blindleia.

Lyngholmane
Chart 9   58° 08.5′ N, 8° 16′ E

A useful anchorage just at the S end of the Blindleia. Approach from the S or the W, and anchor in 10–12 m, soft mud, about midway between the SW points of the two largest islands in the group. Complete shelter. When approaching from or leaving to the S, keep well in to Jenholm as there are shoals off the S side of the SE island of the group. No facilities.

Lillesand
Chart 8   58° 15′ N, 8° 23′ E

This is a completely sheltered harbour available in all weathers. It is the farthest SW of the main harbours in the favourite SE coast cruising area, which extends from the Blindleia to Oslo. Approach from the S between Reierskjær Light and the varde on Langboerne shoal (awash), and steer on Saltholm Light, which is left close to port, after which the entrance between Skogerøya and Langøya is open and clear. The approach from the N is described (in reverse direction) in the general Passage notes at the beginning of this section.

There are three pontoons projecting from the shore providing berths for visitors: beware a 0.9 m shoal 10 m off the front of the middle one at its N end. It is also possible to anchor in the bay at 11–15 m.

With a population of 4500 (1992), Lillesand is a pretty town, but it is very much a tourist resort with beautifully restored old buildings and correspondingly high prices. Fuel from the Esso quay on the E side of the harbour. Good shopping, laundromat, restaurants, etc. Buses to Kristiansand airport.

Grimstad
Chart 8   58° 20′ N, 8° 36′ E

A largish town offering a completely sheltered harbour, but some tricky pilotage in the approaches if major detours are to be avoided. From the S, leave Håbøskjaer and Stangholm lighthouse 1 cable to starboard. From here, a course just W of N leads to Rivingen lighthouse, which is left close to port, after which the fjord to the N is clear apart from two rocks (1.5 m and 2 m) that are clearly marked by perches. From the N, the shortest route is by the Smørsund, which leads from close S of Svartskjær varde WNW between Rossekniben and Indre Maløya. The channel is clearly marked by buoys and perches, but it is narrow and tortuous and carries only 2.5 m of water, so it should not be attempted in swell or onshore winds. In that case, the best entrance is between Ostre and Vestre Svertingen, taking care to leave the buoy NE of the latter to port. Thence steer midway between Teistholm and Ytre Leiholm, then close N of the buoy to the NNW and S of the varde on the islet beyond, whereafter one is in clear water in the main fjord. This passage can be used in all but strong winds from the SE quarter, when the only safe approach is right round to the S of Håkallen.

Berth in the marina W of Torskeholm (check depths) or W of or on the wooden jetty in the northern part of the harbour. Another possibility is inside the breakwaters N of Torskeholm at the N end of the land side. Good shopping, hotels, etc, and an interesting Ibsen museum. The population of 15 000 rises to nearly double that during the summer. Buses to Arendal and Kristiansand. A mile S of the harbour, a beautiful anchorage will be found between Indre and Ytre Maløya. Entering from the W, the channel carries 7 m, and from the N 2 m. Anchor in 12 m, mud. Look out for a reef extending SW into the bay from the wooded part of Ytre Maløya. Toilets and gash bins ashore: may be crowded in summer, especially at weekends.

Fevik
Chart 8   58° 22′ N, 8° 41′ E

A more useful harbour than the apparently more obvious choice of Grimstad, because the latter requires a considerable detour if there is any swell, when the short cut to the N of Indre Maløya becomes inadvisable.

Approach from the S is straightforward, and once Torsken has been left to starboard a course can be steered on the lighthouse which clears all dangers until the town and harbour open up, when course is altered to enter. From Arendal and the NE, the best route is N of Sperrholm (lighthouse) and then between Fevikboen and Vrageboen, both well marked, after which course can be altered to enter the bay. In the NE corner, Bagatell Camping has a marina with 20 visitors' berths: it is also possible to anchor off. Fuel, water, shop, showers, etc. More shops and bank in the main town: up to the road, turn right, left up the steps, then right along the main road. Boatbuilder in the bay. Good shelter, but some swell in strong southeasterlies.

Arendal
Chart 7   58° 27.5' N, 8° 46.5' E
A protected inland harbour in a largish town (pop 12 150 in 1992). The approaches are straightforward via the Galtesund from the S or the Tromøysund from the NE: neither presents any problem. Enter the more easterly of the two basins (Pollen) and berth as space allows anywhere along the E side of the basin. The W basin is not recommended. The town has good shops and facilities: do not miss the Rådhus, one of Norway's largest wooden buildings, dating from 1811. Walk W along the N end of Pollen and continue until a wide main road is reached, when it will be seen across the road and to the left. Directly S of Pollen on the N point of the island of Hisøya is Kolbjørnsvik, with a small marina in the NE corner where fuel can be obtained. This, and the quay at the S end of the bay, is also a better berth in strong southerlies. Ferry to Arendal centre.

Dalskilen
Chart 7   58° 31' N, 8° 56' E
Time for another quiet anchorage after all these noisy towns! This is a most pleasant one on the SW end of Flostaøya, and protected in all weathers. Keep well to the port side of the narrow entrance, as the starboard half is shoal. Anchor in the middle, 6 m, soft mud. This is one of the few places where a CQR will probably serve best in strong winds. Provisions from village ½ mile to the NE: climb up to the road and turn right. A pretty place. Toilets and gash bins ashore. Numerous mooring bolts.

Tvedestrand
Chart 7   58° 37' N, 8° 57' E
This small inland port lies at the head of a short fjord; the approach is through typical Sørland scenery and is a most beautiful example of the softer beauty of this part of Norway. The approach requires care, but the hazards are well marked. There is a pontoon near the head of the fjord with visitors' berths, water, showers, etc. Diesel at Christensen's Marina on the E side S of the T-shaped restaurant jetty. Good shops, bank, etc up the steep hill in the high part of the town, which also has a church overlooking a considerable lake. Pleasant walks in the surrounding country.

Lyngør
Chart 7   58° 38' N, 9° 09' E
Lying between four islands, this anchorage is protected in all weathers, and gives access to one of the best preserved old towns in Norway. There may be a possibility of a berth on the sailmaker's T-shaped pontoon on the NW curve of Lyngør itself, or on the restaurant pontoon on the islet to the N. Sailmaker (see above), restaurant (ditto), shop, fuel and water. A most attractive place.

Risør
Chart 6   58° 43' N, 9° 15' E
A town of some 7000 inhabitants in 1992, Risør is known as the white town because most of its houses are painted white. The S-most jetty projecting NE from the shore is intended for visitors (bows on, stern to anchor), otherwise moor as space allows and with local advice. The harbour can be crowded in summer, especially in August, when a rally for veteran wooden boats is held. Fuel is available just inside the inner harbour, just SW of the root of the N-most of the long jetties: showers and laundrette here too. Good shops, bank

and fish stall. A handsome and interesting town.

Kragerø
Chart 6   58° 52' N, 9° 25' E
A completely sheltered harbour and a town of about 5000 inhabitants. The approach from the SW is covered in the Passage notes for this section: from the NE the approach is by the narrow and beautiful Langårsund and N of Berøya. The harbour is divided by a low bridge to Øya, the not very imaginatively named island E of the town. In the E part of the harbour N of the bridge there is a pontoon for visitors, choppy in NE winds. In the W part, reached between Øya and Gunnarsholmen to its SW, there are several visitors' quays and pontoons with perfect shelter: sound carefully and take advice for some have time restrictions on length of stay. Fuel, water and repairs available. Good shopping and wonderful views from the top of the hill. Some 4 miles to the S, Portør offers sheltered anchorage in pretty surroundings: JA also recommends Jomfruland, 6 miles the E, for attractive

Approaching the N end of Langårsund.

walks with unusual birds and plants. Several anchorages along its NW side, or among the islands to the NW.

Langesund
Chart 5   59° 00′ N, 9° 45′ E

This town of about 3300 inhabitants offers good shelter in all but southerly winds, when swell penetrates the sound. The approach and entrance is simple, steering N on the conspicuous Langøytangen lighthouse (sketch on chart 5), and then passing to the W of it and continuing up the sound, keeping over to the E side until abreast of the steamer pier. There is a visitors' berth at the end of Kongshavn, the inlet running to the S, and farther N is a marina with 40 guest berths, fuel and water. Sound carefully, as not all the berths are deep. Good shops, bank, hotels, etc. Coastal museum near the steamer pier. This is a good base from which to explore the islands and fjords to the E and N, through which boats with an air draft under 12.75 m can even reach Dalen, some 60 miles inland, via a canal from Skien (pronounced 'Shane') that passes through very beautiful country (photo p. 151).

Jordsbukta
Chart 5   59° 01′ N, 9° 49′ E

This perfectly sheltered cove on the W side of Håøya has good holding, sand and mud, in idyllic surroundings. The main anchorage is inside the outer skerry, but it is even possible to work in behind the inner islet with suitable draft. A beautiful wild anchorage with rewarding walks ashore.

Stavern
Charts 2, 5   59° 00′ N, 10° 02′ E

This is the port at the seaward end of the Larvik Fjord, and there seems little reason to go up to Larvik unless there are special circumstances. Approach from the S is straightforward as long as the vessel is kept S of a line E from Tvistein Light until the light and whistle buoy marking the SE corner of the Rakkeboene is identified. From this buoy a course can be held on Stavernsodden Light, but if the stream is setting to the W, course must be laid off to the E to ensure that the course does not veer W of N. When closed, the light is left to starboard, and the entrance is clear. From the E, the easiest way if coming from the Tønsberg Fjord is to keep close in to the Holskjaer Light, close S of Flaten and Melleskjaer, and then inside Svarteskjaer and out through the Båtleia. This route is not without hazards, but so heavily marked as to present no difficulty.

On entering, new guest pontoons will be seen to port, and there may also be berths available in the older marina farther N. In any but strong N winds there is also good anchorage to the N of Stavernsøya, about ½ mile SE of the main harbour entrance. Mooring bolts. It is a smallish town (pop 3900) with some nice old buildings, good shops, chandlery, and an interesting war memorial. Fuel and water in the marina.

Larvik
Charts 2, 5   59° 03′ N, 10° 02′ E

This is a considerable town (pop 12 700 in 1992) and the large commercial port was never a good place for a yacht. However, a marina has now been built about 2 miles SE of the main harbour, approached by passing E of Otterøya. This has ten guest berths with fuel, water and all facilities. However, it is quite a hike from the centre, which is not especially attractive when you get there, and the best excuse for a visit is probably the train service to Oslo, which takes about 3 hours.

18 Larvik to Oslo and the Swedish Border

County: Oslo-fjorden

PASSAGE

Charts 2, 3, 4, 1

Proceeding E and N from Larvik towards Oslo, the main decision is whether to take the open water route by the main Oslo Fjord, or sail inland up Tønsberg Fjord, passing out into the main Oslo Fjord either between Tjøme and Nøtterøya, or farther N, E of Tønsberg itself. There is little to choose for distance, and most people are likely to choose one of the inshore routes as they are of much greater scenic interest.

The offshore route is best started by steering on the island of Svenner from just S of Malmøya, the island at the E of the entrance to Larvik Fjord, until the Seiboen buoy is identified about a mile N of Svenner. Pass 1 cable S of this buoy, after which a course just N of E clears all dangers. Proceed for about 16 miles, passing not less than a mile S of the conspicuous Færder lighthouse to avoid the Treisteinergrund shoal, marked by a buoy, which lies ¾ mile SSW of the light. Once E of the light, it is safe to turn NNE up the fjord.

Using the inshore routes, proceed up the Båtleia to just S of Holskjær Light, as described in the entry for Stavern p. 152. From here, steer NE to pass close N of Lyngholm, and through the well buoyed channel leading close up the E side of Tønsberg Tønde to Trubberodden Light. From here sail ENE, passing just N of the buoyed Exellensenboen (on which one must assume that some unfortunate ambassador was once wrecked), on past the southern Nylandsboen buoy, and then N up the W side of Tjøme in clear water.

The route divides here. To avoid Tønsberg and its bridge turn E into Vrengen, under the conspicuous bridge (33 m clearance). Proceed along the well buoyed channel and up the E sides of S and N Årøy and Bkerkøya, and out through some well marked rocks into the clear waters of the Oslo Fjord. Otherwise continue E of Håøya and on N in shallowing water to the elbow of the fjord, where a narrow buoyed channel leads to Tønsberg. A swing bridge here leads to another buoyed channel, leading out N of Jusøya. Turn N here and follow the buoyed channel round N of Torgersøya and out into Oslo Fjord.

The passage up the fjord to Oslo is hereafter a matter of perfectly easy pilotage, although unobservant yachtsmen have been known to come to grief on the shoal that projects westward from Ferjested (59° 40′ N, 10° 36′ E), before it runs N and joins the S end of Kaholm. This shoal is quite plainly marked on the chart, but it is easy to miss it, and depths of 1–1.5 m are ideal

Quay at Tønsberg.

for catching the unwary! Keep well over to the E side past Drobak and for the next mile or so to avoid problems.

The passage from the E side of the mouth of Oslo Fjord to the Swedish border needs little comment. Apart from visits to harbours, it is simplest to keep fairly close W of the Misingen Islands (watch out for the reef extending about ½ mile S and slightly W of the main island) and Struten. Give the N and S Søstrene a berth of about ½ mile, and Akerøya and its offlying islands rather more. Then pass S of Tresteinene Light, N of the Båskjaerne (the NE-most islands of the Tisler group), and N of the buoys marking the Hatten and Skreia rocks. A mile to the SE the vardes of Tjurholm come into line, and you cross into Swedish waters some 5 miles from Strømstad.

CURRENTS

Currents in Tønsberg and Oslo Fjords are quite unpredictable, as they depend

LARVIK TO OSLO AND THE SWEDISH BORDER

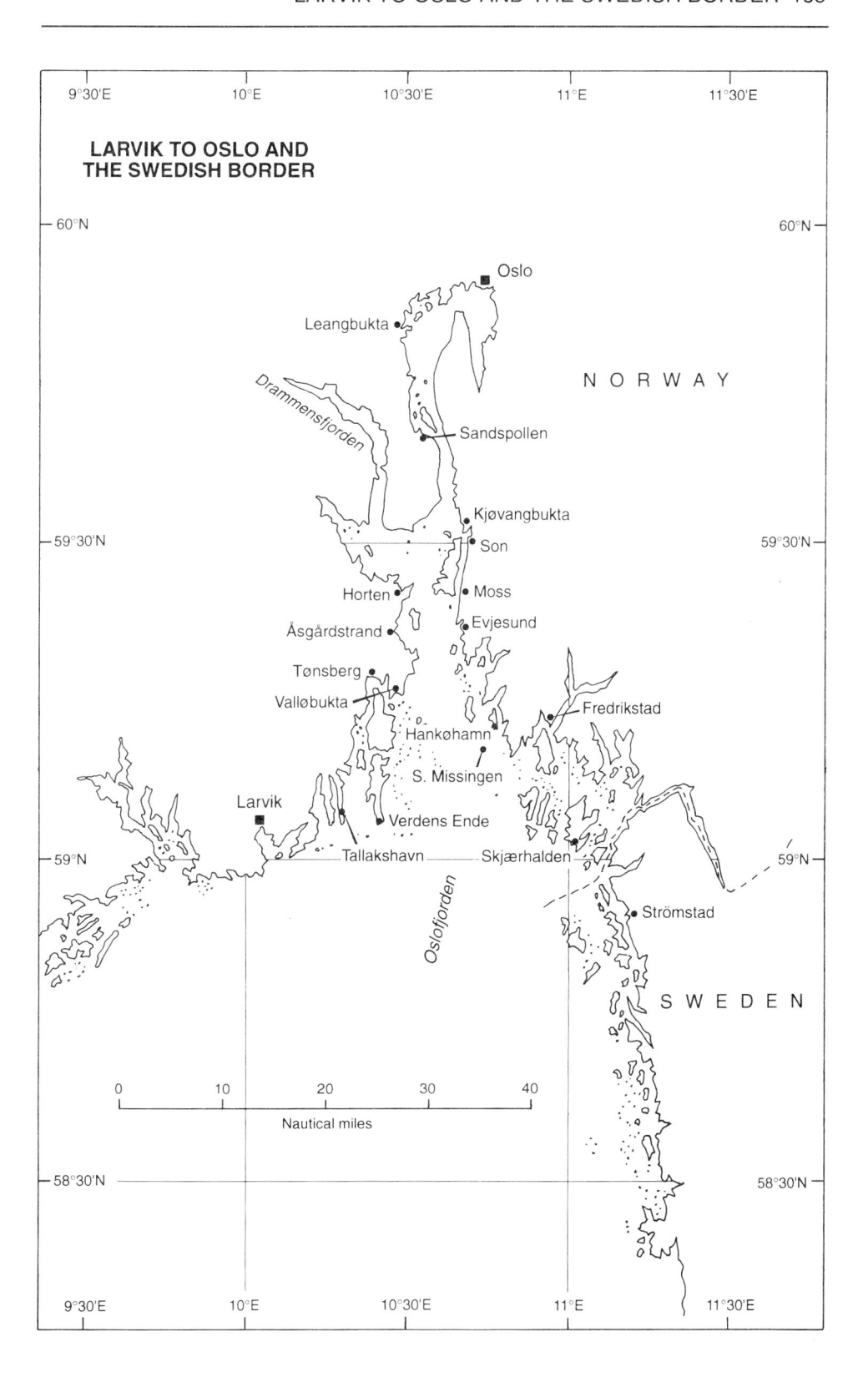

on wind and barometric pressure. They can be quite strong in places, however, and a careful lookout should always be kept to make sure that one is not being carried off course.

HARBOURS AND ANCHORAGES

Tallakshavn
Chart 2   59° 04.5′ N, 10° 19′ E
A roomy, secluded and beautiful anchorage near the entrance of Tønsberg Fjord. Enter via the buoyed channel at the NE end of the bay and anchor W of the protecting skerries, 3–4 m, sandy bottom, mooring rings on the mainland shore. Completely sheltered in all weather except in strong SE wind, when there is some swell. No facilities.

Verdens Ende
Chart 2   59° 03.4′ N, 10° 24.8′ E
On the S tip of Tjøme, this harbour is approached from the N end of Sandholmen, from where two leading marks will be seen to the WNW. The harbour is protected to the S by two moles with a skerry in the middle, and visitors berth along these bows on. Water, toilets and waste bins. Restaurant and shop, showers and washing machine. A pretty place, and useful when going N as one can depart for Tønsberg Fjord or the sea passage equally easily. **Krukehavn**, 1 mile to the NE, has a pilot station where information about the whole area can be sought.

Tønsberg
Chart 3   59° 16′ N, 10° 25′ E
This is an attractive medium-sized town (13 000 inhabitants in 1992) whose good communications with Oslo make it the ideal place to leave a boat for a day or two while visiting Oslo, if the long sail up the fjord and back rules out a visit by water. Approach and entrance are dealt with in the general Passage notes for this section. Approaching from Tønsberg Fjord, the recommended berths are on the port hand before or, better, after the harbour office building, but before the large marina. *Den Norske Los* suggests Strandpromenaden, the first quay to port before the harbour has narrowed, but better shelter will be found farther in if space allows. There may also be a berth free in the marina itself. Fuel and water in the marina, all supplies and facilities in the town. The bridge allowing passage to the E opens four times a day: otherwise there is a NKr 40 fee. Call the bridgemaster on Ch 12. Tønsberg is the oldest town in Norway, and many fine old buildings are preserved near the harbour. Regular train service to Oslo.

Valløbukta
Chart 3   59° 16′ N, 10° 30′ E
A small marina has been built at the N end of this bay, well sheltered except for some swell in S winds. Fuel, water, small shop, 7 ton crane, engine repairs. Industrial surroundings: Esso refinery to the S.

Åsgårdstrand
Chart 3   59° 21′ N, 10° 29′ E
A useful staging point on the W side of the Oslo Fjord, this is a mole harbour with three basins. The southern basin is too shallow for most yachts, and the recommended berth for visitors is in the centre basin, immediately to port on entering, bows on to the mole. The pleasant town has a number of restored old houses, and is a popular holiday resort. Edvard Munch (1863–1944) lived here, and it is the scene of some of his paintings. Shops, PO etc in the town.

Horten
Chart 3   59° 25′ N, 10° 29′ E
Horten is a town of about 15 000 inhabitants (1992) and includes the

Karljohansvern Naval Base. The new guest harbour is towards the S of the harbour, just after the conspicuous Ro-Ro jetty. Larger boats berth alongside the pier that projects into the middle of the basin: 3.3–2.2 m. Toilets, showers, fuel, small shop and open air restaurant. It is also possible to berth in the Fyllinga yacht harbour farther N, on either side of the jetty immediately inside the entrance on the starboard side, or past the pontoons on a quay just to the E of the canal entrance. The town has the shops and services one would expect from its size, but is of no great interest, although the maritime museum is worth a visit. Ferries to Moss, buses to Oslo.

Sandspollen
Chart 4   59° 40′ N, 10° 35′ E
A pretty but often crowded anchorage in a landlocked bay W of Drobak. From the S, the islands of N and S Kaholm must be rounded before turning W and S to reach the anchorage, although there is said to be a channel close in to the Ferjested shore that readers might like to try in really settled weather (but do not risk grounding, as a change in barometric pressure might leave one hard aground for an indefinite time). Anchor in about 5 m W of the entrance. There is a shop among the houses to the N of the anchorage.

Leangbukta
Chart 4   59° 50′ N, 10° 29′ E
This bay in the NW corner of Oslo Fjord offers a quiet anchorage a few hours' sail from Oslo. Anchor in the branch S of the Tangegrund shoal (marked by beacon) with a line to a tree ashore; the N branch is full of private moorings. Bus to Oslo every ½ hour. Supermarket about 1 mile to the NE.

Oslo
Chart 4   59° 54.5′ N, 10° 42′ E
The capital of Norway, and with a population of 468 000 in 1992, Oslo is a beautiful town and one with several good yacht harbours. The traditional place to go was always Dronningen, HQ of the Royal Norwegian YC, but it is as well to call them first on VHF Ch 68 to enquire about the availability of berths. Dronningen is a conspicuous peninsula 3 cables NNW of the very eye-catching pyramidal museum buildings on the E-most point of Bygdøy, the large green peninsula to the W of Oslo. Pass outside the buoy that marks the shoal extending NNE from Dronningen and turn W and S into the yacht harbour. Moor alongside on the clubhouse quay (not the pier leading to Bygdøy) and enquire at the clubhouse, which occupies the upper floor of the building, if the club boatman is not in evidence. Note that the club entrance is at the back of the building and straight up a flight of stairs: the front entrance leads into a public restaurant and opens at different times. Just opposite Dronningen on the Oslo shore is the Kongen visitors' harbour, which has fuel, water and electricity. Visitors' berth in the S part. Finally, for those in a 'Who cares what it costs?' mood, Aker Brygge, Herbern Marina, has 70 visitors' berths with all mod cons – including cable TV! It is in the centre of Oslo at 10° 43.8′ E. In Oslo, do not miss the Vigeland sculpture park in the Frogner Park to the NW of the city, and the *Fram* and *Kon-tiki* museums mentioned above on the E point of Bygdøy. Walk from Dronningen or ferry from Oslo.

Kjøvangbukta
Charts 3, 4   59° 32.5′ N, 10° 40′ E
A useful anchorage on the E side of Oslo Fjord, although somewhat exposed in

strong westerlies. Anchor in the NE corner of the bay, mud, 10 m, mooring rings. Note the submarine cable in the outer part of the bay. Toilets and rubbish bins ashore.

Son
Charts 3, 4   59° 31.5′ N, 10° 42′ E

The large marina at the N end of Son is said to have *a* visitor's berth among its 700 or so private ones, but there is now a guest marina farther S, with showers. Good shopping, banks, etc. Son is the Norwegian Olympic training centre until the end of 1996: they rotate every two years.

Moss
Chart 3   59° 26′ N, 10° 40′ E

As the bascule bridge over the canal that cuts through the isthmus connecting Jeløya with the mainland no longer operates, it is now a fixed bridge with 4.5 m clearance, cutting off Mossesundet from Værlesundet for any normal yacht. However, there are two marinas on the W side of Værlesundet, both with visitors' berths, water and electricity, and as Værlesundet is relatively short, this is the direction from which most yachtsmen will wish to approach the town. It is a large (pop 25 000) industrial and commercial town, and has little to recommend it for the cruising man except a good railway service to Oslo, useful perhaps if a crew member needs to fly home. Good shops, but some way from the berths.

Evjesund
Chart 3   59° 21.5′ N, 10° 40′ E

A landlocked inlet offering good anchorage in complete shelter. Enter the inner harbour midway between the quay and the islet, and anchor in 3–5 m. Mooring rings on shore.

Hankøhamn
Charts 1, 3   59° 12′ N, 10° 47′ E

This harbour lies at the SW end of Hankø. Enter from the S, passing E of N Garnholm (lighthouse and varde), and proceed close round the E shore of the island to the NE, which is clean apart from one off-lyer that is clearly visible. Once past the skerry in mid-channel, with its two off-lyers to the NW and NE, cross sharply E to avoid the rock (1 m) to the N. Anchor in the middle of the bay, 2–4 m, sand. This entry is not as hairy as it sounds because the dangers, though numerous, are almost all awash and visible, but proceed with caution all the same. Stores from Hankø Bad ³/₄ mile to the NNE. There is also a large harbour there; indeed, it is one of the most important Norwegian yachting ports, with marinas both in the bight on the E coast of Hankø and opposite on the mainland. There are visitors' berths in both, a considerable yacht club, and fuel from the marina on the islet connected to the mainland. However, these berths are disturbed by constant ferry traffic between Hankø and the mainland. Good boatyard in the bay on the mainland side ¹/₂ mile farther S. Hankøsund is a nice, jolly place to spend a day, but for a night's sleep the recommendation must come down in favour of the anchorage first mentioned.

Søndre Missingen
Charts 1, 3   59° 10.2′ N, 10° 43′ E

This remote small-island anchorage lies between S Missingen and the small skerries to its S. Enter from the E on the line of two black triangles, points together, on the N of the skerries, and anchor in the bay on the S coast of the main island, 5–6 m, sand and clay. Mooring bolts and toilets ashore, unusual lava deposits on the islet to the SW. A bird reserve: the restrictions during the breeding season are displayed on noticeboards ashore.

Fredrikstad
Chart 1   59° 12' N, 10° 57' E

A considerable town (pop 26 500 in 1992) and suitable for clearing Customs into or out of Norway. The harbour, at the mouth of the River Glomma (the longest in Scandinavia) can be approached E or W of Kråkerøy. There is a lifting bridge over the arm of the river that runs round the N of Kråkerøy, which opens at 0600, 0900, 1200, 1500, 1800 and 2100 as long as there are yachts waiting, and between 2100 and 0600 if called on Chs 12 or 14. There are several marinas, one (unvisited) SE of the lifting bridge, but mostly in the harbour to its N and W. Fjellberg Båthavn, in the bay at the extreme N of the harbour, has fuel, water and toilets: depths from 1.7 m. Excellent shopping, communications, etc; the old fortress town on the E bank is well worth a visit. There is also a fort on Isegran, the promontory that projects from E Kråkerøy into the river mouth, with Nøkledypet marina behind it, and a restored water-wheel on its point.

Skjærhalden
Chart 1   59° 01.5' N, 11° 02.5' E

At the S end of the large island of Kirkøy, this small harbour has several small marinas and visitors' pontoons. It is well sheltered, and water and diesel are available alongside, and also laundry, toilets and showers. It is a bare 2 miles from the Swedish border, but if coming from there it may be easier to clear Customs at Fredrikstad (above).

PART 5

The Swedish Coast between Norway and the Sound

The N part of this coast is not unlike the E Norwegian coast, except that the islands are mostly bare and rocky, without the trees that are such a feature of Norway. As far as Göteborg, most of the distance can be covered inside the skärgård (the Swedish spelling), but S of there the coast is rather bleak, with suitable harbours far apart until the protection (and overcrowding) of the Sound is reached. Strömstad is a convenient place to clear Customs and the office there is efficient and helpful. Prices tend to be somewhat lower, and a higher proportion of restaurants are licensed to serve alcohol. Vardes are still in common use as sea marks, but in Sweden they are known as *kummel* and marked as such on the charts (abbreviation Kl).

CHARTS

The quite excellent Swedish charts are available for most of their coastal waters in two forms: very large single sheets, or books of approximately quarter-sized sheets, printed from the same plates. The latter are very much easier to cope with in the cockpit of the average yacht, and I would recommend them where available.

Unfortunately, *Båtsportkorts* now only cover the area southwards from 57° 50′ N, so Swedish charts 935, 934, 933 and 932 will be needed anyway, but south of that I would recommend *Båtsportkorts* S 32, 31 and 30, which cover the remaining coasts dealt with in this book. For those who prefer the big charts, the same area is covered by Swedish charts 931, 925, 924 and 923. Another solution for the whole area would be British Admiralty charts 880, 889, 890, 891 and 892 at 1:50 000, with chart 2114 covering the relatively open S part at 1:260 000. However, inevitably these are less frequently updated, and I would always prefer the local version. Going S, these are easily found in Strömstad, the most northerly Swedish port covered, and itself covered by Norwegian chart 1.

PASSAGE

In the N part of the passage there are numerous alternatives, and space does not allow me to deal with them all in what is, after all, a book about Norway! I shall therefore tend to confine my description to only one of the inshore passages: the open sea is of course always one alternative, but I apologise if I have left out any reader's favourite channel.

From Strömstad, leave Halsörholm, Likholm and Käbblingarna Lights close to starboard, and proceed S down

Kosterfjord until W of the Bramskär lighthouse. (Alternatively, one can enter the Bisserännan between Store-Snart and Bissen, and emerge via the Havstenssund.) From here, pass N of Djupskär Light and then steer SSE down the well marked fairlead into the Hamburgsund. Continue S, E of Hornö and Ulön, and on down the well marked channel past Hunnebostrand and into the interesting Sotenkanal, a partly artificial channel about 2 miles long and spanned by a swing bridge. Coming from the N, sound Z (— — · ·), and from the S, G (— — ·), for the bridge to open, which it does promptly. At the S end of the Kanal turn E and S through Kungshamn, E close inshore past Fisketaangen, and SSE between Brandskär and Kornö. Continuing S past Lysekil and W of Skäfto, take the narrow but well marked and interesting channel E of Harmanö (on a special enlarged inset). In good weather visit the charming harbour of Käringön, and then turn SE, or in westerly wind keep E of Saltö, either way passing between Vannholm and Bråtö, the Kyrkesund, and then outside

The lifting bridge over the Sotenkanal.

THE SWEDISH COAST BETWEEN NORWAY AND THE SOUND

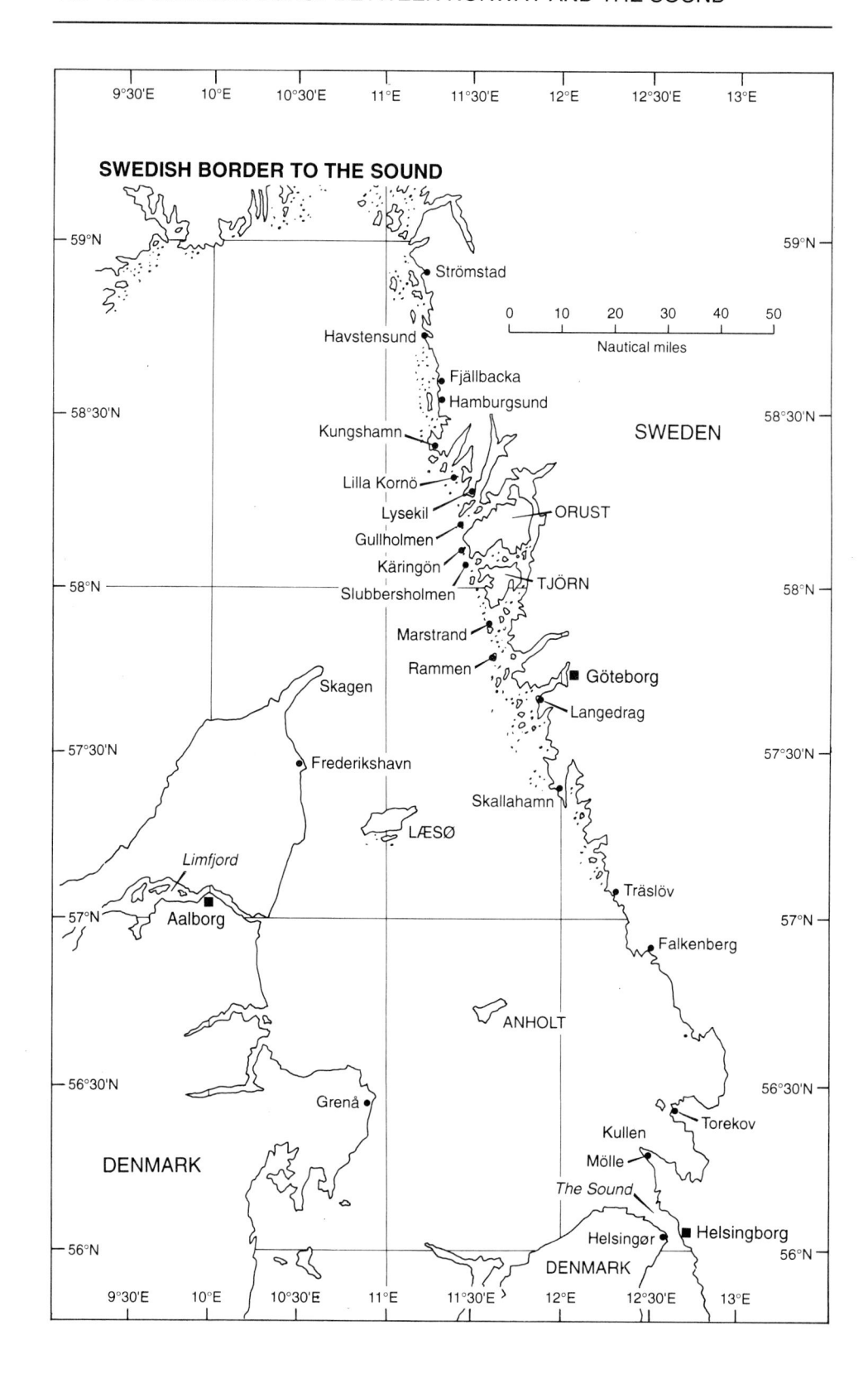

SWEDISH BORDER TO THE SOUND

THE SWEDISH COAST BETWEEN NORWAY AND THE SOUND

the islands until turning sharp E between Bratten and Eggskär (kummel, sketched on chart). Bear S again and enter the sound for Marstrand. Continue SE N of Klaverön through a fascinating narrow channel, then down the marked fairlead E of Langö, Brunskär and Björkö, then SE between Lille and Store Varholm into the main Göteborg channel.

After Göteborg (probably visited by tram from Langedrag yacht harbour, see the harbour entry note), take the marked channel passing E of Asperö, Köpstadsö, Donsö and Valö, where one finds oneself in open sea apart from a few isolated islands for the next few miles.

The rest of the passage needs no comment, consisting merely of running down an open coast, except for a passage of about 30 miles cutting across to the great promontory of Kullen. Once past the point, it is plain sailing into the Sound.

HARBOURS AND ANCHORAGES

Strömstad
(Swedish) Chart 935
58° 56.5′ N, 11° 10.5′ E
A first rate harbour only 5 miles by sea from the Norwegian frontier, and the obvious place to clear Swedish Customs if coming home through the Baltic and Kiel Canal or Limfjord. Approach is intricate but easy. From about ½ mile N of Klövingarna Light steer E, passing close N of the Axelbrottet buoy, and on to enter the heavily buoyed channel between Holmengrå and Flatskär (kummel).

Enter the S harbour, passing S of the end of the long breakwater, and round the jetty projecting NW from the SE side of the harbour. Berth either on the NE side of this jetty, or at the quay straight ahead. When crowded it may be necessary to lie bows on with a stern anchor. Water, toilets and showers: fuel from Myrens Marina, ½ mile to the S, which may have a visitor's berth. Good shopping in the town; Customs at the S side of the N harbour.

Havstenssund
Chart 934 (inset)   58° 45′ N, 11° 11′ E
Good anchorage just S of the peninsula on which the village stands in 12 m, clay. Go E to clear the fairway, but do not anchor in less than 10 m, as the bottom becomes soft mud and poor holding. Stores from village.

Fjällbacka
Chart 934   58° 36′ N, 11° 17′ E
This pretty town has a large guest harbour with water, toilets, showers and electricity. If it is crowded, there are numerous good anchorages nearby. Guest berths are on the outside of the outermost jetty projecting from the W pier, or between the two N-most jetties on the shore side. The berths can be uncomfortable in rough weather. Supermarket and chart counter in bookshop at the top of the hill.

Hamburgsund
Chart 934 (inset)   58° 33′ N, 11° 10′ E
It is possible to anchor in several places in this short sound, or there is a small yacht harbour just S of the main village on the E side of the sound: water and showers. PO and small shop, also restaurant.

Kungshamn
Chart 933   58° 21.5′ N, 11° 15′ E
A protected harbour in a small town. Approach from the N: see Passage notes above. From seaward, from a position E of Hallö Light two white lighthouses are conspicuous E of the conspicuous bridge. Keep them in line on about 020°

until the two triangular white marks W of the bridge come in line. Hold this line until the harbour entrance opens up. Moor alongside the quays as space permits, or bows on and stern to anchor if necessary. Water, fuel and all stores. A pleasant and useful stopping place. **Smögen**, 1 mile to the W, is a famous and picturesque fishing town. It is a bustling place with great atmosphere: while often too crowded for an overnight stay, it is well worth a visit by anyone in the vicinity.

Lilla Kornö
Chart 933   58° 18.5′ N, 11° 22′ E
This pleasant little fishing village harbour is only inhabited in the summer, and is seldom crowded. Moor immediately to starboard on entry or farther down on the port side on the outside of the big T-shaped jetty. Exposed in northerlies. Toilets, showers and water.

Lysekil
Chart 933   58° 16.5′ N, 11° 26′ E
Approach from the N or S as in Passage notes above. From the sea, the approach is straightforward, and the town is easily identified by its tall church spire. Use the harbour to the S of the town; it has a yacht basin at its S end just N of Slägga. Customs, fuel and all the facilities of a considerable town. The fishing harbour, farther N, is also used as a visitors' basin during the high season, and is closer to the centre.

Gullholmen
Chart 932   58° 10.5′ N, 11° 24.5′ E
Sweden's oldest fishing village and most picturesque, the advice is to moor on the long pontoon to the S of Gullholmen, passing first between it and the islet to its S. Toilets, showers and water. If crowded, it may be necessary to moor stern on bows to anchor. Yachts also moor N of the bridge. The museum near the S end of Gullholmen is worth a visit.

Käringön
Chart 932   58° 07′ N, 11° 22′ E
A delightful small offshore island harbour providing full shelter in all weathers. For approach from S or N, see Passage notes; from seaward, pass close S of Måseskär (kummel), and steer NE for the first buoy of the well marked channel. The entrance is narrow, facing N into protected water, but if blowing hard from that direction enter slowly under engine, as there is often no room to manoeuvre, and it can prove difficult to stop. Moor alongside as space permits: most unusually for Scandinavia, one may find oneself outside three or four others, but nobody seems to mind and it is a thoroughly jolly place. One modest shop.

Slubbersholmen
Chart 932   58° 03.5′ N, 11° 27′ E
Protecting a bay in the larger island of Mollön, Slubbersholmen creates a wild anchorage nearly ¼ mile square. Good holding and mooring bolts ashore. In W and NW winds, go as far N as possible. There is a little sandy beach at the E end of the Slubbersholm N shore, popular with children.

Marstrand
Chart 931   57° 53.5′ N, 11° 35′ E
A protected and popular harbour in a sound: the Swedish equivalent of Burnham-on-Crouch, perhaps. Approach from the N or S as in Passage notes; from seaward, the castle of Carlstens Fastning W of the town is conspicuous. Moor alongside the pontoons on the W (Marstrandsön) side at the S end of the town if space permits, but anywhere near high season it will be bows on and stern to anchor. All shops and facilities: fuel from the small basin S of the ferry stop on the E (Koön) side.

THE SWEDISH COAST BETWEEN NORWAY AND THE SOUND

Rammen
Chart 931   57° 47′ N, 11° 38′ E
A useful island anchorage some 12 miles from Långedrag. Enter from the W on the marked transit to avoid the reefs to starboard, and turn SE into the bay once the inner shore opens up. Mooring bolts both on the peninsula and the mainland. Good shelter from all but NW winds.

Långedrag, Göteborg
Chart 931   57° 40′ N, 11° 51′ E
This protected artificial yacht harbour is the HQ of the Royal Göteborg YC. Approach from the N or S as in Passage notes; from seaward, the main channel leads in N of Vinga and is clearly marked and made obvious by continuous heavy traffic (large scale inset on the *Båtsportkort*). Enter S of the conspicuous long breakwater and N of the short one running N from Ägnholm, moor at the end of a pier, and report to the harbour office (in a round tower like a lighthouse) which will allot a berth, probably stern to post and bow to quay. My harbourmaster spoke virtually no English. Water on every pier, fuel on the S of the entrance between the two outer pontoons. No local shops, only a large and expensive restaurant. Tram (200 m) goes to shops (one stop) and on to the centre of Göteborg. It is very slow – 30 minutes to the centre – but frequent, about four or five an hour. Göteborg is a nice town with all possible facilities. It is also possible to proceed up the river to Lilla Bommen, a small marina on the S bank only a short walk from the city centre. It has water and electricity on the pontoons and a small shop; 200 m to the centre of Göteborg.

Skallahamn
Chart 925   57° 21.5′ N, 12° 00′ E
A tricky but invaluable anchorage on this rather bleak coast, protected from all directions though swell penetrates in SW gales. Anchor S of the permanent moorings at the top of the bay in about 6 m. Holding is thick weed on stiff clay, and I motored my fisherman anchor backwards several times across the bay without it catching. A 35 lb CQR, however, engaged, and would then have held in a hurricane. No facilities, as far as I know. In SW gales, the bay to the W, Malöhamn, is said to afford more shelter. It has a cruising club buoy at its SW end. For normal use it is a wide and windy place, and Skallahamn is to be preferred.

Träslöv
Chart 924 (inset)   57° 03.5′ N, 12° 16.5′ E
This is a better place for yachts than the larger **Varberg** 3 miles to the N. Enter past the outer breakwater and, if under 12 m overall, turn S into the narrow buoyed channel into the yacht harbour. Fuel, water, toilets and showers. Larger yachts should continue into the main inner harbour and berth as opportunity offers on the S or E side (the N side is shoal): probably alongside a fishing boat, or continue still farther into an inner harbour and berth where possible. Fuel at the S quay of the main harbour. Good shops in the village, boatyard with slip, engine and hull repairs.

Falkenberg
Chart 924   56° 54′ N, 12° 30′ E
A rather commercial harbour at the mouth of the River Ätran, protected by moles and breakwaters. Enter between the moles (leading lights) and proceed up the well buoyed channel. There is a small marina on the E side, or one may be able to berth alongside on the NW side clear of fishing boats: this is nearer town than the marina. Good small shops and bank, and the museum is worth a visit, as is the old town. Keep an eye out for current from the river while manoeuvring.

Torekov

Chart 923   56° 26′ N, 12° 37.5′ E

A pretty but overcrowded harbour, which is however useful for those who wish to break the long passage from Falkenberg or beyond to the Kullen. The entrance, which lies E of the S end of Hallands Väderö, is well marked and lit, with two sets of leading lights at night. Enter by the buoyed channel (inset on chart 923) and proceed into the inner harbour (2.5 m) to berth as space permits, and there isn't a lot! Dues are charged. Shop and PO, water from tap only.

Mölle

Chart 923   56° 17′ N, 12° 30′ E

This artificial harbour lies on the S side of the magnificent promontory of Kullen, some 2 miles ESE of its point. Coming from the N, remember that in good visibility Kullen looks like an island, as the land E of the W 4 miles is low lying. Identification can always be confirmed by the radio beacon, which has a 100 mile range and transmits KUL continuously on 344 kHz. Approach from well N of W, or in the white sector of the main light at night, to avoid the shoal that extends WNW from the pier. Its end is marked by a buoy; once this is identified, pass close N of it and then steer straight for the pierhead. Inside the pier turn sharp to starboard into the harbour. Do not go beyond the smaller pier to the E, as it is shoal inside it. There is 3 m alongside, berth as space allows alongside or bows to and stern to anchor. The harbourmaster may well appear and direct. Toilets open 24 hours, good and clean; it is an offence to use a marine toilet in the harbour. Good shop up the main road leading SE from the middle of the harbour; water from hose by harbour office. Fuel. A pleasant, typically Swedish village, looking freshly scrubbed and shining.

Sixteen miles to the SE lies the harbour of Elsinore (interestingly, the road to the shop in Mölle is called Guildensternallee: the Rosenkrantzes are commemorated everywhere, but that is the only memory I noticed of the unfortunate Guildenstern!), and another 23 miles brings you to Copenhagen itself.

These waters are well covered in other books, so we will leave the reader here in the hope that these modest notes will prove helpful in planning and carrying out an exploration of one of the most beautiful stretches of the coast of Europe, if not the world.

PART 6

Cruise Planning Information

Sailing Distances between Principal Ports

This section is designed to help the aspiring visitor to Norway, who may not have all the charts available, to plan his or her cruise. It consists of a table of distances (in nautical miles) between the most important ports dealt with in the foregoing sections, divided into a table for the N section and one for the S, which can be used in conjunction. Do please read the note printed under the S table carefully before using it, as otherwise you may obtain misleading results.

To have included the Hardangerfjord ports would have made the main table unwieldy, and also introduced considerable mathematical complexity, owing to the alternative routes available. A separate table of distances from Leirvik (included in the main table) to the Hardanger ports has therefore been added. I have also included distances for the Lysefjord, and from the E coast ports to Strömstad, the Swedish port nearest to the Norwegian border, and on from there to Denmark, from where I imagine most readers will know the way home!

Distances between Kviturspollen, Leirvik and the Hardangerfjord ports

89	80	80	57	32	32	Kviturspollen
77	68	68	45	15	Leirvik	
64	55	55	32	Uskedal		
36	29	29	Norheimsund			
33	10	Ulvik				
33	Eidfjord					
Odda						

Note: Distances between Kviturspollen and the Hardanger ports are by the Lokksund and Bjørna and Raune Fjords. Use as with the main table – thus from Leirvik to Kviturspollen via Uskedal, Ulvik and Odda is 15 + 55 + 33 + 89 = 192 nautical miles.

Lysefjord

Stavanger to entrance 12 miles. Entrance to Vika 3½ miles. Vika to Lysebotn 17½ miles.

Distances to Strömstad: direct routes

From Risør 61 miles; Kragerø 55 miles; Stavern 35 miles; Tønsberg 32 miles; Horten 39 miles. Proceeding S, Strömstad to Skagen 81 miles. Strömstad to Lysekil

168 CRUISE PLANNING INFORMATION

N Norway: approximate sailing distance (nm) between principal ports: shortest recommended route

```
1089  975  923  864  834  710  662  627  534  488  479  422  341  228  168   98   48  Kirkenes
1040  929  875  816  788  661  617  581  489  440  432  376  294  180  122   53  Vardø
 994  881  828  768  740  614  569  534  441  393  385  328  247  133   74  Berlevåg
 923  810  757  699  670  545  498  464  370  322  314  257  175   63  Honningsvåg
 865  754  701  640  612  487  440  406  313  265  256  201  119  Hammerfest
 748  633  581  521  494  368  322  286  195  147  139   80  Tromsø
 671  561  508  449  419  294  248  213  120   71   64  Harstad
 670  556  503  445  415  291  245  208  117   68  Narvik
 612  500  448  389  360  233  188  153   61  Svolvær
 558  444  391  330  303  177  130   96  Bodø
 460  347  295  236  208   81   36  Sandnessjøen
 427  311  260  199  171   47  Brønnøysund
 380  267  212  155  126  Rørvik
 317  204  150   90  Trondheim
 228  116   63  Kristiansund
 166   54  Ålesund
 112  Måløy
Bergen
```

S Norway: approximate sailing distance (nm) between principal ports: shortest recommended route

```
524 492 477 452 434 420 397 379 364 344 329 313 284 245 244 230 211 185 153 142 103  75  31  Skjolden
511 479 464 439 421 407 384 366 351 331 316 300 271 232 231 217 198 172 140 129  90  62  Årdalstangen
449 417 402 377 359 345 322 304 289 269 254 238 209 170 169 155 136 110  78  67  28  Vikum
423 391 376 351 333 319 296 278 263 243 228 212 183 144 143 129 110  84  52  41  Eivindvik
382 350 335 310 292 278 255 237 222 202 187 171 142 103 102  88  69  43  11  Bergen
371 339 324 299 281 267 244 226 211 191 176 160 131  92  91  77  58  32  Kviturspollen
339 307 292 267 249 235 212 194 179 159 144 128  99  60  59  45  26  Leirvik
313 281 266 241 223 209 186 168 153 133 118 102  73  34  33  19  Haugesund
296 264 249 224 206 192 169 151 136 116 101  85  56  17  16  Skudeneshavn
293 261 246 221 203 189 166 148 133 113  98  82  53  14  Stavanger
279 247 232 207 189 175 152 134 119  99  84  68  39  Tananger
240 208 193 168 150 136 113  95  80  60  45  29  Egersund
211 179 164 139 121 107  84  66  51  31  16  Listahavn
195 163 148 123 105  91  68  50  35  15  Lindesnes (The Naze)
183 151 136 111  93  79  56  38  23  Mandal
165 133 118  93  75  61  38  20  Kristiansand
148 116 101  76  58  44  21  Lillesand
127  95  80  55  37  23  Arendal
104  72  57  32  14  Risør
 97  65  50  25  Kragerø
 72  40  25  Stavern
 47  15  Tønsberg
 32  Horten
Oslo (Dronningen)
```

(outside) 49 miles; Lysekil to Göteborg 47 miles. Göteborg to Varberg 44 miles; Varberg to Mölle 51 miles; Mölle to Copenhagen 36 miles.

Total Strömstad to Copenhagen (via the above ports) 227 miles. Direct distance 207 miles.

Note on the use of the tables

All figures (in nautical miles) are given for the distance between the two ports chosen by the shortest of the routes mentioned in the text, and without the detours involved in visiting intervening ports. Thus, Skudeneshavn to Tananger is 17 miles, but Skudeneshavn to Stavanger is 16, and Stavanger to Tananger 14 miles: total 30 miles. To find the total distance between one port and another, visiting others on the way, the distances between each successive port to be visited should be looked up and added together. This will almost certainly be more than the shortest route between the two extreme ports. For example, Bergen to Oslo direct is 382 miles, but visiting all the quoted intervening ports increases this to 415. Try it!

Coastal Radio

The coastal stations are usually most cordial and helpful, and often refreshingly informal. The staff are generally happy to show guests their facilities and explain their operations, and if one is stopping in a harbour near a station, a call to ask about a visit may lead to an unusual and interesting tour.

The radio channel maps on the following pages show the VHF and MF coverage for the areas covered in this book. One should not call up the coastal station on VHF Ch 16 unless unable to reach them on a working channel, and at call-up one should state the name of the coastal station called and the working channel number used, as well as the yacht's name and callsign.

Before sailing 'foreign', one should establish with the marine radio authority a charge code and provisions for payment of charges; the coastal station may assume such a charge code even if not given one, send in charges where there has been no provision for payment, and then blacklist the call sign for non-payment. In principle, the coastal stations are required to charge for all services, but they will often ignore charges for a quick and simple service, and they tend to be quite kindly in their timing of link calls. If one asks for an entire weather forecast to be read, there will probably be a charge, but if one asks only for the local area forecast (eg: 'Echo 4' for Lofoten), there may well be no charge. Norway permits VHF-to-VHF link calls (with a double charge to cover both ends of the hookup) and this can be very convenient (although not cheap) for communication with another yacht that is outside direct VHF range. Bjørnøya Radio, as of 1994, was not equipped to handle telephone link calls, but for a modest cash charge one can make a call in person from the shore station.

The channels most commonly used for ship-to-ship communication are 06, 08, 10 and 69. There is very little traffic on Ch 16, and it is wise (legally required, in fact) to listen for announcements of gale warnings, navigation warnings and traffic list broadcasts, which will then be made on the working channels; these broadcasts do not seem to follow the scheduled times closely, and it works out much better just to listen for the announcements on Ch 16 than to try to catch them at a specified time. All announcements, except those relating to local fishing regulation, are made first in English and then Norwegian.

Many of the aerials are located on mountains, with a surprising reach offshore and into fjords and leads. Bergen Radio has Chs 16, 21 and 87 on the Oseberg oil platform at 60° 29′ N, 2° 50′ E, and Florø Radio has Chs 16, 65

COASTAL RADIO

and 85 on the Gullfaks oil platform at 61° 10′ N, 2° 11′ E, giving coverage nearly to Lerwick in Shetland. If outside VHF coverage, one may be able to communicate on MF or HF via Rogaland (for Rogaland HF channels, see the UK *Admiralty List of Radio Signals Vol 1(1)*; this publication also gives the lat/long position for each aerial).

To make a shore-to-ship link call, telephone the following numbers and give the yacht's name, callsign and approximate position. See table opposite.

Norway should soon have coverage along the entire coast for automatic direct-dial ship-shore telephone calls, which are very much cheaper than calls handled by a shore operator. If you have the necessary equipment for handling such calls, the Coast Radio can advise you concerning procedure.

Station	International No	Freephone from within Norway
Göteborg Radio	(46) 31 89 73 00	—
Tjøme Radio	(47) 33 39 02 20	120
Farsund Radio	(47) 38 39 08 12	130
Rogaland Radio	(47) 51 67 30 11	122 (and 135 for HF traffic)
Bergen Radio	(47) 55 32 73 90	136
Florø Radio	(47) 57 74 15 00	137
Ørlandet Radio	(47) 72 52 33 47	125
Bodø Radio	(47) 75 52 46 61	126
Vardø Radio	(47) 78 98 72 28	129

172 CRUISE PLANNING INFORMATION

VHF Channels for Norway

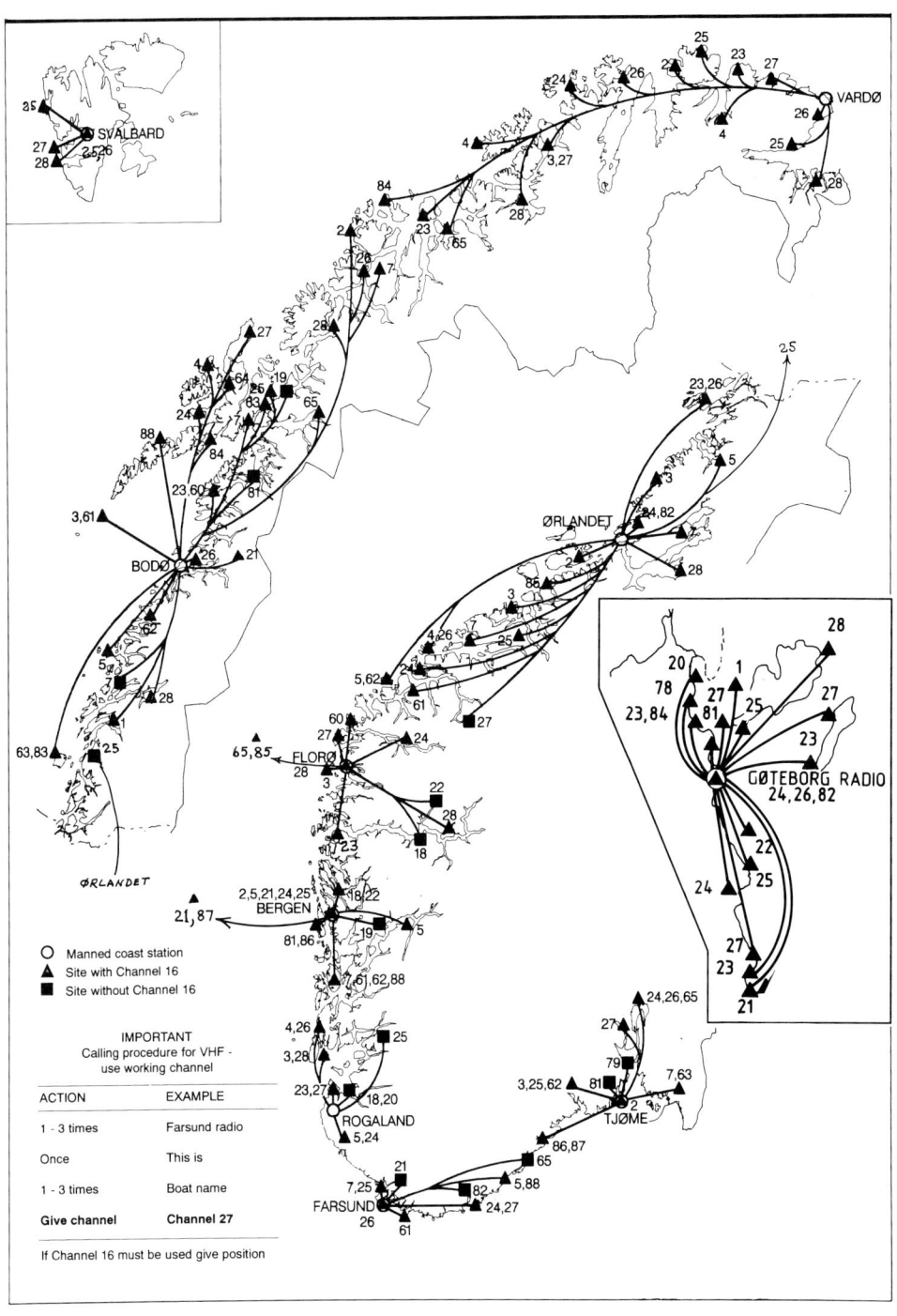

ACTION	EXAMPLE
1 - 3 times	Farsund radio
Once	This is
1 - 3 times	Boat name
Give channel	Channel 27

IMPORTANT
Calling procedure for VHF - use working channel

If Channel 16 must be used give position

○ Manned coast station
▲ Site with Channel 16
■ Site without Channel 16

Reproduced with permission from Norwegian Telecom.

COASTAL RADIO

MF Channels for Norway

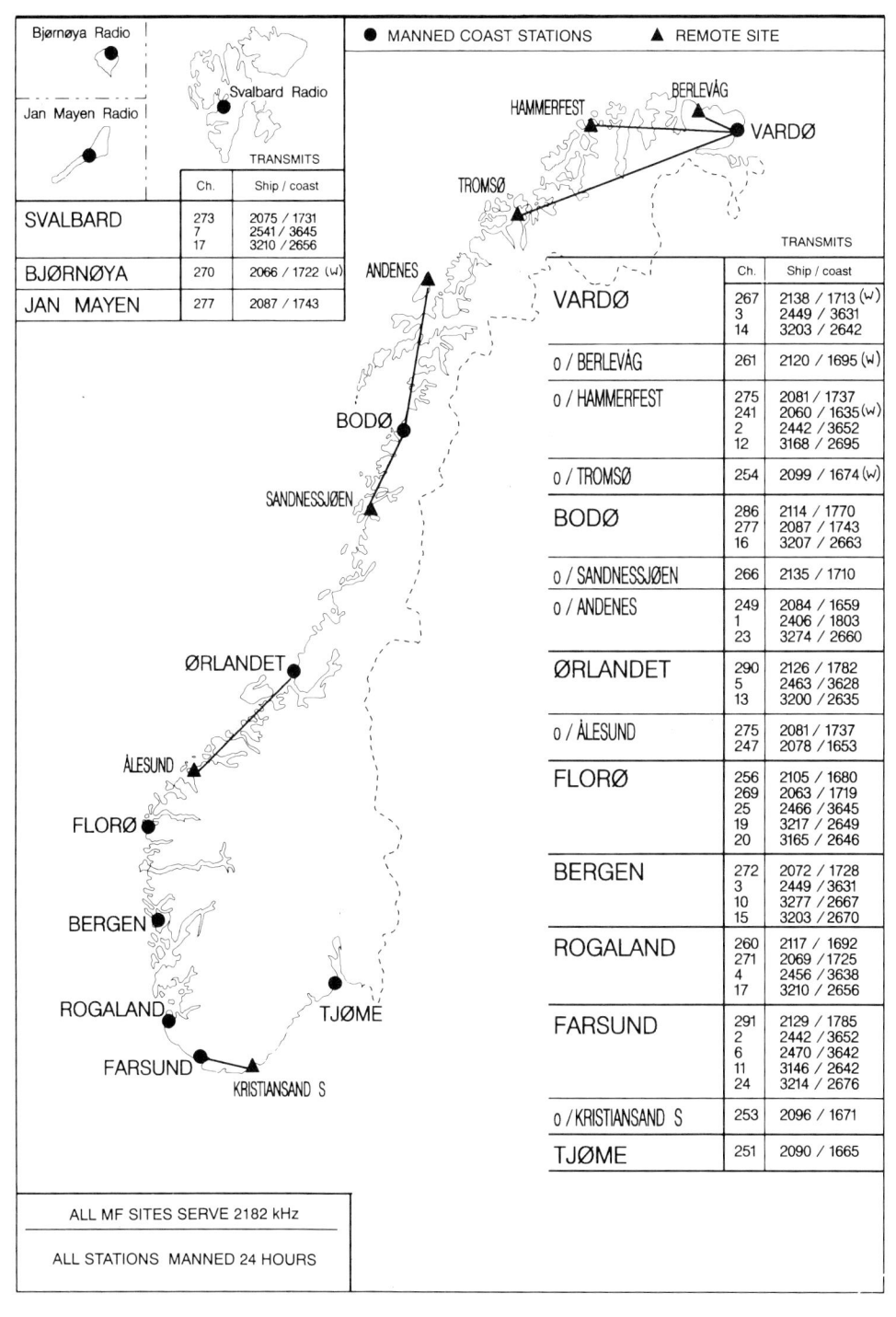

	TRANSMITS	
	Ch.	Ship / coast
SVALBARD	273 7 17	2075 / 1731 2541 / 3645 3210 / 2656
BJØRNØYA	270	2066 / 1722 (w)
JAN MAYEN	277	2087 / 1743

● MANNED COAST STATIONS ▲ REMOTE SITE

	TRANSMITS	
	Ch.	Ship / coast
VARDØ	267 3 14	2138 / 1713 (w) 2449 / 3631 3203 / 2642
o / BERLEVÅG	261	2120 / 1695 (w)
o / HAMMERFEST	275 241 2 12	2081 / 1737 2060 / 1635 (w) 2442 / 3652 3168 / 2695
o / TROMSØ	254	2099 / 1674 (w)
BODØ	286 277 16	2114 / 1770 2087 / 1743 3207 / 2663
o / SANDNESSJØEN	266	2135 / 1710
o / ANDENES	249 1 23	2084 / 1659 2406 / 1803 3274 / 2660
ØRLANDET	290 5 13	2126 / 1782 2463 / 3628 3200 / 2635
o / ÅLESUND	275 247	2081 / 1737 2078 / 1653
FLORØ	256 269 25 19 20	2105 / 1680 2063 / 1719 2466 / 3645 3217 / 2649 3165 / 2646
BERGEN	272 3 10 15	2072 / 1728 2449 / 3631 3277 / 2667 3203 / 2670
ROGALAND	260 271 4 17	2117 / 1692 2069 / 1725 2456 / 3638 3210 / 2656
FARSUND	291 2 6 11 24	2129 / 1785 2442 / 3652 2470 / 3642 3146 / 2642 3214 / 2676
o / KRISTIANSAND S	253	2096 / 1671
TJØME	251	2090 / 1665

ALL MF SITES SERVE 2182 kHz

ALL STATIONS MANNED 24 HOURS

Reproduced with permission from Norwegian Telecom.

Weather Forecasts and Ice Reports

In the waters covered by the *Norwegian Cruising Guide,* the actual weather seems to follow the forecast even less often than in some other parts of the world. Especially in Spitsbergen, the weather seems often to bear little similarity to the forecast or even to the real-time computer generated surface chart. Also, the local weather may be greatly influenced by terrain, with substantial changes in wind direction, precipitation and visibility, so that even if the overall forecast is valid one's local experience may be quite different. None the less, nearly everyone is always eager to know what the meteorologists have to say, and forecasts in English are widely available for Norway and Sweden.

Forecasting for southern Norway is from Bergen, Tel: (47) 55 23 66 00, and for northern Norway from Tromsø, Tel: (47) 77 68 40 44. New 24-hour forecasts are issued to the coastal radio stations by telex at 0600 and 1800 UT, and are usually available upon request one to two hours after these times. These forecasts are for (portions of) the areas A1...A2...H3...I3, as shown on the map of offshore forecast areas. Generally, one should request the forecast only for the area of immediate interest, for example 'Echo 4' for Lofoten or 'Hotel 3' for the Bergen area; such an abbreviated forecast will often be given without charge by the coastal radio station. To obtain a five-day forecast one can make a link call to Bergen or Tromsø, and although usually such a forecast will be given without charge (although one must pay for the radio link call), after repeated requests payment may be required for further forecasts.

Scheduled broadcasts of the offshore weather forecast are made from Vardø Radio and Bjørnøya Radio on their VHF working channels and on their MF channels marked with (W) on the MF-channels map, and from Rogaland on HF, as follows:

UT	Station	Frequency	Channel
0905	Bjørnøya	1722 kHz	270
1033	Vardø	1713	267
1033	Vardø/ Berlevåg	1695	261
1033	Vardø/ Hammerfest	1635	241
1033	Vardø/ Tromsø	1674	254
1205	Rogaland	8749, 13158	811, 1228
1215	Rogaland	8749, 13158	811, 1228 (coastal forecast)
1305	Bjørnøya	1722	270
2005	Bjørnøya	1722	270
2233	Vardø & satellites as for 1033		
2305	Rogaland	6507, 8749	603, 811
2315	Rogaland	6507, 8749	603, 811 (coastal forecast)

WEATHER FORECASTS AND ICE REPORTS

Rogaland Radio	0148	0548	0948F	1348	1748	2148F
Bodø Radio	0018F	0418	0900	1218F	1618	2100
Vardø Radio	0300	0700	1100F	1500	1900	2300F

Gale warnings, for Force 7 near gale and higher, are broadcast appropriately on working channels after announcement on Ch 16 and 2182 KHz.

Navtex broadcasts are made on 518 kHz as shown above; all times are UT. Gale warnings are broadcast upon receipt and at all scheduled times; forecasts are broadcast twice daily at the times marked by 'F'. Vardø Radio broadcasts a Navtex ice report Tuesday at 1500 UT.

The BBC shipping forecast for N Utsire and S Utsire can be useful for the southern areas covered in this book: UT 0455, 1255, 1650 and 2333 in summer, UT 0033, 0555, 1355 and 1750 in winter, on LW 198 kHz (AM).

There is good weatherfax coverage for Norway and Sweden from Offenbach, Bracknell and Northwood. Many of the charts do not go far enough N for Svalbard, but the Offenbach 36-, 48-, 60-, 72-hour forecast charts, and Bracknell 48- and 72-hour charts, do include Svalbard, and they are often well received at those latitudes.

The North Atlantic Ice Chart, which includes Svalbard, is broadcast daily on weatherfax from Bracknell at 1602 UT and repeated by Offenbach at 2021 (1994 schedules).

One can often get extensive weather forecast information from local TV or FM radio stations, including a daily five-day forecast, with help from a Norwegian-speaking sailor who knows the language, broadcast schedules and radio frequencies.

More detail is available in the UK *Admiralty List of Radio Signals, Vol 3: Radio Weather Services*.

The following table may be useful in interpreting Norwegian and Swedish forecasts and in discussing weather with local sailors:

Beaufort	Knots	English	Norwegian	Metres/second
0	0	Calm	Stille	0–0.2
1	1–3	Light air	Flau vind	0.3–1.5
2	4–6	Light breeze	Svak vind	1.6–3.3
3	7–10	Gentle breeze	Lett bris	3.4–5.4
4	11–16	Moderate breeze	Laber bris	5.5–7.9
5	17–21	Fresh breeze	Frisk bris	8.0–10.7
6	22–27	Strong breeze	Liten kuling	10.8–13.8
7	28–33	Near gale	Stiv kuling	13.9–17.1
8	34–40	Gale	Sterk kuling	17.2–20.7
9	41–47	Strong gale	Liten storm	20.8–24.4
10	48–55	Storm	Full storm	24.5–28.4
11	56–63	Violent storm	Sterk storm	28.5–32.6
12	64+	Hurricane	Orkan	32.7+

Note that 1 'sekund-metre' (m/sec) of wind is very close to 2 knots; it is very easy to confuse Force 5, 5 knots, and 5 m/sec.

176 CRUISE PLANNING INFORMATION

Coastal weather forecast areas

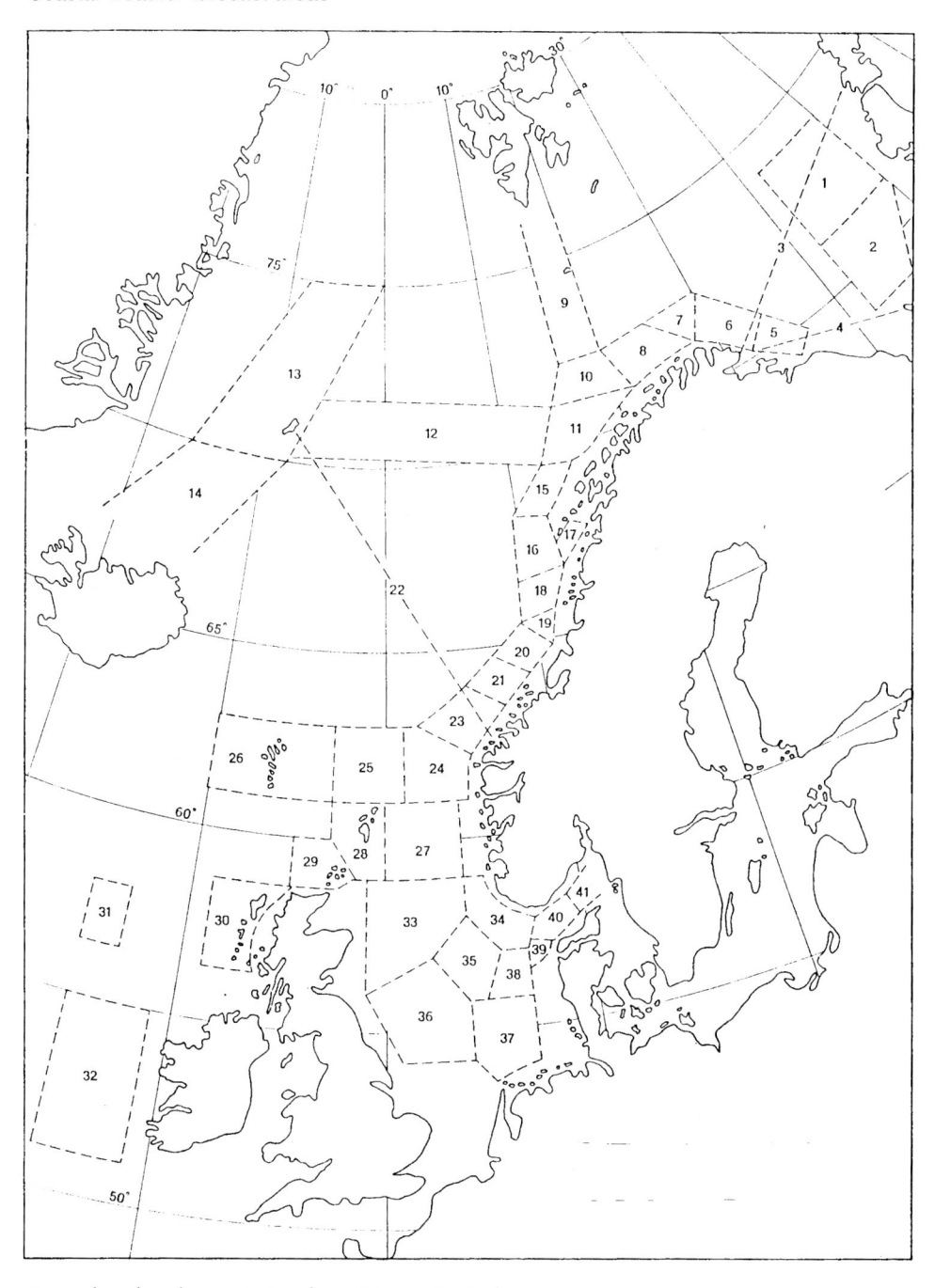

Reproduced with permission from Norwegian Telecom.

Weather Forecast Sea Areas
1 Østisen ved Gåslandet
2 Østisen ved Kapp Kanin
3 Overfarten Vardø – Gåslandet
4 Overfarten Vardø – Kapp Kanin
5 Kildinbanken
6 Nordbanken
7 Nordkappbanken
8 Hjelmsøybanken
9 Overfarten Tromsøflaket –
  Bjørnøya – Sørkapp
10 Tromsøflaket
11 Bankene utenfor Troms
12 Overfarten Troms – Jan Mayen
13 Vesterisen fra 70° N til 75° N
14 Vesterisen fra Kapp Nord til 70° N
15 Vesterålsbankene
16 Røstbanken
17 Ytre Vestfjorden
18 Trænabanken
19 Sklinnabanken
20 Haltenbanken
21 Frøyabanken
22 Overfarten Ålesund – Jan Mayen
23 Storegga
24 Aust-Tampen
25 Vest-Tampen
26 Fæøybankene
27 Vikingbanken
28 Shetlandsbankene
29 Orknøyene
30 Hebridene
31 Rockall
32 Fiskefeltene vest for Irland
33 Fladengrunn
34 Revet Lindesnes – Jæren
35 Store Fiskebank
36 Doggerbank
37 Kvitbanken
38 Lille Fiskebank
39 Jyske Rev
40 Ytre Skagerak
41 Indre Skagerak

178 CRUISE PLANNING INFORMATION

Offshore weather forecast areas

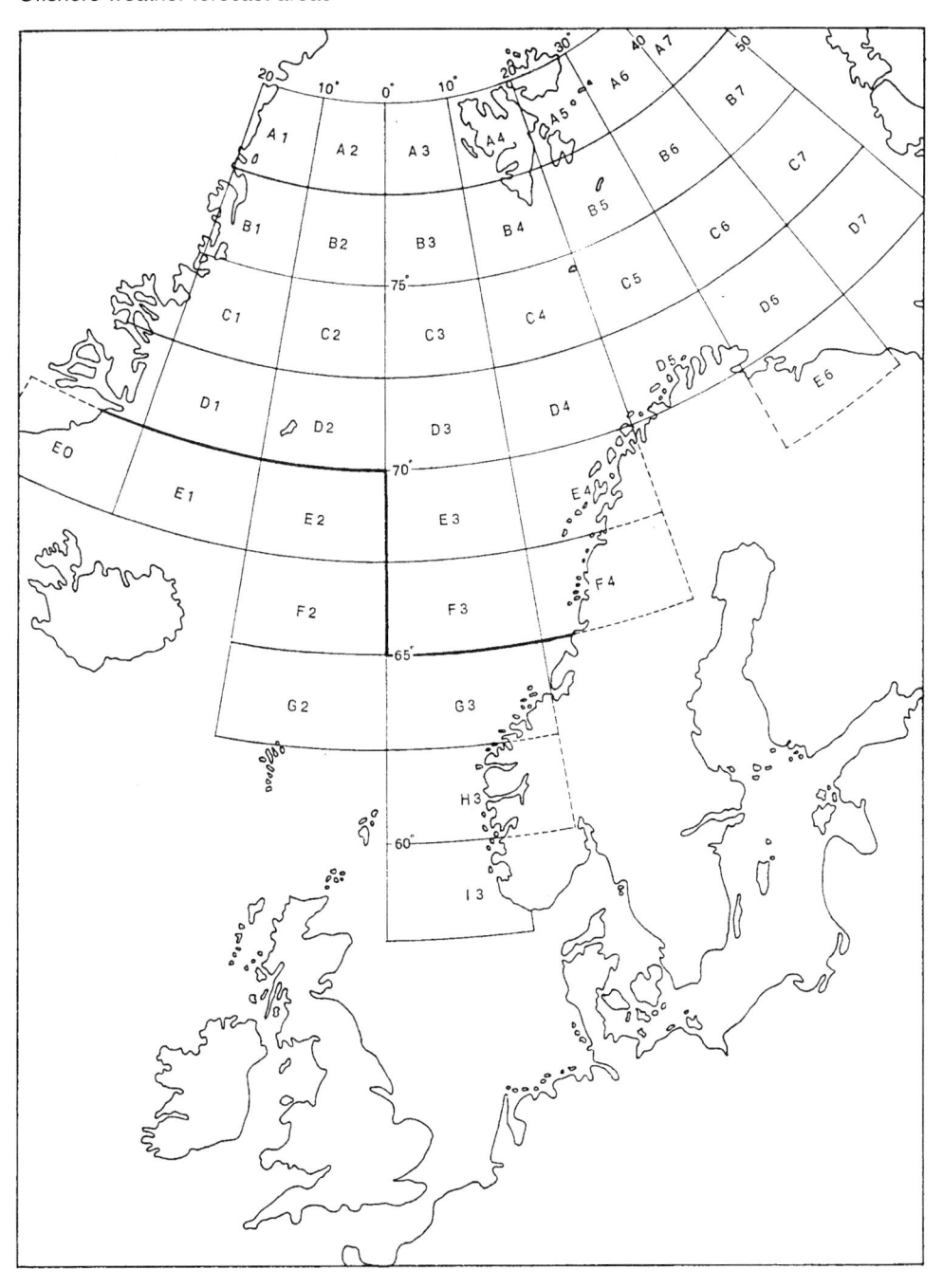

Reproduced with permission from Norwegian Telecom.

Coastal Danger Areas

The Norwegian Hydrographic Office identifies 23 areas of the coast likely to have exceptionally high, steep or chaotic seas, sometimes dangerous to ships and boats, under certain conditions of wind and tidal stream. It is believed that particular bottom contours, even at substantial depth, and coastal topography can interact to produce sea-state conditions much more severe than would be expected. The maps indicate these areas with shading; triangles indicate locations where vessels, often large fishing ships, are believed to have foundered because of these unusual conditions. The Hustadvika, area 11, is mentioned as Norway's most dangerous coastal area.

Area	Wind/Waves	Stream/Current	Depth
1	N	–	several hundred m
2	NW	ebb	–
3	NW	–	27–70 m
4	NW–NE	W-going	30–150 m
5	SW–NW–NE	expect irregular strong flow	0–400 m
6	SW–NW–NE	NE current generally	400 m
7	NW–NE	N–NE current generally	200 m
8	SW–W	ebb	300–450 m
9	NW	ebb	300–500 m
10	NW–SW	ebb	100–150 m
11	SW–NW–N	ebb	90–100 m
12	W–NW	ebb	–
13	SW–N	2–4 kt flow occurs	60–150 m
14	W–NW	ebb (1–2 kt)	–
15	SW–NW	ebb, esp. with snow-melt	–
16	SW–NW	ebb, over small area	250 m
17	SW–NW	1–1.5 kt flow occurs	16–40 m
18	SE–S–NW	expect variable flow	10–100 m
19	–	ebb	300 m
20	–	–	–
21	SW–W	W-going	–
22	SW	W-going	<100 m
23	SW–SE	W-going 1–1.5 kt	50–100 m

Source: *Den Norske Los* (Sailing Directions) Volume 1, 1986. Reproduced with the permission of the Norwegian Hydrographic Service 163/94.

Coastal Danger Areas

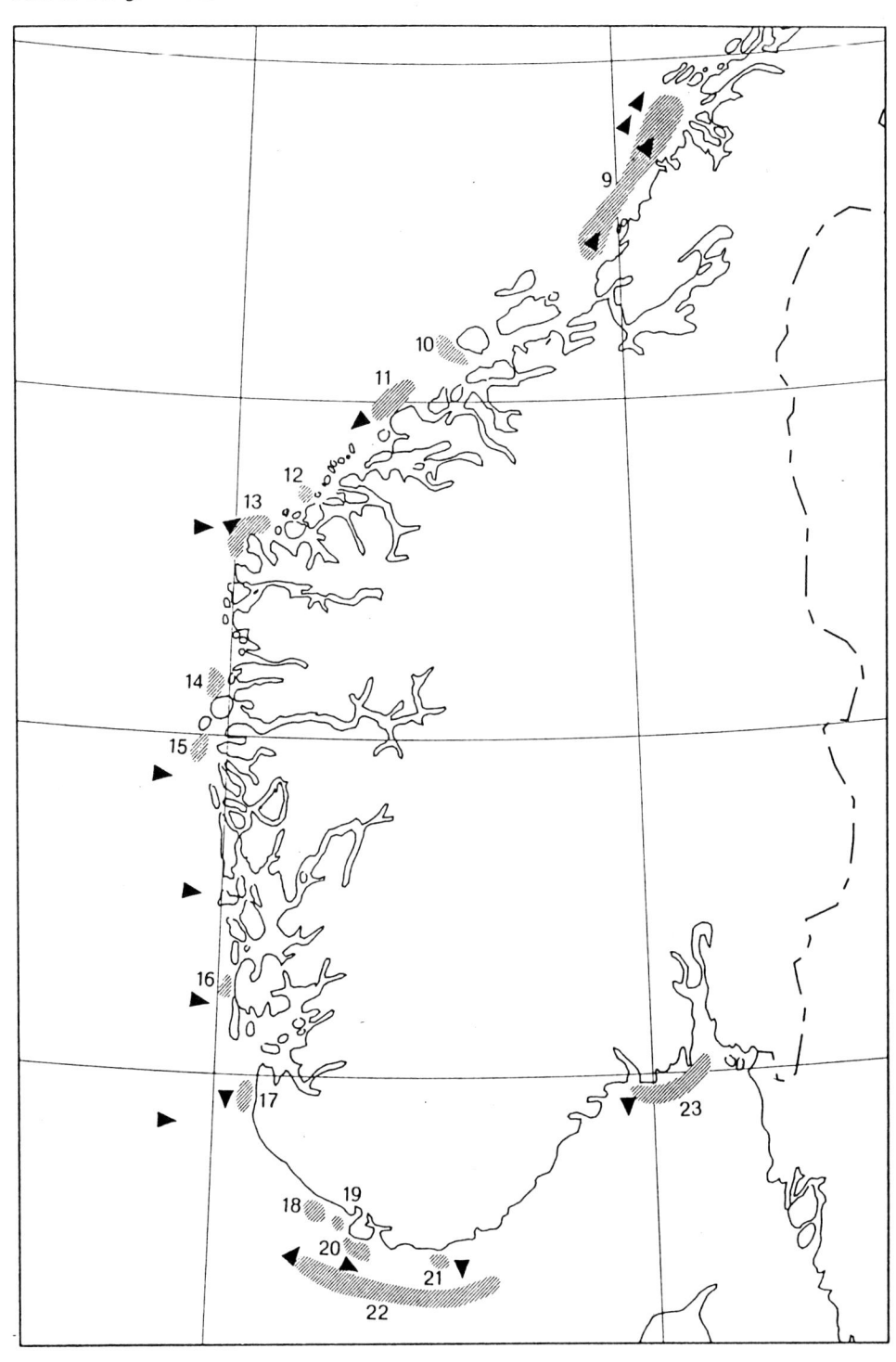

COASTAL DANGER AREAS 181

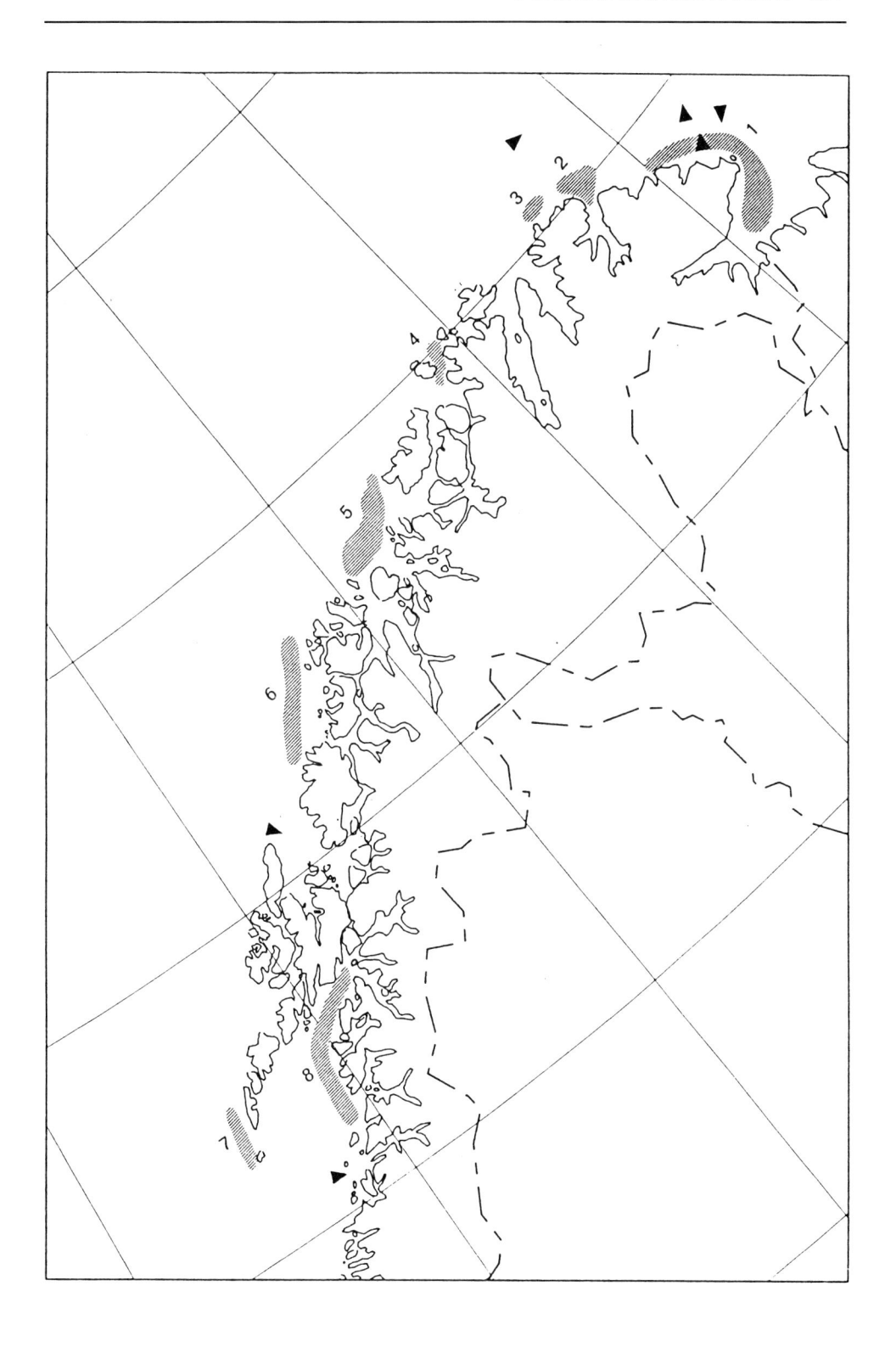

Glossary

Words and abbreviations from charts and *Den Norske Los*

It is often very useful to understand Norwegian words and place-name endings used on charts and in pilots and guides that are not in English. Because of noun word endings used in the Norwegian language, it is sometimes difficult even to be sure which word one is seeing. Without attempting a proper or comprehensive grammar, commonly found word forms are given here that may help in decyphering the text. For nouns, where it might aid in recognition of a word, the singular and plural, indefinite and definite forms are given (abbreviated for longer words). For example: **bølge, bølgen; -r, -ne** stands for **bølge, bølgen; bølger, bølgene**, which is in English: **wave, the wave; waves, the waves**. For words that are distinct whatever the ending, only the first form is given; for simplicity, only the English singular is given.

Norwegian chart and pilot abbreviations now follow international English usage, but one may encounter an obsolete usage, and these are shown in [brackets]. A slash '/' indicates alternatives/equivalents.

Note that sometimes there is no exact conceptual equivalency between the two languages, and a simple word substitution is not possible.

Abbreviation	Norwegian	English
	advarsel, varsel	warning, notice
ankpl	ankerplass	anchorage
Ø, au, E	austre, øst, østre, østlig	east, eastern, easterly
	av	of
bb	babord	port side, on the port hand
-bg, -bgt	berg, berget; berg,-ene, -a	mountain, rocky hill
	betongkai, -en; -er, -ene	concrete quay
Wd	bladtare	kelp
Fl, [bl]	blink	flashing (light)
Wd	blæretang	bladder-wrack
so	bløt	soft
Bu	blå	blue
	boe, boen; boer, boene	covered rock/shoal
	bog, bogen; -er,-ene/bøger,-ene	shoulder, saddle
	bratt	steep
	bre, breen; breer, breene	glacier
Br	bredde, bredden; bredder,-ene	latitude

Abbreviation	Norwegian	English
Br	bro, broen; broer, broene	bridge
	bru, brua; bruer, bruene	bridge
	brygge, bryggen; -r, -ne	quay
	båe, båen; båer, båene	covered rock/shoal
-bkt, -bkta	bukt, bukta/bukten; -er, -ene	bay, cove, bight
	bunkers	fuelling point
	bunn, bunnen; bunner, bunnene	bottom, seabed
	by, byen; byer, byene	town
	bølge, bølgen; -r, -ne	wave
	bøye, bøyen/bøya; -er, -ene	buoy
	båe, båen; båer, båene	sunken rock
B	båke, båken; båker, båkene	beacon, day-mark
	båt, båten; båter, båtene	boat
	båtverksted	boatyard
	dag, dagen; dager, dagene	day
	drivstoff	fuel
	dusj, dusjen; dusjer, dusjene	shower
	dybde	depth
	dypgående	draught
	dønning	swell
	eller	or
	elv, elva/elven; elver, -ene	river
	er	is
Efs	Etterretninger...	Notices ... (to Mariners)
Fabr	fabrikk	factory
	fallende	falling
	fare, farene	danger
	fare, farende	go, travel, travelling
	fartøy, fartøyer; -a, -ene	vessel, craft, boat
	farvann	fairway, waters
F	fast	fixed (light)
	ferjekai, -en/-a; -er, -ene	ferry quay
	fiskeoppdrett	fish farm
-fj,-fjt	fjell, fjellet, fjell, -ene,-a	mountain
R	fjellbunn, -en; -er, -ene	rocky bottom
	fjern	far away
	fjære	ebb, ebb-tide, LW
	flak, flaket; flak, flakene	shoal, 'flat'
	flere	several, more
	flo	flood, flood-tide, HW
-fl,-flene	flu/flue, flua, fluer, fluene	shoal that uncovers
	fly, flya/flyen; flyer, -ene	plateau
	flytekai, flytebrygge	pontoon
f eks	for eksempel	for example
	forbudt	prohibited
	forbudt sjøområde	restricted sea area

Reminder: alphabetical order is a b c...x y z æ ä ö ø å

Abbreviation	Norwegian	English
Oc, [fm]	formørkelser	occulting (light)
R	fortøyningsbolt	mooring bolt on shore
	fortøyningsbøye	mooring buoy
R	fortøyningsring	mooring ring on shore
	fortøyningsstenger	mooring bar, post on shore
	fortøyningssøyle	mooring pillar on shore
	fra	from, of
	friareal, -et; -, -ene	recreation area
	fri seilingshøyde	vertical clearance over max HW
	fuglereservat	bird sanctuary
	fyr, fyret; fyr, fyrene	lighthouse
gml	gammel, gamle	old
	gasolje/gassolje	diesel fuel oil
	gjestebrygge, -en; -r, -ne	visitor's berth
	gjesteplass, -en; -er, -ene	visitor's berth
	god	good
o	grad, graden; grader, gradene	degree of arc (or °C)
	gradnett	coordinate system, datum
c	grovkornet	coarse (sand)
-gr, -grne	grunne, grunnen; -r, -ne	shoal, ground, rock
	grunt, grunn	shallow
G	grus	gravel
	gruve, gruven/gruva; -r,-ene	mine
G	grønn	green
Y	gul	yellow
	halvøy, halvøya/-en; -er, -ene	peninsula
	handel, landhandel	small grocery shop
	haug, haugen; hauger, -ene	small hill
	havbruk, -et; -, -ene	fish farm
	havn/hamn, -a/-en; -er, -ene	harbour
	havnekontor	harbourmaster's office
	havneskisse	harbour sketch
	holdebunn	holding (bottom quality)
-hl, -hlne	holme, holmen; holmer, holmene	islet
	hoved	main, primary
	huk, huken; huker, hukene	point, headland
	hvert	every
W, [h]	hvit, hvitt	white
	høgd, høgda; høgder, -ene	hill
	høstjevndøgn spring flo	Sept equinox spring tide
Hd	høyde	height
HW	høyvann	high water (tide)
	ikke, ingen	not, none
in	indre	inner
	indrelei, indreleia; -er, -ene	inshore channel
	innenfor	within, inside

Reminder: alphabetical order is a b c...x y z æ ä ö ø å

Abbreviation	Norwegian	English
	innløp, innløpet; -, -a/-ene	inlet, entrance
	innseiling	approach
	is, isen; is, isene	ice
	jernbane	railway
	jernstang	iron perch (pole)
kbl	kabellengde	cable length (0.1 miles)
	kai, kaien; kaier, kaiene	quay
	kam, kammen; kammer, -mene	ridge
	kanal, kanalen; -er, -ene	channel
	kapp, kappet; kapp, kappene	cape
	kart, kartet; kart, kartene	chart
CD	kartnull	chart datum
	kirke, kirken; kirker, kirkene	church
Fl, [kl]	klipp	flashing (light)
	klippe, klippen; klipper, -ne	cliff
	klokka	clock, o'clock (the time)
	knaus, knausen; knauser, -ene	knoll
kn	knop, -en; -, -ene	knot
	kran, -a/krane/-n; -er, -ene	crane, hoist
	kuling, kulingen; -er, -ene	strong wind (Force 6–8)
	kun	only
	kurs, kursen; kurser, -ene	course, heading
	kyst, kysten; kyster, -ene	coast
	lagune, -n; -r, -ne	lagoon
LW	lavvann	low water, ebb
	lei, leia; leier, leiene	(recommended) lead
Cy, [L]	leire	clay
	lengde, lengda/-n; -r, -ne	longitude, length, distance
l, sm	liten, lille, litle	little, small
	linje, linja/-n; -r, -ne	line
	livsfarlig	mortally dangerous
	loddskudd, -et; -, -a/-ene	sounding
	los, losen; loser, losene	pilot
	luftspenn, -et; -, -a/-ene	overhead cable
	lydbøye, -n; -r, -ene	sound buoy
	lykt, lykta/lykten; -er,-ene	light
	lys, lyset; lys, lysa/lysene	light
	lysbøye, -n; -r, -ene	light buoy
	løp, løpet; løp, løpa/løpene	channel, passage
	maskinolje, -en; -er, -ene	lubricating oil
	med	with
	mellom	between
	merke, merket; merker, -ene	mark
MSL, [MW]	middelvann	mean sea level
m	midtre	middle, centre
	minste dybde	least depth

Reminder: alphabetical order is a b c...x y z æ ä ö ø å

Abbreviation	Norwegian	English
m	minutt, minuttet; -er, -ene	minute
	misvisning	magnetic variation
m.m.	med mer	etc {with more}
	molo, moloen; moloer, -ene	mole, breakwater
	munning, -en; -er, -ene	mouth, estuary
	mudret	dredged
Obscd, [mk]	mørk, skjult	dark, hidden (light obsc)
	målestokk	scale (of chart)
	måne, månen; måner, månene	moon
	måned, måneden; -er, -ene	month
M	nautisk mil, -en; -, -ene	nautical mile
'	nautisk minutt,-et; -er,-ene	minute of a great circle
"	nautisk sekund,-et; -er,-ene	second of a great circle
	nes, neset; nes, nesene	point, cape, ness
ned	nedre	lower
N	nipp	neap (tide)
N, n	nord, nordre, nordlig	north, northern, northerly
	ny	new
	nær	near
	odde, odden; odder, oddene	point, headland
	og	and
	olje; oljer, -ene	lube oil, diesel fuel oil
	område, området; -r, -ne	area
omtr, ca	omtrentlig	approximately
	oppmerket	marked
	oppmåling, -a/en: -en, -ene	survey, registration
	os, osen/oset; os, osene	river mouth, outlet
ldg	overrettlinje	leading line
ldg	overrettlykter	leading lights
ldg	overrettmerker	leading marks
	peiling, -en; -er, -ene	bearing (angle)
	pelebukk, -en; -er, -ene	dolphin piling
	pir, piren; pirer, pirene	pier
	poll, pollen; poller, pollene	bay, cove
	postårpneri	small post office
	postkontor	large post office
	proviant	provisions
-pt, -ptn	pynt, pynten; pynter, pyntene	point, headland
	på	on, upon, in, at
RG	radio peilestasjon	radio direction finding station
RC	radiofyr, -et; -, -ene	radio beacon
[RS]	redningsstasjon	rescue station
	red, reden; reder, redene	roadstead
	renne, renna/rennen; -r, -ene	channel
	retning, retningen; -er, -ene	direction
	rettvisende	true heading

Reminder: alphabetical order is a b c...x y z æ ä ö ø å

Abbreviation	Norwegian	English
	rutebåtkai, -en; -er, -ene	coastal route boat quay
	rev, revet; rev, revene/-a	reef, bar
	rygg, ryggen; rygger, ryggene	seamount, ridge
R	rød	red
	sakte fart!	slow speed!
S	sand, sanden	sand
	(å) seile, seiler, seilt	to sail, sailing, sailed
s	sekund, sekundet; sekunder, -ene	second
Sg	singel	shingle (bottom)
	sjø, sjøen; sjøer, sjøene	sea, wave, lake
	sjøkabel, -en; -er, -ene	underwater cable
Wd	sjøplante, tang, tare	seaweed
Wd	sjøgress, sjøgras	sea-grass
sh, [Sk]	skjell, skjellet; -, -ene/-a	shell
	skjær i vannflaten	covering rock
-skj, -skjt	skjær, skjæret; skjær, -ene/-a	skerry, rock not covering
	skjærgård	archipelago, skerries
M, [Sl]	slam, mudder, søle	mud
	slette, sletta; -r, -ene	plain (flat land)
	slipp, slippen; -er, -ene	slipway
	smal	narrow
	små	small
	småbåthavn	pleasure-boat harbour
p, [Sg]	småstein	pebbles
	sol, sola	sun
S	spring flo; -	spring (tide)
	stake, staken; staker, -ne	spar buoy
	staur, stauren; -er, -ene	sea-stack (literally = 'pole')
	sted, stedet; steder, stedene	place
St	stein, steinen; steiner, -ene	stones, rock, shoal
	stengt	closed
	sterk	strong
	stigende	rising
	stjerne, -n/stjerna; -r, -ne	star
st	stor, store	large, great
	strand, -en; strender, -ene	beach
	strøm, strømmen; -mer, mene	current, flow
	strømskifte	change of flow direction
stb	styrbord	starboard
-sd, -sdt	sund, sundet; -, -ene	sound
B, [sv]	svart	black
S, s	sør, syd, søndre, sørlig	south, southern, southerly
Wd	tang, tangen, stortang, tare	kelp
	tange, tangen; tanger, tangene	lowpoint, spur, peninsula
	tegn, tegnet; -, tegnene/-a	symbol, character, sign
	tent	lighted

Reminder: alphabetical order is a b c...x y z æ ä ö ø å

Abbreviation	Norwegian	English
	tid, tida/tiden; tider, tidene	time (but not o'clock)
	tidevann	tide
	tidevannsstrøm	tidal stream
	til	to, towards
	tilleggsside	alongside berth
h, [t]	time, timen; timer, timene	hour
-td, -tdne	tind, tinden; tinder, tindene	sharp peak
WC	toalett, -et; -/-er, -ene	toilet
	topp, toppen; topper, toppene	summit, peak
	trang	narrow
	trekai, -en; -er, -ene	wooden quay
	tvers	abeam
	tørrfall, falle tørr	drying foreshore
	tørketrommel	tumble dryer
	urent farvann	foul ground
	uten	without
	utenfor	off, outside
	utløp, utløpet; -, -ene	mouth, outlet, estuary
	utstikker, -en; -e, -ne	jetty
	uvær, uværet; uvær, -ene/-a	squall/storm, w/rain, snow
	vann, vannet; -, -ene	water, lake
	vannfylling	water tap
	vannledning	water pipe
	vannstand	water (sea) level
V	varde, varden; varder, -ne	cairn (of specific shape)
	varsel, advarsel	warning
	vaskemaskin	washing machine
vn, vnt	vatn, vatnet; vatn, -a/-	lake, water
Al, [vks]	vekslende	alternating (light)
	vesle	little, small
V, v, W	vest, vestre, vestlig	west, western, westerly
vk	vik, vika/viken; viker, -ene	bay, cove, creek, inlet
	vind, vinden; vinder, vindene	wind
	vindretning	wind direction
	vinkelkai, -en; -er, -ene	L-shaped quay
Wk, Wks	vrak, vraket; vrak, vrakene/-a	wreck
	vær, været	weather
	(å) være	to be, exist
	våg, vågen; våger, vågene	(small) bay
	vårjevndøgn spring flo	March equinox spring tide
yt	ytre	outer
Ø, au, E	øst, østlig, østlige	east, eastern, easterly
	øy, øyen/øya; øyer, øyene	island
øv	øvre	upper
	åpen	open
	år, året: år, årene/-a	year

Reminder: alphabetical order is a b c...x y z æ ä ö ø å

Glossary of Wildlife

A common topic of conversation with coastal residents and sailors is the new wildlife one sees, and often a Norwegian with a surprisingly large English vocabulary may not know the English names for birds, fish and mammals found along the coast. It is hoped that this list will bridge that gap; the Latin names are given to assist in using field-guides in different languages. Note that the common names for fish are far from exact and consistent.

Birds

Alke	Razorbill	Alca torda
Alkekonge	Little Auk, Dovekie	Alle alle
Canadagås	Canada Goose	Branta canadensis
Dvergmåke	Little Gull	Larus minutus
Fiskemåke	Common Gull	Larus canus
Fjelljo	Long-tailed Skua	Stercorarius longicaudus
Fjæreplytt	Purple Sandpiper	Calidris maritima
Grønlandsmåke	Iceland/Kumlien's Gull	Larus glaucoides
Gråhegre	Gray Heron	Ardea cinerea
Gråkråke	Gray Crow	Corvus cornix
Gråmåke	Herring Gull	Larus argentatus
(gås)	(goose)	–
Havhest	Northern Fulmar	Fulmarus glacialis
Havsule	Northern Gannet	Sula bassana
Havørn	Sea Eagle	Haliaetus albicilla
Havelle	Long-tailed Duck	Clangula hyemalis
Hettemåke	Black-headed Gull	Larus ridibundus
Hvitkinngås	Barnacle Goose	Branta leucopsis
Ismåke	Ivory Gull	Pagophila eburnea
(jo)	(skua)	–
Kongeørn	King Eagle	Aquila chrysaetos
Kortnebbgås	Pink-footed Goose	Anser brachyrhynchus
Kråke	Crow	Corvus corone & cornix
Krykkje	Kittiwake Gull	Rissa tridactyla
(lire)	(shearwater)	–
Lomvi	Common Guillemot	Uria aalge

Reminder: alphabetical order is a b c...x y z æ ä ö ø å

Lunde, Sjøpapegøye	Puffin, Atlantic Puffin	Fratercula artica
Makrelterne	Common Tern	Sterna hirundo
(måke)	(gull)	–
Polarjo	Pomarine Skua	Stercoraius pomarinus
Polarlomvi	Brünnich's Guillemot	Uria lomvia
Polarmåke	Glaucous Gull	Larus hyperboreus
Polarsvømmesnipe	Grey Phalarope	Phalaropus fulicarius
Praktærfugl	King Eider	Somateria spectabilis
Ravn	Raven	Corvus corax
Ringgås	Brent Goose	Branta bernicia
Rødnebbterne	Arctic Tern	Sterna paradisaea
Rosenmåke	Ross' Gull	Rhodostethia rosea
(rype)	(ptarmigan)	–
Sabinemåke	Sabine's Gull	Larus sabini
Sandlo	Ringed Plover	Charadrius hiaticula
Sandløper	Sanderling	Calidris alba
Sildemåke	Lesser Black-backed Gull	Larus fuscus
Sjøpapegøye, Lunde	Puffin, Atlantic Puffin	Fratercula artica
(skarv)	(cormorant)	–
Smålom	Red-throated Diver	Gavia stellata
Snøspurv	Snow Bunting	Plectrophenax mivalis
Steinvender	Turnstone	Arenaria interpres
Storjo	Great Skua	Stercorarius skua
Storskarv	Great Cormorant	Phalacrocorax carbo
Svalbardrype	Svalbard Ptarmigan	Lagopus mutus hyperboreus
Svartbak	Great Black-backed Gull	Larus marinus
Svartkråke	Black Crow	Corvus corone
Teist	Black Guillemot	Cepphus grylle
(terne)	(tern)	–
Tjeld	Oyster Catcher	Haematopus ostralegus
Toppskarv, Småskarv	Shag Cormorant	Phalacrocorax aristotelis
Tyvjo	Arctic Skua	Stercorarius parasiticus
Ærfugl	Common Eider	Somateria mollissima
(ørn)	(eagle)	–

Fish

Breiflabb	Monkfish, Goosefish	Lophius piscatorius
Brosme (torsk)	Cusk, Tusk	Brosme brosme
Hyse	Haddock	Gadus aeglifinus
Kveite, Helleflyndre	Halibut	Hippoglossus 'oglossus
Laks	Salmon	Salmo salar
Lyr	Pollock	Pollachius pollachius
Makrell	Mackerel	Scomber scombrus
Makrellstørje	Tuna (yellow-fin)	Thunnus thynnus
Rødfisk, Uer	Redfish, Ocean perch	Sebastes marinus

Reminder: alphabetical order is a b c...x y z æ ä ö ø å

Rødspette, Kongeflyndre	Plaice	Pleuronectes platessa
Sei	Saithe, Coalfish, Pollock	Pollachius virens
Sild	Herring	Culpea harengus
Torsk	Cod	Gadus morrhua
(ørret)	(trout)	–

Shellfish

Akkar	Squid	
Blåskjell	Blue Mussel	
Haneskjell	Icelandic Scallop	
Hjerteskjell	Cockle	
Hummer	Lobster	
Kamskjell	Scallop, Clam	
Krabbe	Crab	
Reke	Prawn, Shrimp	
Sandskjell	Soft Clam, Sandgaper	
Sjøkreps	Norway Lobster	
(skjell)	(mussel, clam, scallop, cockle)	

Mammals

(bjørn)	(bear)	–
Elg	Elk (Europe), Moose (US)	Alces machlis
Fjellrev, Polarrev	Arctic Fox	Alopex lagopus
Grønlandshval	Bowhead Whale	Balaena mysticetus
Grønlandsel	Harp Seal	Phoca groenlandica
(hval)	(whale)	–
Hvalross	Walrus	Odobenus rosmarus
Hvithval, Kvitfisk	White Whale, Beluga	Delphinapterus leucas
Isbjørn	Polar Bear	Ursus maritimus
Kaskelott	Sperm Whale	Physeter macrocephalus
Klappmyss	Hooded Seal	Cystophora cristata
Kvitnos	White-beaked Dolphin	Lagenorhynchus albirostris
(kobbe)	(seal)	–
Narhval	Narwhal	Monodon monoceros
Polarrev, Fjellrev	Arctic Fox	Alopex lagopus
Pukkelhval	Humpback Whale	Megaptera novaeangliae
(rev)	(fox)	–
Ringsel, Snadd	Ringed Seal	Phoca hispida
Spekkhogger	Killer Whale (Orca)	Orcinus orca
Spermasetthval	Sperm Whale	Physeter macrocephalus
Steinkobbe, Fjordsel	Harbour Seal	Phoca vitulina
Storkobbe, Blåsel	Bearded Seal	Erignathus barbatus
Svalbardrein	Svalbard Reindeer	Rangifer tarandus platyr.
Vågehval	Minke Whale	Balaenoptera

Reminder: alphabetical order is a b c...x y z æ ä ö ø å

Bibliography

This section discusses the additional publications that you may wish to obtain or consult. It is by no means complete, but covers the most important sources available at date of publication.

A 70-page *Catalogue of Norwegian Charts* is available at no charge from: Norges Sjøkartverk, Postboks 60, N-4001 Stavanger, Norway. This catalogue also describes the other publications available from the Norwegian Hydrographic Office.

Symbols and Abbreviations used on Norwegian Charts, in Norwegian and English, is available from chart agents. Rather than purchase the official tide tables, you can often pick up from a fuel dealer or chandlery a small booklet distributed gratis by Esso, Shell or Statoil: *Båtbok* or *Kysthåndboken,* which includes one- or two-year tide tables as well as other useful information. You can also use Dover if you have tide tables for the UK; HW occurs at Bergen 1 hour earlier than at Dover (remember that Norway is in time zone -1, and also observes summer time between late March and late September). If you are sailing in the late autumn or winter, the *Norwegian List of Lights* would be useful.

Den Norske Los (The Norwegian Pilot) is available in seven volumes. Volume 1, in Norwegian, contains much interesting general information, the most useful and critical of which has been adapted and included in this book. Volume 7 is the Arctic Pilot, in both Norwegian and English, highly recommended for a voyage to Svalbard. Volumes 2a (Svenskegrensen–Langesund), 2b (Langesund–Jærens Rev), 3a (Jærens Rev–Bergen), 3b (Bergen–Statt), 4 (Statt–Rørvik), 5 (Rørvik–Lødingen and Andenes), and 6 (Lødingen and Andenes–Grense-Jakobselv) cover the coast from the Swedish border to the Russian border, giving objective descriptions of harbours, and pilotage information, useful for both large ships and small boats. Harbour plans, aerial photographs and large scale chartlets of intricate leads are often included. The latest editions of volumes 2a, 2b, 3a and 3b are in both English and Norwegian, but volumes 4, 5 and 6 are in Norwegian only. These are excellent publications, each volume around 300–400 pages, published by *Statens Kartverk*.

The Norwegian *KystGuiden* is available in three volumes, in Norwegian, giving information on harbours, fishing, accommodation and tourist information for land and sea travellers S of Sognefjorden in Norway and in SW Sweden. Each volume consists of around 120 large-format pages with maps and photographs, and is published by *Statens Kartverk*.

Norske Drømmehavner (dream harbours) consists of three magazines, advertisements intermixed with descriptions (in Norwegian) and harbour sketches of 205 harbours between the Swedish border and Bodø. These are oriented towards motorboats, sometimes with less concern for overhead clearances and depths than is needed for a sailing yacht. Available from Båtmagasinet, attn: Mr Ingvar Johnsen, Postboks 250 Økem, 0510 Oslo, Norway, Tel: (47) 22 63 60 00, Fax: (47) 22 63 61 75.

Norges Sjøatlas is an elegant publication, in Norwegian, for the Norwegian coast S of Sognefjorden, with 1:100 000 and 1:350 000 chart reproductions, many colour photographs and selected harbour descriptions. Published by Nautisk Forlag (address below) and Statens Kartverk 1987, 350 large-format pages, ISBN 82-90335-02-4.

Lofoten, in Norwegian, English and German, is a fine photographic study of the culture and coast of Lofoten in all seasons: by Jenssen, 207 large-format pages, published 1994 by Lopo Media Forlag, ISBN 82-7626-004-7.

Til Sjøs i Nordland, in Norwegian, an attractive introduction to the coast of Nordland, contains interesting photographs and useful information on 200 harbours; published by Nordland Fylkeskommune, 1994, 134 pages, ISBN 82-91138-02-8.

For the SW Swedish coast, there are two volumes, new in 1995, *Svensk Kusthandbok, Del. 1a and 1b (Svinesund-Kullen)*, in Swedish, for pilotage information and descriptions of major harbours, published by Svenske Sjöfartsverket. For descriptions and sketches of smaller harbours, there are two volumes, *De Stora NP Hamnlotsen (Lysekil-Norska Gransen) and (Varberg-Lysekil)*, each around 120 large-format pages, published in 1993 and 1994 by Nautiska Publikationer, ISBN 91-972033-0-0 & 91-972033-1-9.

An attractive, useful and inexpensive small booklet with many colour aerial photographs is *Lofoten og Vesterålen*, in English, French, German and Norwegian; 32 pages, published by Aune Forlag, ISBN 82-90633-17-3.

Climbing in the Magic Islands is a technical rock climbing guide to Lofoten, in English; by E Webster, 1994, 391 pages, ISBN 82-993199-0-0, published by Nordnorsk Klaterskole, N-8330 Henningsvær, Norway.

There are several books in English of interest to voyagers to Svalbard: *Guide to Spitsbergen*, by Umbreit 1991, ISBN 0-946983-33-X, 208 pages; also available originally in German, and being revised in German in 1994. Another guide is *Exploring Spitsbergen*, by Baardseth, 1993, ISBN 82-516-1409-0, 64 pages, published by Schibsted. *Svalbard, Det Arktiske Norge*, in Norwegian, English and German, has many beautiful colour photographs; published by Aune Forlag, 1990, 64 pages, ISBN 82-90633-13-0. Also available is *Norway's Polar Territories*, by Barr, 1987, published by Aschehoug, 92 pages, and *Jan Mayen*, by Barr, ISBN 82-516-1353-1. Although available only in French, *En Voyage au Spitsberg, Terre Polaire*, by C Kempf, *Espaces 1992*, is a magnificent (and expensive) book, and contains an extensive multilingual bibliography gleaned from the Polar Institute in Oslo. *Friluftliv på Svalbard* is in Norwegian only, but gives a view of Svalbard more from an adventurer's viewpoint than a tourist's, and contains many superb photographs; by J Grønseth, 1994, published by Teknologisk Forlag, 144 pages, ISBN 82-512-0459-3.

These books are available, as well as charts and advice on the latest price information and availability of newly issued guides and other nautical publications, from Nautisk Forlag,

Drammensveien 130, Postboks 321, Skøyen N-0212 Oslo 2, Norway, Tel: (47) 22 55 84 80, Fax: (47) 22 56 23 85. It is difficult to advise regarding the purchase of these books: none are essential, but even though they have all been consulted in the preparation of this book, they contain more detailed information than is possible to include here, and are nice to have if the budget permits. The ideal would be to inspect them before purchase, or buy with return privileges. If purchasing *Den Norske Los*, be certain that the volume in the bookshop is the latest edition and not old stock.

A tourist visitors' guide to Norway and/or Sweden is useful for an overview and general information. One excellent choice is the World Travellers Series, by Moorland Publishing in England (Hunter in the USA).

Once you reach Norway or Sweden, you will find that the larger bookshops display many large-format photographic books covering the scenery, culture and history of the coast, mostly only in Norwegian. These are interesting to browse through, even if you do not wish to purchase them. You will find also several handsome books, in Norwegian, on Svalbard and on polar bears.

The libraries in the larger towns and cities also have photographic books you might wish to look at, as well as English novels that might be useful for onboard reading. There is usually no problem getting a library card, and books can be renewed by telephone after four weeks and can often be returned to another library farther along on your voyage (ask about this first, though). You may be able to borrow volumes of *Den Norske Los*, although perhaps not the latest editions (which, as well as in some cases being bilingual, are also much improved).

Vast numbers of brochures are produced to promote tourism, and these often contain fine colour photographs as well as useful information. By taking the trouble to post requests to the addresses below, you can be deluged with publications that may help in cruise planning, and perhaps provide good stimulus for dreaming over during the preceding winter. These publications are also a good way to get an advance perspective of the areas you expect to visit. Once on the spot, you can pick up even more brochures from local tourist offices, as well as useful city or regional tourist maps. A good tourist guidebook will list the address and telephone number for each local information office, as well as the regional offices that are given below; also listed below are other addresses of special interest:

Norwegian Tourist Board, POB 499 Sentrum, N-0165 Oslo 1, Norway

Norwegian Tourist Association, Storgingsgt 28, N-0161 Oslo 1, Norway

Norwegian Tourist Board, Charles House, 5 Lower Regent St, London SW1Y 4LR, UK, Tel: (0171) 839 6255

Norwegian Tourist Board, 655 Third Ave, NY, NY 10017, USA

Svenska Turistforenningen, Drottninggatan 31-33, Box 25, 10120 Stockholm, Sweden

Rutehefte NORWAY (Timetables, for air, rail, bus, boat), from foreign Norwegian tourist offices and probably from the Tourist Information Office, Rådhuset, N-0037 Oslo 1, Norway

FLY Ruter i Norge, the complete air timetable, from SAS, Fornebuvn 40, Oslo Lufthavn, Norway

Braathens SAFE, POB 55, 1330 Oslo Lufthavn, Norway (for Svalbard brochure, and brochure on the 'Visit Norway Pass'; special low fares on internal flights for non-Scandinavian residents)

Norwegian Government Seamen's Service, POB 8123, N-0032 Oslo, Norway (for 'Guide to Norwegian Ports')

Ofotens & Vesteraalens Dampskibbsselskab, POB 57, N-8501 Narvik (for colour brochure on Hurtigruten Coastal Voyage)

Akershus Tourist Board, POB 6888, N-0130 Oslo 1, Norway (E of Oslo)

Oslo Tourist Information Office, Rådhuset, N-0037 Oslo 1, Norway (Oslo)

Vestfold Tourist Board, Storgt 55, N-3100 Tønsberg, Norway (W of Oslo)

Telemark Tourist Board, POB 743–Hjellen, N-3701 Skien, Norway (W of Oslo)

Vest-Agder Tourist Board, POB 770, N-4601 Kristiansand, Norway (S coast)

Aust-Agder Fylkeskommune, Fylkeshuset, N-4800 Arendal, Norway (S coast)

Rogaland Reiselivsråd, Øvre Holmegt 7, N-4006 Stavanger, Norway (SW coast)

Hordaland & Bergen Tourist Board, Slottsgt 1, N-5003 Bergen, Norway

Sogn and Fjordane Travel Assn, POB 299, N-5801 Sogndal, Norway (for *Båtguiden*; and information on Sognefjorden and Nordfjorden)

Norwegian Glacier Centre, N-5855 Fjærland, Norway (Sognefjorden)

Luster Tourist Office, N-5820 Gaupne, Norway (for Nigardsbreen glacier, Sognefjorden)

Svanøy Stiftelse avd Kvalstad, N-6965 Svanøybukt, Norway (nature reserve at listed harbour Svanøybukta/ Kvalstadbukta)

Stryn Reiseliv A/S, N-6880 Stryn, Norway (Nordfjorden)

Geiranger Turistråd, N-6216 Geiranger, Norway (Geirangerfjorden)

Ålesund Reiselivslag, Rådhuset, N-6025 Ålesund, Norway (incl bird island Runde)

Møre og Romsdal Reiselivsråd, POB 467, N-6501 Kristiansund, Norway

Sør-Trøndelag and Trondheim Tourist Information, POB 2102, N-7001 Trondheim

Nord-Trøndelag Tourist Information, N-7870 Grong, Norway (area S of Rørvik)

Nordland Reiselivsråd, POB 434, N-8001 Bodø, Norway

Sør-Helgeland Reiselivslag, Boks 315, N-8901 Brønnøysund, Norway

Polarsirkelen Travel Assn, HTS, N-8801 Sandnessjøen, Norway (incl. Træna)

Minol/Esso, POB 84, N-8801 Sandnessjøen, Norway (for Nordland folder)

Lovund Turistheim, 8764 Lovund, Norway

Myken Fyr Holiday, Gro Bygdevoll/Helge Eriksen, N-8199 Myken, Norway

Lofoten Tourist Board, POB 210, N-8301 Svolvær, Norway

Røst Tourist Information, N-8064 Røst, Norway

Nyvågar/Lofoten, POB 183, N-8310 Kabelvåg, Norway (tourist centre)

Nordnorsk Klatreskole, N-8330 Henningsvær, Norway (climbing guides)

Vesterålen Reiselivslag, POB 243, N-8401 Sortland, Norway (incl. Møysalen climb)

Øksnes Turistinform, POB 33, N-8430 Myre, Norway (Tinden, Nyksund, Øksnes)

Stø Whale Watch, POB 284, N-8430 Myre, Norway

Andøy Whale Safari, POB 58, N-8480 Andenes, Norway

Gratangen Boat Museum, N-9470 Gratangen, Norway

Troms Tourist Information, Storgata 61/63, N-9001 Tromsø, Norway

Finnmark Travel Assn, POB 223, N-9501 Alta, Norway

Info-Svalbard, POB 323, N-9170 Longyearbyen, Norway

Svalbard Polar Travel, 9170 Longyearbyen, Norway

Spitsbergen Travel, POB 548, N-9170 Longyearbyen, Norway

Svalbard Næringsutvikling, POB 460, N-9170 Longyearbyen, Norway

Index

Entries referring to main articles about the port selected are printed in **bold** type, entries referring to photographs appear in *italic*. When using the index, remember the order of the Norwegian alphabet, see bottom of every page.

Abelvær, 40
Aberdeen, 4
Albertøya, 108
Aldevågen, 24
Alicehamna, 110
Alstahaug, 44
Alsøyvågen, 45
Alta, 80
Alverstraumen, 120
Anchoring, 11-12, 95-6
Andenes, 75
Ankenes, 61
Anservika, 103
Ansnes, 36
Antonio Pigafettahamna, 99
Anvil of the Gods, *55*, 62
Arendal, 150
Asen, 39
Askvoll, 24
Aurlandsfjorden, 115
Aurora Borealis, *18*, 80
Austervåg, 98
Axeløya, 100

Ballstad, 56
Barentsburg, 102
Bellsund, *89*, 89
Bergavik, 135
Bergen, 6, **122**
Bergsfjord, 79
Berlevåg, 85
Bessaker, 39
Bibliography, 192-195
Bird Reserves, 16
Bjarkøya, 68
Bjonhamna, 103
Bjørn, 44

Bjørnhamna, 108
Bjørnnesholmen, 112
Bjørnsund, 31
Bjørnøya, 89, 93-4, **96-8**
Bleik, 75
Bliksvær, 49
Blindleia, *vi*,11, **144-5**
Blokken, 68
Blomstrandhamna, 106
Blomvåg, 122
Bockfjorden, 110
Bodø, 49
Bogen (N Salten), 64
Bogen (Ofoten), 61
Bogøyvær, 37
Bolla, 72
Borebukta, 104
Borgvær, 56
Borøysundet, 37
Bossekop, see Alta
Brakstad, 40
Breibogen, 110
Breidvik, 80
Breivikbotn, 80
Brekstad, 38
Bremsteinen, 44
Brepollen, 100
Bringsinghaug, 28
Brønnøysund, 41, 43
Bud, 31
Bugøynes, 86
Bulandet, 24
Bulbrebukta, 104
Buoyage, 9-11
Bustadhamn, 81
Buvågen, 54
Byfjord, 118, 120

Båke, 9-10
Bårdsetøya, 34
Båtsfjord, 85
Båtsportkart, 7, 160

Charts, 7-8, (also at the beginning of every section)
Colesbukta, **102**
Currents, 6-7

Dahlbrebukta, 105
Dalen, 152
Dalskilen, 150
Danger Areas, 179-81
Digermulen, 58
Distance tables, 167-69
Djupvågen, 69
Dunøyane, 100
Dyrvika, 37
Dyrøyhamn, 69

Ebeltofthamna, 107
Edøy, 36
Egersund, **140**, *141*
Eidestranda, 34
Eidembukta, 104
Eidet, 69
Eidfjord, 128
Eidsfjorden, 73
Eivindvik, 120
Engelsbukta, 105
Engen, *47*, 48
Engenes, 69
Esbjerg, 5
Esefjord, 115
Espevær, 130

Reminder: alphabetical order is a b c...x y z æ ä ö ø å

Evjesund, 158

Falkenberg, 166
Farmhamna, 104
Farsund, 142
Fedje, 5, 122
Fevik, 149
Fimreite, 116
Finnasandbukta, 135
Finnsnes, 69
Fjortende Julibukta, 107
Fjærland, 3, 116
Fjærlandsfjorden, 115
Fjällbacka, 163
Flag Etiquette, 15
Flakstadvåg, 71
Flakstadøya, 54-55
Florø, 26
Fløtningsviken, 57
Food, 12-14
Forlandsrevet, 105
Fosnavåg, 28
Fredrikstad, 159
Fresvik, 117
Fridtjovhamna, 89, 101

Gamvik, 83
Gas, 15
Gash, 14-15
Gashamna, 100
Gasøyane, 103
Gaukværøya, 73
Geiranger, 29
Geirangerfjorden, 23, 29
Gibostadt, 70
Gimsøystraumen, 51
Gjerdsvika, 28
Gjersheimholmane, 128
Gjesvær, 81
Glomen, 48
Glomfjorden, 48
Glomset, 29
Glossaries, 182-91
Godøysund, 126
GPS, 8
Gratangen, 72
Grimstad (near Bergen), 125
Grimstad (SE coast)), 149
Grip, 23, 32
Grundfjorden, 58
Grunnesundet, 120, 123
Grunnfjorden, 62
Gryllefjord, 71
Gryvikta, 98

Grøtøya, 64, 85
Gudvangen, 117
Gullholmen, 164
Gullvika, 59, 79
Guns, 91-2
Göteborg, 163, 165

Hagevika, 29
Halsa, 48
Halten, 37
Halvardsøya, 71
Hamarøya, 51, 63-4
Hamburgbukta, 107
Hamburgsund, 163
Hamiltonbukta, 110
Hammerfest, 80
Hamn, 71
Hamnaholmen, 27
Hamningberg, 85
Hamnøy, 54
Hamsund, 63
Hankøhamn, 158
Hansbreen, (glacier), 99
Hardangerfjord, 124, 125, 128-9, 130
Harstad, 72
Harsvika, 39
Harwich, 4
Hasvik, 79
Haugestranda, 142
Haugesund, 131
Haugsholmen, 28
Havnøya, 44
Havstenssund, 163
Havøysund, 81
Helgeland, 6
Helgoland, 5
Helgøysund, 134
Hellesylt, 29
Hellfjord, 73
Helligvær, 65
Helløya, 69
Hennes, 58
Henningsvær, 56
Henøysundet, 26
Herand, 129
Hersøy, 72
Herwighamna, 98
Hinnøya (61° 21' N), 26
Hinnøya (68° 28' N), 58-60, 66-8, 72
Hjartøya, 44
Hjellestad, 126
Hjelløya, 64

Hjeltefjord, 118, 120
Holandsfjorden, 41, 47, 48
Holmiabukt, 110
Honningsvåg (71° N), 81
Honningsvågen (62° 12' N), 28
Honskår, 27
Hopen, 48
Hopsjøen, 36
Hornbækpollen, 111, 111
Hornelen, 23, 27
Hornsund, 89, 94, 99-100
Hornvika, 82
Horten, 156
Hovden, 74
Hurtigruten, 20, 68
Hustadvika, 24, 31
Husøy, 71
Håholmen, 31
Håja, 72

Igerøya, 44
Immigration Rules, 18-19
Indre Pollen, (SW Rognsundet), 80
Ice reports, 174-9
Ingelsfjorden, 58
Inndyr, 48
Isbjørnhamna, 99
Isfjord, 89, 102-4
Isøyane, 100

Jan Mayen, 88-90
Jordsbukta, 152
Josephbukta, 100
Jostedalbreen (glacier),17,27
Jotunkjeldane, 112
Jøkelfjordbotn, 79

Kabelvåg, 57
Kaiser Wilhelm II, 58
Kalvåg, 26
Kamøyvær, 81
Kapp Linne, 102
Kappp Wijk, 104
Keiservarden, 58
Kinsarvik, 128
Kirkefjorden, 17, 55
Kirkehamn see Kjerkehavn
Kirkenes, 86
Kirkholmen, 69
Kirkøy, 44
Kjelbotn, 65
Kjelkenes, 26

Reminder: alphabetical order is a b c…x y z æ ä ö ø å

INDEX

Kjerkehavn, 142
Kjerringvika, 72
Kjerringvågen, 24
Kjerringøy, 64
Kjøllefjord, 83
Kjøpsvik, 62
Kjøtta, 72
Kjøvangbukta, 157
Klauva, 69
Klosterøyna, 135
Klubben, 27
Klungsvågen, 28
Knarriagsund, 36
Kobbebukta, 98
Kobbefjorden, 109
Kobbholet, 81
Koksøysundet, 122
Kolbjørnsvik, 150
Koløystø, 126
Kongsfjord (Finnmark), 85
Kongsfjorden (Svalbard), 106-7
Kongsvoll, 38
Kopervik, 134
Korshamn, 143
Korsnes, 62
Kragerø, 145, 151
Kristiansand, 146
Kristiansund, 32
Kristoffervalen, 77
Krokvika, 110
Krossfjorden, 107
Kummel, 160
Kungshamn, 163
Kunna, 55
Kvalrossbukta, 96
Kvalstadbukta, 26
Kvalsundet, 77
Kvalsundvika, 80
Kvalvåg, 126
Kvaløsæter, 39
Kvankjosen, 59
Kvarøya, 46
Kvedfjordbukta, 107
Kvenvær, 36
Kvernhusvika, 36
Kvitsøyna, 134
Kviturspollen, 118-9, *119*, 122, 126
Kya, 37
Käringön, 164
Kårhamn, 80

Landnøringsvika, 98

Landrøyvåg, 126
Langesund, 152
Langfjordbotn, 79
Langårsund, 151, *151*
Larvik, 152
Lavik, 115
Leknes, 56
Leangbukta, 157
Leirangspollen, 135
Leirvik, 129
Lerwick, *5*
Liefdefjorden, 110-11, *111*
Liland 61
Lilla Kornö, 164
Lillesand, 148
Lindesnes, 3, 138, 140
Lingbukta, 110
Lista Light, 138
Listahavn, 142
Listraumen, 24
Loen, 27
Lofoten, 6, 51-61
Lognvika, 98
Lokksund, 128, *130*
Longyearbyen, 90-1, 103
Lonkanfjorden, 58
Lovund, 45
Lunkevika, 98
Lustrafjorden, 115
Lyngholmane, 148
Lyngvær (Vågøen), 43
Lyngvær (W Lyngværøya) 46
Lyngør, 150
Lyngøya, 43
Lysebotn, 137
Lysefjorden, 6, 124, 135-7, *136*
Lysekil, 164
Lødingen, 60
Långedrag, 165

Magdalenefjorden, 108, *109*
Magerøysundet, 77
Mandal, 146
Mariaholmen, 101
Marstrand, 164
Mastrevik, 120
Mausundvær, 37
Mehamn, 83
Melbu , 73
Meværet, 79
Midnight Sun, 17-18
Mjosund, 34

Moffen, 110
Molde, 31
Moskenesøya, 53-4
Moskenstraumen, 51
Moss, 158
Mosselbukta, 112
Mosterhamn, 130
Murmansk, 83, 86
Mushamna, 111
Myken, 46
Mölle, 166
Møllerhamna, 107
Mølstrevågen, 130
Måløy, 27

Narvik, 61
Nature Reserves, 16-17
Naze, The, see Lindesnes
Nesabukta, 31
Nesna, 45
Nesseby, 86
Nordeidet, 70
Nordenskjøld (glacier), 104
Nordfjord (Syltefjorden), 85
Nordfjorden, 23, 27
Nordfjordholmen, 46
Nordhamna, 98
Nordkapp, 82
Nordnesøya, 46
Nordskot, 64
Norheimsund, 128
Norskøysundet, 109
North Cape, see Nordkapp
Northern Lights, see Aurora Borealis
Nusfjord, 55
Ny Hellesund, 146
Ny Ålesund, 106
Nyksund, 74, 75
Nykvåg, 74
Nyvågar, 56
Nærøyfjorden, 115

Odda, 128
Offersøen, 60
Ofoten, 6, 51, 61-5
Olden, 27
Oldenborg, 32
Omastranda, 128
Ona, 23, 31
Onøya, 46
Ornes, 117
Orpholmsund, 146
Ortnevik, 117

Reminder: alphabetical order is a b c...x y z æ ä ö ø å

INDEX

Osen, 62
Osholmen, 65
Oslo, 6, 157
Oslofjorden, 6, 153-4

Passages (to Norway), 4-5
Peirsonhamna, 107
Peterhead, 4
Polar Bears, 81, 91-2
Polish Polar Station, 99
Prestøya, 148
Prins Karls Forland, 104
Pronunciation, 21
Pyramiden, 104

Radio, Coastal, 170-3
Raftsundet, 50-1, 58
Rammen, 165
Ramsundet, 61
Ramsvik, 120
Randesund, 144
Randvika, 102
Raudfjorden, 110
Refsvik, 53
Regnardneset, 107
Reine, 54
Reinholmen, 100
Rekvedbukta, 107
Renga, 47
Revingsund, 134
Ringberget, 37
Ringholmen, 34
Risvær, 60
Risør, 150
Risøyhamn, 68
Roan, 39
Rognaldsvågen, 26
Rognan, 71
Rognsvåg, 122
Romdalsfjorden, 31
Rosendal, 129
Rubbish, 14-15
Rugsund, 27
Runde, 28
Ryfylkefjordane, 132
Rødsand, 71
Rødøya, 47
Rødøyvågen, 44
Røedvika, 98
Rørvik, 40
Røssøya, 64
Røst, 53

Saltstraumen, 41

Sand, 69
Sandfjord, 83
Sandland, 79
Sandnessjøen, 44
Sandshamn, 28
Sandspollen, 157
Sandviken, 48
St Laurentiusbukta, 108
St Sunniva Klostervågen, 27
Sauøya, 37
Scheibukta, 108
Seglvik, 79
Selfjorden, 54
Seljevågen, (-hamna), 28
Selvågen (Fleina), 49
Selvågen (Svalbard), 105
Selsøyvik, 47
Selvbukta, 38
Senje-Hopen, 71
Shetland, 5
Signehamna, 107
Silavågen, 45
Silda, 27
Sildevåg (Fedje), 122
Sildevågen (Risnesøya), 24
Sildpollen, 62
Sirevåg, 140
Sistranda, 37
Sjøvika, 44
Skallahamn, 165
Skansbukta, 104
Skarsfjord, 72
Skarstad, 61
Skarsvåg (67° 58' N), 64
Skarsvåg (71° 07' N), 81
Skeishamna, 43
Skien, 154
Skipøøsen, 59
Skjervøy, 78
Skjervøya, 39
Skjolden, 119
Sklinna, 43
Skjøtningberg, 83
Skærbukta, 80
Skjærgård, 2, 4
Skjærhalden, 159
Skjærvær, 44
Skomvær, 51
Skrolsvik, 69
Skudeneshavn, 4, 6, 134
Skutvik, 64
Sleneset, 45
Slettvik, 26
Slubbersholmen, 164

Slåtøya, 73
Smeerenbukta, 109
Smögen, 164
Sognefjorden, 2, 6, 113-17
Solsemsvågen, 43
Sommarøy, 71
Son, 158
Sortland, 68
Sotenkanal, 161
Specimen cruises, 6, 50-1
Speidarneset, 107
Spitsbergen, 87-96, 99-112
Stamsund, 56
Stattlandet, 4, 23, 28
Stattvågen, 28
Stavanger, 135
Stavern, 152
Stefjord, 55, 62
Stefjordbotn, 62
Steinsø, 59
Steinvikbukta, 39
Stetind, 55, 62
Stockmarknes, 68
Stokksund, 39
Store Ekkerøya, 86
Storfossnavågen, 38
Storjorda, 62
Stormbukta, 94
Storsundet, 125
Stranda, 29
Stranden, 48
Straumen, 36
Straumshamn, 63, 63
Straumsholmen, 31
Straumøya, (Helgeland), 43
Straumøya, (Lofoten), 55
Streams, 6
Stryn, 27
Strömstad, 163
Stø, 75
Stølen, 129 (Rosendal)
Støtt, 48
Sula, 37
Sund, 55
Sunndal, 129
Svalbard, 87-112
Svanøybukta, 26
Svartisen (glacier),17, 47, 48
Sveabreen (glacier), 104
Sveagruva, 101
Sveggsundet, 32
Svellingen, 60
Svenskegattet, 109
Svolvær, 57

Reminder: alphabetical order is a b c...x y z æ ä ö ø å

Sysselmann, 90, 99, 103, 108
Sæbuøya, 36
Sætervika, 39, *40*
Sætre, 29
Søndre Ospesund, 24
Søndre Missingen, 158
Sørdalsbukta, 111
Sørfjord, 128
Sørgjerøyvågen, 47
Sørgjæslingan, 40
Sørhamna (Trondheimsleia), 37
Sørhamna (Bjørnøya), 96
Sørkapp, 89, 94
Sørnesøya, 46
Sørvær, 80
Sørvågen, 54

Tafjord, 29
Tallakshavn, 156
Talvik, 80
Tananger, 4, 6, 140
Tansøya, 26
Tannvikvågen, 37
Teltvika, 98
Tengelfjord, 58
Thyborøn, 5
Tides, 6, 93
Tinayrebukta, 107
Tind, 54
Tinden, 74
Titran, 36
Tjellsundet, 61
Tjøtta, 44
Tofte, 72
Torekov, 166
Tornes, 31
Torsken, 71
Torsvåg, 71
Tovik, 72
Tranesvågen, 68
Trinityhamna, 108
Trollfjorden, 50, 57
Tromsø, 70
Trondenes, 73

Trondheim, 38
Trovåg, 24
Tryghamna, 104
Træna, 45
Träslöv, 165
Tufjord, 81
Tvedestrand, 150
Tverfjord S, 79
Tysfjorden, 51, *55*, 61-2
Tyttebærvika, 70
Tømmervik, 62
Tønsberg, *154*, 156

Ulvik, 128
Ungsmaløya, 61
Uskedal, 129
Uthaug, 39
Utstein Kloster, 135
Utvorden, 40
Uvågen, 73

Vadsø, 86
Vallavik, 128
Valløbukta, 156
Van Keulenhamna, 100
Van Muydenbukta, 101
Vannvåg, 70
Varberg, 165
Varde, 9, 10
Vardø, 85
Variation, Magnetic, 8-9
Vartdalsfjorden, 29
Vatlestraumen, 125
Veidholmen, 36
Veidvåg, 122
Vennesund, 43
Verdens Ende, 156
Vestervågen, 100
Vesterålen, 6, 50
Vestfjorden, 50, 61
Vestpollen, 59
Vestvågøya, 56
Vettøysundet, 64
Vik, 117
Vika, 137
Vikevåg, 135

Vikingevågen, 120
Vikum, 6, 115, *116*
Villa Havn, 39
Vingen, 26
Virgohamna, 108
Vottesnes, 73
Vulkanhamna, 112
Værøy, 53
Vågsvågen, 45

Weather, 1, 174-8
Whale Safari, see Andenes
Whale Watch, see Stø
Wijdefjorden, 112
Woodfjorden (unnamed anchorage), 112
Worsleyhamna, 111

Ymerbukta, 104
Ystabøhamn, 134
Ytre Kiberg, 86
Ytre Norskøya, 110

Øksfjord, 80
Øksfjorden, 51, 59
Øksnes, 75
Ørnes (Helgeland), 48
Ørnes (Ofoten), 62
Østervågen, 81
Østnesfjorden, 57
Østvågøya, 56-8

Æfjorden, 61
Æsøya, 56

Å 54
Ålesund, 23, 30, *30*
Åndalsnes, 31
Ånfjordbotn, 75
Åram, 28
Årdalstangen, 117
Årviksand, 77
Åsgårdstrand, 156
Åvik, 146